BOUND IN THE BOND OF LIFE

"This remarkable collection is a powerful testament to how individuals and communities cope with an act of unbelievable violence."

—*PUBLISHERS WEEKLY*

"What does it take to mend the world? Parts prayer, howl, remembrance, and meditation, the essays in *Bound in the Bond of Life* go beyond the initial shock and grief of October 27 to examine the meaning of community and the power of faith under attack. Rather than make sense of hate, the Pittsburghers here wisely try to find perspective on a moment evil struck too close to home."

—STEWART O'NAN, author of *Emily, Alone* and *City of Secrets*

"Taking its place in the somber tradition of heart-rending Jewish chronicles, *Bound in the Bond of Life* memorializes the Tree of Life synagogue massacre, the most deadly act of antisemitism in all of American Jewish history. Filled with first-person accounts, this book fulfills a sacred commandment: to recall the tragedy that befell Pittsburgh on October 27, 2018, and never to forget it."

—JONATHAN D. SARNA, Joseph H. & Belle R. Braun Professor of American Jewish History, Brandeis University

"It is a depressing reality that, in America today, mass shootings come and go with the news cycle in a blur of sameness, marching us from one shattered community to the next. Parkland. Charleston. Newtown. Orlando. Las Vegas. Yet people who cherish each of these communities are left to step into each new day differently, along different streets, through different histories, and toward different tomorrows. It's important to know them as unique places with unique people. This anthology provides that for the tragedy at the Tree of Life synagogue by uniting a range of talented local writers who explore the loss of eleven lives and the special community that Squirrel Hill was and is."

—JENNIFER BERRY HAWES, author of *Grace Will Lead Us Home*

"This sterling collection of essays by writers from Pittsburgh reflecting on the October 27, 2018, massacre of Jews at the Tree of Life synagogue gives us just the company we need as we work through our collective grief, together and alone. I was stunned by their deep, generous insights into how this tragedy affected this dynamic and diverse city and by the writers' compassion for both the victims and survivors. By turns devastating and consoling, each of these reflections takes us a little further down the path to healing, despite community wounds and losses that can never be fully mended or compensated."

—JAMES E. YOUNG, author of *The Stages of Memory,*
At Memory's Edge, and *The Texture of Memory*

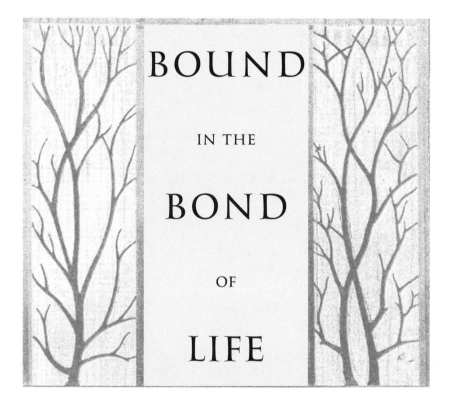

BOUND

IN THE

BOND

OF

LIFE

PITTSBURGH WRITERS REFLECT
on the TREE *of* LIFE TRAGEDY

EDITED BY BETH KISSILEFF AND ERIC LIDJI

UNIVERSITY *of* PITTSBURGH PRESS

A portion of the proceeds of the sale of this book will support Jewish Family and Community Services of Pittsburgh: https://www.jfcspgh.org/

Published by the University of Pittsburgh Press, Pittsburgh, Pa., 15260
Copyright © 2020, University of Pittsburgh Press
All rights reserved
Manufactured in the United States of America
Printed on acid-free paper
10 9 8 7 6 5 4 3 2 1

Cataloging-in-Publication data is available from the Library of Congress

ISBN 13: 978-0-8229-4651-9
ISBN 10: 0-8229-4651-3

Cover photograph: Rabbi Jeffrey Myers and Rabbi Jonathan Perlman lead a gathering in Hanukkah songs after lighting a menorah outside the Tree of Life Synagogue on the first night of Hanukkah, Sunday, December 2, 2018, in the Squirrel Hill neighborhood of Pittsburgh. AP Photo / Gene J. Puskar

Cover design: Alex Wolfe

תנצבה

In Memory of the kedoshim of the Tree of Life Tragedy
October 27, 2018, Pittsburgh, Pennsylvania

אֵל מָלֵא רַחֲמִים שׁוֹכֵן בַּמְּרוֹמִים, הַמְצֵא מְנוּחָה נְכוֹנָה, עַל כַּנְפֵי הַשְּׁכִינָה בַּמַּעֲלוֹת
קְדוֹשִׁים וּטְהוֹרִים כְּזוֹהַר הָרָקִיעַ מַזְהִירִים, אֶת נִשְׁמוֹת קְדוֹשֵׁי פִּיטְטסבּוּרג

אידית בלציא בת אבא מנחם	Joyce Feinberg
יוסף בן חיים	Richard Gottfried
רייזל בת אברהם	Rose Mallinger
יהודה בן יחזקאל	Jerry Rabinowitz
חיים בן אליעזר	Cecil Rosenthal
דוד בן אליעזר	David Rosenthal
בילא רחל בת משה	Bernice Simon
זלמן שכנא בן מנחם מענדל	Sylvan Simon
דניאל אברהם בן ברוך	Daniel Stein
משה גדול בן יוסף	Melvin Wax
יצחק חיים בן מנחם	Irving Younger

שֶׁנֶּהֶרְגוּ עַל קִדּוּשׁ הַשֵּׁם, בַּעֲבוּר שֶׁאָנוּ מִתְפַּלְלִים לְעִלּוּי נִשְׁמוֹתֵיהֶם. וְזֹכֹר לָנוּ עֲקֵדָתָם וְתַעֲמֹד לָנוּ וּלְכָל יִשְׂרָאֵל זְכוּתָם. אֶרֶץ אַל—תְּכַסִּי דָמָם וְאַל—יְהִי מָקוֹם לְזַעֲקָתָם.

לָכֵן בַּעַל הָרַחֲמִים יַסְתִּירֵם בְּסֵתֶר כְּנָפָיו לְעוֹלָמִים, וְיִצְרוֹר בִּצְרוֹר הַחַיִּים אֶת נִשְׁמוֹתֵיהֶם. ה' הוּא נַחֲלָתָם, בְּגַן עֵדֶן תְּהֵא מְנוּחָתָם, וְיַעַמְדוּ לְגוֹרָלָם לְקֵץ הַיָּמִין, וְנֹאמַר אָמֵן.

God full of mercy, who dwells on high, establish proper rest upon the wings of the Divine Presence, on the levels of the holy and pure ones [who] shine like the splendor of the firmament, for the souls of the Kedoshim of Pittsburgh, murdered *al kiddush Hashem*, because we pray for the elevation of their souls, and remember for us their sacrifice and let their merit stand for us and for all of Israel. Let the earth not cover their blood and let there not be a place [sufficient] for their cries.

Master of mercy, cover them in the cover of His wings forever and bind their souls with the Binding of life. God is their inheritance, may their rest be in *Gan Eden* and let them rest in peace upon their places of repose, and let them stand for their fate in the end of days. And let us say Amen.

—Traditional memorial prayer for martyrs
adapted by Rabbi Daniel Yolkut, Passover 2019

CONTENTS

FOREWORD

David M. Shribman

I DIDN'T HEAR THE SHOTS THE FIRST TIME. I hear them all the time now.

I suspect I am not alone. So many of us—whether Jewish or not, whether from Squirrel Hill or not, whether in Pittsburgh that morning or not—hear those shots still. They were the modern-day shots heard 'round the world. But they also are shots that continue to be heard around our world, whether we heard them the first time or not.

We hear them, to be sure, when we round the corner of Shady and Wilkins Avenues. But we hear them, too, echoing from other places and at other times. When shots ring out in Dayton, or in El Paso, or in Poway. When hurtful words are shot across the country, or the world. When the calendar turns to October and the black-crepe anniversary that needs no further explanation, at least in our precincts. We will hear them for as long as we shall live.

These are the shots that try our souls. The phrase is adapted from Thomas Paine, from a pamphlet called The Crisis. For those shots were the opening shots in our contemporary crisis of hurt and hate. Only a few of us heard the shots when they actually rang out, and some eleven were slain by them. But we were all injured by them.

We all have our stories. You may have been a neighbor. The fellow over there was at the Giant Eagle. The woman across the street was coming out of Five Points Artisan Bake Shop. I was the editor of a newspaper. My colleagues covered these shootings, covered them with grace, with feeling, with compassion, with comprehensiveness. One of us, there at the paper, has a mother who ate lunch with two of the victims almost every day. Another lost a revered family doctor. A third lives right by Tree of Life. My own home was three blocks away. Each of us was marked by the shots, deaths, vigils, services, funerals. It was, for all of us, one of those before-and-after moments, like Pearl Harbor, the death of Franklin Roosevelt, the assassination of John F. Kennedy, and the terror attacks of September 2001. In each of those, there was life before, and then life after, and nothing was the same in the after. We are living life after October 27, 2018, trying to recapture life before the Shabbat without shalom. Nothing is the same.

This book is a tale of life before, and of life after, and the difficulty—the impossibility—of reconciling the two. It includes accounts of how we learned, how we processed, how we grieved, how we carried on. Ann Belser writes about covering a neighborhood tragedy, Andrew Goldstein about how a young reporter was shaped by the biggest story of his career, unfolding on familiar streets. Peter Smith recounts how he witnessed and chronicled the aftermath, Jane Bernstein shares her feelings about driving by a neighborhood scene transformed into a crime scene. Lisa D. Brush tells us how she got through the ordeal, Avigail Oren about how the shots activated her activism. Abby Schachter talks about the power of ritual in recovery, Tony Norman about how shocking, and yet so ordinary, was the tragedy. And so many others share their thoughts, each offering between these covers an affecting essay, each screaming with passion and power to match the moment. It will take patience and persistence to read every page here. The hurt may be too much to bear. The shots may seem too close, too loud.

In the two years that have passed I have been called upon repeatedly as a columnist to address the sad parade of mass shootings and antisemitic acts. From time to time on these occasions I have called Rabbi Jeffrey Myers to reflect on his own role in these episodes, and, with deadline pressing, we always return to the phrase "Never again," and to its sad corollary for our times, "Yet again."

Prompted by these commentaries, as in the remarks of Rabbi Myers, I have wondered what can be done to prevent these tragedies from occurring yet again. Because the vigil at the corner of Forbes and Murray, hard by that beloved clock tower with the time recorded in Hebrew letters, did not do it. The mass meeting at Soldiers and Sailors Memorial Hall did not do it. The series of funerals, with rabbis from around the country and the world, did not do it. The visit of the president did not do it. The protests over the president's visit did not do it. The one-year commemorations did not do it. Nor did anything that any of us wrote, not even the work of our neighbor Bari Weiss, who published a whole book on antisemitism and how to prevent it. None of this did it. None of it came close.

I am sometimes asked how it came to be that the *Post-Gazette* led the paper the Friday following the shooting with the first four words of the Mourner's Kaddish, in Hebrew script. For the answer I defer to the opening scene of the Broadway play Fiddler on the Roof, where Tevye confronts the question of why Jews wear head coverings and prayer shawls. He answers: "I'll tell you. I don't know." That's my answer: I'll tell you. I don't know. It came to me in the middle of the night. Wonder of wonder, miracle of miracles.

But do I know it was the right call, even though there were those who doubted it when I told them what the front page would look like the next morning. My explanation was that if words were failing us, and by that time they were, then perhaps we were thinking in the wrong language. The real language of the Kaddish, of course, is Aramaic, and it somehow seemed right to employ a tenth-century prayer for a twenty-first-century tragedy. The headline also prompted me to write perhaps the most extraordinary correction in the history of American journalism, explaining that because original prayer was written in Aramaic, the final letter of the fourth word should have been rendered with an aleph rather than with the hay we published that day. It was then, as it is now, essential—in all moments, but in that moment especially—to get things exactly right. But here is one of the lessons of Tree of Life: repairing the word is one thing, repairing the world quite another.

So in moments like these—and moments like these occur often in times like these, when we hear the shots, at Tree of Life, and at places not yet famous for their sadness—it might be wise to recall these words, appearing in the new (2009) prayer book used by Reform Jews and adapted from the work of Michael Walzer, professor emeritus at the Institute of Advanced Studies at Princeton, New Jersey:

> Standing on the parted shores of history
> we believe what we were taught
> before ever we stood at Sinai's foot;
>
> that wherever we go, it is eternal Egypt
> that there is a better place, a promised land;
> that the winding way to that promise
> passes through the wilderness.
>
> That there us no way to get from here to there
> except by joining hand, marching
> together.

We march together, hand joining hand, in Pittsburgh and beyond. But still we hear the shots.

INTRODUCTION

Eric Lidji

"MAY THE SOUL BE BOUND IN THE BOND OF LIFE" is a Jewish prayer. It first appears in the Book of Samuel, where Abigail says it to her future husband David, after preventing an act of bloody vengeance by assuaging his anger. "Though a man rises to pursue thee, and to seek thy soul: yet the soul of my lord shall be bound in the bond of life with the Lord thy God; and the souls of thy enemies, them shall he sling out, as out of the hollow of a sling" (1 Samuel 25:29). The phrase has since become essential to the Jewish mourning liturgy. It was incorporated into the prayer *El Malei Rachamim* (God, full of mercy), recited graveside at funerals and at subsequent memorial services. A five-letter Hebrew acronym of the phrase traditionally anchors the bottom of Jewish gravestones.

The "bond of life" surely refers to divine protection. But just as surely, humans have taken it as an imperative. So much of Jewish custom and culture—especially its manifestation in North America by families of Ashkenazic descent—is built around remembering the dead: the annual yahrzeit commemoration marking the anniversary of the death of a loved one, the memorial yizkor service recited at four major Jewish holidays, the illuminated bronze memorial plaques covering almost every synagogue, the recycling of the names of deceased ancestors for newborn children, the auspicious days established on the death dates of the righteous, the public commemorations of sorrow enacted in ancient times on Tisha b'Av and in modern times on Holocaust Remembrance Day, and all the many miniature ways the dead are incorporated into the patterns of life. There is a sense within Judaism that the dead depend on the living. Our actions somehow help them navigate the mysterious realms beyond this world. It is customary on the yahrzeit of a loved one to learn a little Torah or to bless a meal and then to add, "The neshama should have an aliyah." "The soul should ascend." *Through the merit of these good deeds I have done down here on earth, the soul of this person should be elevated through the heavenly spheres.* Beyond the religious realm, there has long been a strong cultural tradition among the Jewish people to push the act of remembrance from thought into action, be it charitable, artistic, or political. The bond of life is a vital and eternal connection between the dead and the living. It exists through our memory of them.

The attack at the Tree of Life synagogue on October 27, 2018, created more death than any Jewish community in America has ever faced at one time. Eleven people from three congregations were murdered. Eleven funerals were held. At each of those funerals, the prayer was recited: *May the soul be bound in the bond of life.* What do those words demand of us, the living? And more specifically, what do those words demand for the millions of people who stand beyond the immediate blast of the attack?

The attack sent two shock waves through the world. The first was the private pain felt by those who knew the victims personally. The second struck everybody else. It was felt all over the world, and it brought people from all over the world here to Pittsburgh, to mourn and to bear witness. Eventually they departed, leaving the city to reckon with the aftermath. The writers who contributed to this book have all taken part in that reckoning in different ways. Some have been involved through their work as journalists, historians, teachers, archivists, activists, and rabbis, or through their personal connections to the people and institutions attacked that morning. Some were involved emotionally, through the perspectives gained by reckoning with personal tragedies. With the notable exception of Rabbi Jonathan Perlman, who leads New Light Congregation and lost three of his congregants that morning, all of the authors occupy middle ripples in the "concentric circles" of grief. None of the other writers were inside the synagogue that awful Saturday morning, and none of them lost an immediate loved one in the attack (although many of them knew at least one of the victims, as is inevitable in a city like Pittsburgh, with its many interwoven communities). And yet, as locals, they feel they have a closer connection to the attack than someone who watched it from another place.

Perhaps that feeling of closeness is an illusion. Perhaps living near a tragedy is really no different from living far from one. Soon after the attack, "Pittsburgh" became convenient shorthand for a range of interrelated topics: the growth of violent antisemitism and other racially and religiously motivated attacks, the call to strengthen coalitions of targeted groups, the rise in gun violence and the ways of preventing it, and the need to improve security at Jewish institutions, among others. The power of that shorthand increased with subsequent antisemitic attacks in Poway, Halle, Jersey City, and Monsey, and with attacks motivated by similar hatreds in Christchurch, El Paso, and many other places. (These attacks are now so frequent that this list will likely be outdated by the time it appears in print.) With each of these attacks, Pittsburgh becomes increasingly fixed as an archetype, so that today, a great American city, a city with 182 years of continuous Jewish settlement and all the resulting variety of life experiences implied by those years, has been reduced in the minds of many to a single terrible event. A city has become a way of having a conversation. It is a necessary conversation, and the writers in this book have been participating in that conversation, too. But they have also been having a different conversation, one that is only happening here, one that can only happen here.

A horrifying act cannot easily be reduced to a symbol when it occurs in your neighborhood. To casually pass the site of a massacre on your way to the grocery store—or to consciously avoid it—is a profound and confusing experience. The big questions of human existence lurk within all of us, covered by our daily routines. A place of great destruction has a way of bringing those questions into the open, like salt drawing blood from raw flesh. As the story of Pittsburgh is increasingly told from afar, the editors wanted to create an opportunity for a diverse group of local writers to grapple with these questions in an intimate way. We selected writers who were entangled in the aftermath through their professional or personal obligations. We sought a variety of perspectives within the local Jewish world, and also just beyond it. We are pleased with the results, and yet at the same time we regret the inevitable limits of such a project. So many perspectives are worthy of public consideration. We could compile dozens of volumes like this one. We hope this book will inspire others to share their experiences.

All honest writing is grounded in authority. Any writer can write about any subject, so long as they truthfully define their relationship to it. The contributors to this anthology had to find the authority to write about an attack that most of them did not experience directly. Again and again, closeness is where they find that authority. They describe their visits to the Tree of Life synagogue over the years and their involvement with the three congregations housed within it that morning—Tree of Life Congregation, New Light Congregation, and Congregation Dor Hadash. They describe their prior interactions with the victims at street corners and grocery stores and book clubs and synagogue events throughout Squirrel Hill and the greater Pittsburgh area. They note their physical proximity to the attack. They measure the miles and the blocks, sometimes even the feet, between their homes and the crime scene. They explain how their familiarity with personal tragedy gave them insight into the pain caused by unexpected violence. They describe how their professional or communal obligations have given them intimate access to the unfolding aftermath. Over and over, closeness makes it personal. To read all these essays together shows how a single tragedy can rip through a community, the stunning volume and variety of pain it causes throughout the local population. This is the other conversation, the quiet conversation. And it is being had all over the world, in every community beset by such violence.

Closeness changes how you see an event. It focuses the eye on specifics, away from the big picture. Things are what they are, not what they represent. Closeness also opens the heart. Compassion has a way of expanding to fit its surroundings. That is why public tragedies are different from private ones. They create a class of indirect victims, neighbors who are blown over by the shock waves of a blast they never felt. We are living in an era of public tragedies, where local events become international concerns. Each one inflames debate about causes and about methods of prevention. These debates are important, but they are incomplete. Without a corresponding close view, these debates will inevitably erase the actual victims. They will turn every tragedy into an item on a list.

The bond of life is that close view. It is a commitment to carry actual people and specific experiences in our hearts and in our minds as we move through our lives. We are bound by that commitment. It is an essential responsibility and privilege of being alive.

PART I

HERE

IS

SQUIRREL

HILL

HERE IS
SQUIRREL HILL

Molly Pascal

It is a battered tree, long suffering and much climbed,
held together by strands of wire but beloved of those
who know it. In a way it symbolizes the city: life under
difficulties, growth against odds, sap-rise in the midst
of concrete, and the steady reaching for the sun.

—EB White, *Here Is New York*, 1949

SEPTEMBER 2018

Cecil Rosenthal, giant and smiling, looms in the door in his usual
place as usher and greeter to all who enter, his gentle presence so
constant from year to year that I think of him as a physical element
of the building, a Doric column of a man. I scan the seats, looking
for family and friends. On Kol Nidre, every Jew comes to shul. On
Kol Nidre, we come in droves. Except not anymore. On what should
be the busiest night of the year, the sanctuary looks largely empty. As
I stand at the entrance, I stare and wonder if I've gotten something
wrong. Once upon a time I would not have had a choice of where to sit.
I would have carefully guarded my ticket or searched for a space among
the six hundred to squeeze in. But times have changed. Conservative
Judaism has been on a downswing, with congregations everywhere
losing and fighting for members.

I join my brother Sam and his wife, Andy, in a pew near the front
of the main sanctuary. Audrey, our Lilliputian and Ruth Bader Gins-
burg–lookalike cantor this evening, barely clears the podium. This is
her annual gig, singing the opening vows. She pauses briefly, allowing
us to cough and shuffle, before raising her voice for the crescendo of
the third repetition.

I hear the voices rise around me, chanting the *al chet*, the communal recitation of transgression. *And for the sin which we have committed before You in passing judgment.* As I ask to be sealed in the Book of Life for the next year, I'm not feeling very pious. Instead, I'm thinking that I don't really know this fairly new rabbi up there gracing the bima. I'm thinking about how long it will be before I can sit down and that I'm not even an hour into the fast and I'm thirsty. I'm thinking that modern American sanctuaries are all rather ugly. They bear the architectural hallmarks of postwar modern design: lots of concrete, industrial carpet, and clean lines. The growing darkness of dusk paints the windows, obscuring the gem-colored stained glass. Most of all, I'm questioning why I am here.

For those who are not from here, it is first necessary to explain what *here* is. There are roughly three Pittsburghs. There is the Pittsburgh of the indigenous, the person who was born here and remains here; in that category too are boomerangs, the ones who left for various reasons and intervals, then returned to stay. Second, there is the Pittsburgh of those who moved here, and who, no matter how long their tenure, will always find that demerit part and parcel of their status. Third, there is the Pittsburgh of the diaspora, those who claim a spiritual residence in lieu of a current address.

Pittsburgh is not so much a city as an amalgamation of neighborhoods, formed by immigration and migration: Italian Morningside and Bloomfield, Black Hill District and Homestead, Irish North Side, and so on. While time has softened those definitions and borders, there remain impervious pockets. About four miles east of Downtown live the vast majority of the area's Jews.

Here is Squirrel Hill, an urban shtetl so natural and commonplace that I never knew it was a shtetl. It is pickles and babka and rye. It is statuesque oaks, maples, and London planes clipped in compromise for the electric wires. It is kosher pizza and donuts. It is busy at 7:00 a.m. with morning minyan traffic. It is thirteen congregations of four denominations in two square miles. (Walk another mile and you get another two.) The outdoor *chanukkiyah* is permanent, not one seasonally affixed to a Hasid's car. It is a public clock rendered in

Hebrew; little hand on aleph marks the hour, steeple-high over the Jewish Community Center.

At the age of six I ventured upstreet alone for the first time, following a two-block urban trail from my parent's home on Marlborough Road to Carnegie Library and the candy store. The shortcut required a shimmy past dilapidated garages, then a trespass along the deteriorating condos where Forbes Terrace used to be. The condos have been renovated, the garages torn down.

Now, at forty-six, I walk the same old route. Progress slows at the hiss of a 61C. I slip around the knot of Oakland-bound international students, then I'm forced to stop. I wait, like I've always waited, at a sacrosanct square, the four-way walk and compass points of all who call this home: the intersection of Murray and Forbes. A flash of white, a high-pitched beep, then we all go at once. Right, left, diagonally. One driver has violated the double line, but a pedestrian pushes him back with a punishing scowl. On I go, passing stores (coffee, bikes, candy, books, bagels, banks, bars, ice cream) and restaurants (Lebanese, Taiwanese, Japanese, Thai, Indian, Greek, Turkish, Mexican, pizza, pizza, pizza). I see geriatrics inching toward the Imperial House; lines and pancake gridlock at Pamela's; flocks of yeshiva girls in long navy skirts; strollers battling for sidewalk space; hipsters seeking vintage clothes or vinyl LPs; modern Orthodox boys shooting hoops, trailing tzitzit like spaghetti; cognoscenti at the Manor Theater; revelry on Simchat Torah, parades on Yom Ha'atzmaut and silence on Yom Kippur.

It is our way to describe places by what came before. *That is where Isaly's used to be. By the old Poli's. Where the old Foodland was.* Perhaps even more remarkably, everyone understands. *Used to be* is our geography. It is the semantics of belonging, the archeology of sedentary generations, and the rhetoric of an insular people. For newcomers, the young, and progressives, this attitude can be frustrating and off-putting. But it also speaks to a community who, though slow to pledge, are loyal once they do; who are not so much resistant as cautious with the heart.

In Squirrel Hill, you are always someone's granddaughter or grandson, son or daughter, mother or father, cousin, coworker, doctor, neighbor, or friend. My pediatrician's son became my nephew's pediatrician. We gave birth to our children at Magee; we buried our grandparents, then our parents, at Schugar's. My daughter will go to school where I went to school, where my mother went to school. My childhood friend is the school nurse; my second-grade class photo hangs on the wall in her office. When we meet someone new, we interrogate. *Do you know so-and-so? How about so-and-so? No? Well, you should!* We welcome the stranger, but hasten to dispose of that title.

If New York bestows the gift of loneliness, Squirrel Hill wards against it. Intrusion and concern are its gifts. To live here requires participation, whether you like it or not. New Yorkers are created every day. We require a lifetime.

For those of us who have always lived in Squirrel Hill, your shul is more of an inheritance than a choice. Growing up, Sam and I spent our Saturdays at the "other" Conservative synagogue. My father never advanced beyond that *ish* subset of three-times-a-year Jews, but cancer largely stopped my parents' participation. When Sam married Andy, a Tree of Life girl, we all followed. The rows of Goodmans, Ryaves, and Zimmermans expanded to include Schachners and Pascals, then another generation of each. Over the years, however, I found conventional prayer unsatisfying and yearned for alternative ways of being Jewish. Eventually my husband, Matt, and I enrolled our children in a Jewish day school, a community that increasingly fulfilled both their (and my) secular and religious needs. Sam, however, continued to find comfort in tradition. As the years passed, he attended shul more and more, I less and less. I even flirted with the idea of quitting.

Then, one day, Sam called to tell me that he was going to be president of Tree of Life. "Why?" I asked.

"They asked me if I would. There's no one else."

"But *why?*"

"My wife had her bat mitzvah at Tree of Life. I was married at Tree of Life," Sam said. "I hope my sons could have their bar mitzvahs at Tree of Life."

"You're crazy," I replied. "You can't save Conservative Judaism."

"I'm stubborn," he said. A childhood of irritation offered me a surplus of evidence on that front. "I know some things need to change," he said. "I'm going to try."

"How long is the term?"

"Two years."

I contemplated this. To be stubborn about change is an act of hope. Perhaps I needed to try too. "All right," I said. "I'll give it two more years."

The Squirrel Hill grapevine works quickly. Again and again, friends and acquaintances from the community stopped me to share their opinion about Sam's new role.

"Tell Sam that we're all sorry."

"Should we offer him congratulations or condolences?"

"Uh, Mazel Tov?" It was a good thing Sam had never cared about power or recognition, since he'd taken on a job and position nobody wanted.

The questions about why I am here—at Kol Nidre, at Tree of Life— leave my mind as Rabbi Myers motions for the crowd to sit. Sam heads to the microphone and speaks, pleading with members to tell him how he can help them. As he promises not to ask for the money the congregation so desperately needs to survive, my attention involuntarily returns to the ceiling. It is brown with water damage, pocked with missing panels, and flaking drywall like sunburned skin. Buckets are set out to catch dripping rainwater. My head pings with Sam's words from an earlier, private conversation: "One of the first things we need to do is replace the roof."

OCTOBER 2018

After Simchat Torah I often retreat, not showing up to shul again until Purim. But with my nephew Max's upcoming bar mitzvah, I'm thinking more about my own faith, prayer, and, generally what being Jewish means. Seeking answers, I decide to read from the Torah for the first time. I spend weeks studying *trope* (musical notation for chanting) and practicing. I even pop in to Shabbat services again. My husband, meanwhile, heads to neighboring Frick Park with Sam and Max to plan a course for a *tikkun olam* project, a fundraising race. Everyone has busy and conflicting schedules, but in early October we finally nail down the date: Sunday, October 28. To encourage the Hebrew school classes to attend the race, Tree of Life decides in mid-October to cancel the monthly youth service on Saturday, October 27.

Sam and Max attend services every week, so we plan to meet them afterward to set up the course for the following day. We are eating breakfast when Facebook lights up with an alert. Six words that crack my life into Before and After.

Active shooter at Tree of Life.

I read the words again because they don't make sense. This doesn't happen *here*.

We leave our doors open. We leave cars unlocked. We housed *Mr. Rogers*.

This doesn't happen in *Squirrel Hill*.

I dial Sam's number. *Please answer the phone.* It rings. And rings. Matt switches on CNN. I begin to shake. I redial.

I call and call. *Please answer the phone.* The reporter claims that the shooter is still inside the building. Our leafy trees and quiet streets flash on national TV. This is an agony I have never understood before, an agony I associate with long-past wars, of knowing that there will be a list of dead, and being forced to wait to hear if the ones you love are on it. Helicopters tenaciously chew the air. The footage repeats: SWAT teams, the giant black letters spelling out the congregational name on the facade, and overhead images of the building. I feel like my mother, who, even in the midst of disaster, would apologize, embarrassed, if she had to invite an unexpected visitor into an untidy house. My world is collapsing, but *the roof.* Everyone is looking at the crumbling Tree of Life roof.

Sam finally answers. I can hear him breathing hard. He is running. "We're safe. We were a few minutes late. We were still outside. But we have to get out of here."

"Who's inside?" I ask. My head reels with names. It's a regular week, and early. It couldn't be that many, could it? Sam doesn't answer. Instead, he says, "Tell families to go to the JCC. The meeting point is the JCC." He hangs up.

Every so often the number of dead reported on TV rises. As the scene unfolds, I feel the distance growing between watching and experiencing. Unlike with previous mass shootings, I cannot power off the

TV and walk away. I'm struck, too, by my own familiarity with what will follow. Media has steeped us in the pattern. Sandy Hook, Parkland, Las Vegas. There will be hugging, ululation, an outpouring of thoughts and prayers, then candlelit vigils. But there the script as I know it ends. After the vigil, what happens? We do not get to wake up tomorrow and go to work. We will wake up and go to funerals. From Tuesday through Friday: eleven funerals in four days.

In the course of the night, Sam calls periodically from the JCC, where they've set up an emergency center. I learn things I do not want to know. I will learn why the families will not be allowed to identify bodies in person, but with photographs. I will learn that bullets from assault rifles do not simply enter and exit a body. They are not meant to. They are meant to shatter. I will learn the question that matters most—"Did they feel pain?"—and the relief when the answer is no.

A few high school students put out the word to meet that evening at Forbes and Murray. Thousands go. In the shtetl, we are one family. Tree of Life is Squirrel Hill; Squirrel Hill is Tree of Life. The three congregations that worshiped in the building—Tree of Life, Dor Hadash, and New Light—consisted of hundreds of families from our community. Everyone either has lost someone or knows someone who lost someone. Andy and I put our arms around each other, turning our heads away from the cameras, and sob.

The names are released. My memory singes with that photo hanging in the Colfax Elementary School office, the one with my old friend Howard Fienberg grinning, whose mother Joyce has now been murdered. Why did my family get to live, and not his?

On Sunday, Tree of Life members are directed to the front left at Soldiers and Sailors Memorial Hall. I sit with my brother and his family. To our right and front, the rows fill with the blue and black suit uniform of politicians. To our left, members of clergy. On the far right, the other side of the auditorium, sit members of Dor Hadash and New Light. I wonder if they feel like us, like animals in the zoo. I sense the city's sorrow, but also a perverse adrenaline. The media stares at us.

We listen to words of sorrow, proclamations of support, and panegyrics to unity, but my gratitude is flavored with resentment at this forced public mourning. We peer out from behind bars of trauma and loss. The public leaves, but the animals never can.

We rise and recite Kaddish, the prayer of mourning. Not for the first time, I ponder the words. The Aramaic contains not a word of comfort. It does not even mention death. Instead, the mourner proclaims God's greatness, a final salute of faith at the hour of least faith. Why? Perhaps no prayer could meet expectations for such a moment. Perhaps Kaddish is just the Jewish way of saying that there are no words for pain.

On Monday as I drive the kids to school, they pepper me with questions I've been unable to answer for two days now. *Why do people hate us? Why aren't there laws about guns? Should we pretend we aren't Jewish? Are we safe?*

For a moment I can't speak. I think about the increasingly common instances of mass school shootings and the impossibility of any parent promising that such a thing won't happen, but I know that isn't what my kids are asking. They go to a Jewish day school, a few blocks from what is now the site of the worst antisemitic massacre in US history. Their uncle and cousin ran for their lives. The people they sat next to in shul are dead.

Are we safe?

Yes? Statistically, yes. Rationally, yes. All the doors of the school remain locked. Cameras remain in place. Visitors must show ID. Armed guards vigilantly monitor the desk and grounds. The police and FBI will sweep the area.

No. I can't promise them they will be safe. They are only the latest victims in a steady patter of attacks on Blacks, immigrants, Muslims—anyone *other.* The terrorist ended up at Tree of Life, but he could have attacked anywhere in Squirrel Hill. He wanted to kill Jews, and Jews live in Squirrel Hill. We were all his target. I thought we lived in a shtetl, but it turns out that, all along, it was the ghetto.

I park the car. We walk past the school's Holocaust memorial, a glass Star of David with walls made of transparent bricks containing six million soda can tabs collected by students over the years. We walk past the police. We walk past the armed guard. We walk past the flags, one American and one Israeli, both at half-mast.

"You are well protected," I say. We hold hands as we walk up the path. I hug them. I leave them there.

The Fienberg shiva is at Joyce's apartment. I hug Howard and shake my head, because I don't know what to say to him. We sit and eat and chat about camp and soup dumplings, surrounded by Joyce's belongings. People come and go: neighbors, friends, congregants, a river of community flowing through the room, and on to the next shiva, and the next, and the next.

NOVEMBER 2018

The Tree of Life congregation gathers Friday night—members only— to welcome Shabbat in Levy Hall, which we've borrowed from Rodef Shalom, a nearby synagogue. The door opens and, though the public has not been invited, a Muslim family enters: three men and two women wearing hijabs. They fill the row behind us. We are a congregation in mourning, so we all stand for Kaddish. They stand with us. When the service is over, we turn to say hello, to say thank you. "Shalom," they say. "Salaam," we say.

DECEMBER 2018

I attend my nephew Max's bar mitzvah with a cracked heart. We stand again in Levy Hall, not Tree of Life, surrounded by family, but also survivors, and families of victims. Max commands the service in a suit and a white-and-blue striped silk tallit draped over his shoulders. Rabbi Myers calls out my name, inviting me to the bima. *Yisraela bat Yossel veh Miriam*. Yisraela, after my grandfather Israel, daughter of Yossel and Miriam, daughter of Stephen and Marcia Schachner.

I stand in front of the Torah between the rabbi, a survivor, and the gabbai, Stephen Weiss, a survivor, and gaze out at my community. Suddenly, for a moment, I understand prayer, I understand why I am here. As I look at my mother and daughter, at the generations in the pews, I cease to be just Molly. I am daughter of Marcia, daughter of Betty, daughter of Lena. We are part of tree, whose roots can be traced back generation after generation, across the Atlantic, to Eastern Europe, Romania and Poland, to Treblinka, to Italy, and on, all the way to the tribes of Israel. The biblical tradition of jettisoned surnames lives on in every Jewish neighborhood, in every synagogue, whether two thousand years ago or yesterday. We are daughters of daughters; we are sons of sons. The rabbi calls the honored forward for each aliyah. He calls Andrea Wedner, survivor, daughter of Rose Mallinger. *Chaya bat Razel.* He calls Howard and Marnie Fienberg. *Chananya ben Yisroel Utsheh v' Yedit Baltcha.* Rose is gone. Joyce is gone. But they are not. As their names echo across the hall, they are with us, now, and always.

I pull out my cheat sheet, a copy of my reading that indicates the vowels that are not printed in the Torah itself. As the rabbi hands me the *yad*, he filches my notes and stuffs them in his pocket. "You've got this," he whispers. Afterward, at the kiddush lunch, he pours shots. "L'chaim," he says, raising the glass. "L'chaim," we reply, raising ours. *To life!* We shout the words, for they are not only a hope; they are a scream, a scar, a blessing, and a command. We drink three more.

DECEMBER 2018

In some ways life feels normal, ordinary. I work, take the kids to school, grocery shop. I don't speak about the bouts of loneliness. The blips of being irritable. The sudden, random anger. I'm not even sure who I feel anger toward. I'm reminded of how trauma is largely invisible. Few can see how it eats at our fortitude, like moths in a sweater trunk, creating small, secret holes.

On the bad days I turn to my new friends, fellow members of communities affected by mass violence who have journeyed to Pittsburgh to visit us, offering support and resources. A woman from Columbine invites me to an online support group, where I find thousands like me. *People are telling me to move on,* I tell them. *There's no moving on, only moving forward,* they reply. *So few understand,* I tell them. *We don't want more in this club,* they reply. *We don't want them to understand. But we do, and we are here for you.*

JANUARY–APRIL 2019

On three occasions we return to the building for Sorting Day. This means that someone gathers everything throughout the building— photographs, papers, artifacts, dishware, religious objects—and piles it all on tables in the ballroom. The sorting is my first time back in the building and, for a moment, I stand there and shiver with the pain of it. Panels stretch across the stairs, closing off access to the rest of the building. I look around at the holes, the plywood patched doors, and the still-shattered tempered glass of interior office walls. The foyer holds stacks of pictures with broken frames and broken glass.

Eric Lidji, the Director of the Rauh Jewish Archives, instructs us on how to search the boxes and decide what to keep, for either tax reasons or historical significance. We work quietly, occasionally reading out interesting items here and there. I focus, head down paging through files, carefully ignoring the damage around me. Miscellaneous letters. Bills. *Shred.* A list of items for Passover. $345 in horseradish. *Shred.*

SEPTEMBER–OCTOBER 2019

Rosh Hashanah brings with it the difficult knowledge that a year has passed. The synagogue remains closed, so Calvary Episcopal Church generously offers to host us for the High Holiday services. They hang a black veil over the central crucifix. They cart in the ark and piles of siddurim. The FBI has searched the building multiple times. Police guard the entrances. A security company searches purses and bags.

First on Rosh Hashanah, then on Yom Kippur, I spend services at the door, greeting everyone who arrives and—in stark contrast to the year before—checking tickets. These are needed once again, not because membership has skyrocketed but because we must identify every person who enters the building for security. I indicate where to find prayer books, where to go and where to sit. For as long as I've been at Tree of Life, this job belonged to Cecil Rosenthal and his brother David. Every person who passed through Tree of Life's doors felt their kindness. It is up to us now to emulate them, and by doing so, honor them.

On Kol Nidre, just like the year before, Audrey, a survivor, stands on the bima. Tiny, clad in white, dark ponytail. Once again, our voices rise together in the al chet. *For the sin which we have committed before You by causeless hatred.* Above me the Calvary ceiling soars, the consummate antonym to the one over me the Kol Nidre before. It rises three stories high, majestic with stone arches and flying buttresses. It is beautiful, unravaged, pristine. There are no buckets to catch leaks. It is whole. Its wholeness reminds me of all we have lost.

The one-year commemoration of the attack looms only a couple of weeks away. I both dread it and welcome it, wanting the public show over. Then we will go back to the hard part. The living with it. And yet one does not really learn to live with holes. One coexists with them. For some things there's no learning, only eternal surviving. The survivors pick splinters out of their skin for the rest of their lives.

This is the dilemma: we do not want to ever forget, and yet to heal is to forget a *little*. What a fine balance we seek of honoring memory and not being devoured by it. We go on, we are changed. What will we do with that change? What will be the point of our victimhood unless it propels us to act in such ways, and fight for such laws, as to prevent it from happening to someone else?

I look around, as I did the year before, thirsty and pensive. Do I know any better why I am here? Do I even believe in God? What good has been furtive whispering of the Shema? How has prestidigitation hard-won by application of the thin leather snake of tefillin protected Jews from the kilns or the terrorist's gun? I remind myself that Jewish prayer has never been a method to grant wishes. It is not heaven we seek, but humanity. It is a plea and a request—not to ask more from God, but to ask more from ourselves. What will be my contribution? What will I do to support my community? How will I continue to advocate for gun control? What will I do to fight against racism, xenophobia, or Islamophobia? How will I reach out to my neighbors, as they have reached out to me this past year?

The Kol Nidre service concludes and we quietly exit, murmuring, "G'mar Chatimah Tovah." Those words we utter every year weigh far heavier this day. *May you be sealed in the Book of Life.*

On the way home, I pass Tree of Life. As I look at the still-shuttered building, I wonder: Should we rebuild? How do we rebuild? Who will rebuild? I think of the leveled land where the temple in Jerusalem once stood and it reminds me—Jews are not a congregation, nor a building, not even a land. We might want all of those things, but the lack of them does not change our vow or bond. Our greatest power is not the physical Tree, but the metaphorical one. Jews are a family, and anywhere, together, is home. The attack at Tree of Life awakened us in Squirrel Hill, I hope, not to fear but to the responsibility we have to each other.

CLOSED BECAUSE
OF YESTERDAY

Andrew Goldstein

GROWING UP IN SQUIRREL HILL, Jewish life can be indiscernible from life as a typical Pittsburgher. We did not have to be one way or the other; you could be a Jew and a Pittsburgher at the same time. We belonged in this place. Squirrel Hill's Jews, like its other diverse residents, shop at Giant Eagle, have breakfast at Eat'n Park, and don the Steelers' black and gold on game days. Squirrel Hill, I thought, was just one of Pittsburgh's distinct neighborhoods—it just happened to be where the majority of the city's Jews lived. That didn't mean it wasn't special—we celebrated being the center of the region's Jewish community, but we also took pride in being Mr. Rogers's real-life neighborhood, in the business district along Forbes and Murray Avenues that rivaled any other in the city, and in having Pittsburgh's largest inner-city park.

Jewish life, it seemed, was natural to the neighborhood. Massive synagogues like Beth Shalom and Poale Zedeck fit into the landscape as though they were part of the hills they were built on. Jewish stores like Murray Avenue Kosher, Milky Way, and Pinsker's provided offerings not available anywhere else in the city. High up on the Jewish Community Center, at the corner of Forbes and Murray, a massive clock with Hebrew letters rises above the street. During Hanukkah dozens of vehicles are adorned with menorahs for a holiday parade.

Living most of the twenty-six years of my life in this environment made the atrocity on October 27, 2018, at Tree of Life–Or L'Simcha Synagogue all the more painful. The world will never be able to replace the innocent Jewish lives lost to hatred that morning. Still, there was more taken from us that day than the lives of the eleven martyrs. The massacre was first and foremost an attack on Jews, an offense against the very fiber of who we are and the idea that we belong. But it was also an assault on our beloved neighborhood and the city where we had sanctuary for generations. Like the glass that was broken at the entrance of the synagogue, the belief that Squirrel Hill and Pittsburgh could be immune to such evil was shattered.

My father's side of the family moved from the Hill District to Squirrel Hill in the early 1960s. I was six years old when my parents, brother, and I moved there from Highland Park, where my mother was from. I was raised on Aiello's pizza, and I played at Blue Slide Park. I attended Taylor Allderdice High School, where I first became interested in journalism while working on the student newspaper, the *Foreword*. I went to Point Park University in downtown Pittsburgh, earned a degree in journalism and mass communications, and spent two summers as an intern at the *Pittsburgh Jewish Chronicle*. In 2014 I landed a job as a reporter for the *Pittsburgh Post-Gazette*.

On the day of the shooting I woke up to a phone call from former *Post-Gazette* entertainment editor L.A. Johnson, who was on duty that morning and had heard a report about an active shooter at Tree of Life come over the police scanner. I dressed as quickly as possible, ran out of my house on Forward Avenue, and drove as fast as I could to the synagogue. But my brain was moving faster. I kept thinking one thing: *What am I going to find when I arrive?* I had been a reporter long enough to know that not everything said over the police scanner turns out to be accurate.

Still, this felt different. I kept thinking about my aunt Ellen and uncle Paul Sikov, and their sons, Zachary and Tyler, who belonged to Tree of Life–Or L'Simcha Congregation. I also had friends who attended Tree of Life, and Dor Hadash, one of the other congregations that held services in the building. While I sped along the short distance from my house to the synagogue, something changed inside me. I thought about my relatives and friends who might be in the building.

It took me months to find the right word to describe what I felt in the earliest moments of the massacre, but I eventually determined that it was *violation*. I felt personally violated, and I felt that my family, as well as my community, had been violated. The attack on Tree of Life was an invasion by callous, conscious evil into a place of warmth and goodness—a place I knew.

After discovering that my friends and family were safe, the reality and horror of the situation began to set in. Here, in Squirrel Hill, the terror that so many communities in the United States and across the world had experienced was now our experience, too. Coming to understand that the deadliest attack on Jews in the history of the United States had happened in this friendly, welcoming neighborhood was not something that I ever imagined having to do. And now not only was that experience real but I was in a position that would require me to explain and contextualize what had happened immediately as well as for generations to come: there is an old expression that says journalism is "the first draft of history," and I suspected that historians, students, and other interested people would be reading our coverage of the massacre decades later.

As I stood with a group of reporters and photographers outside the synagogue, I watched SWAT officers with long guns running toward the building where I had attended the bar mitzvah ceremonies of friends and relatives, Purim gatherings, and weddings. I had been to countless crime scenes in my work for the *Post-Gazette*. Each is dreadful in its own way, but they're especially excruciating when the friends or loved ones of victims are around. I have always tried to show sympathy and understanding to those who have lost people they cared about, but this was the first time I understood what it was like to be one of them. At the time, I still didn't know if anyone had been killed or injured, but even so, this was an attack against the Jews of Squirrel Hill—my people, my neighborhood.

In the days and weeks that followed, Pittsburgh embraced the city's Jewish community like never before. Messages of support and shows of solidarity came from nearly all walks of life: Asian Americans and African Americans, Muslims and Christians, musicians, politicians and athletes, and many more. The attack, and Pittsburgh's response to it, made me even more proud to be a resident of the city. And I am particularly proud to be from Squirrel Hill. Before the massacre, when people asked me where I lived, I would sometimes say the "East End." It was an answer I could give that would not immediately lead to me being identified as a Jew. People have asked me if I am Jewish on several instances while I was working. Even without saying where I was from, my last name was often a giveaway. I was not ashamed of being Jewish, but I grew to understand that sometimes saying less could save me some trouble. I never experienced hostility, but people would sometimes look at me with suspicion. I am not concerned about that kind of thing anymore, and I am proud to tell people that I'm from Squirrel Hill.

My sense of violation, I believe, came from the emotional toll of the attack. I have never gone through anything that caused me to experience the same range of emotions. There was the initial panic, shock, and horror. Then came the sadness, despair, and anger. Pittsburgh is, and always has been, a tough community. People around the globe still think of this city as blue-collar even decades after most of the steel mills closed and the jobs left town, and we take pride in that identification. Pittsburgh has also had to cope with its share of sadness from violence. Not even three years before the synagogue massacre, there was a mass shooting in nearby Wilkinsburg in which five people and an unborn child were killed. In 2009, a conspiratorial white supremacist shot and killed three Pittsburgh police officers in the Stanton Heights neighborhood. There have been a number of racially motivated acts of violence over the past few decades in and around Pittsburgh.

The summer before the shooting at Tree of Life, Pittsburgh experienced wave after wave of terrible incidents. Because of my job, I was keenly aware of all of them. Racial tensions were at a breaking point in June when Antwon Rose, an unarmed Black teenager, was fatally shot by white East Pittsburgh police officer Michael Rosfeld. In August 2018 the Pennsylvania attorney general's office released a grand jury report detailing the appalling abuse of minors by priests and other officials in several Catholic dioceses in the state, including Pittsburgh. Budding rap star Jimmy Wopo was shot and killed in the Hill District. Mac Miller, the world-famous rapper and Allderdice alum, died of a drug overdose in Los Angeles, and I covered his vigil at Blue Slide

Park. I graduated from high school with Miller in 2010, and although I wasn't particularly close with him we shared many mutual friends, and his death shocked me as it did many others.

I was involved in the *Post-Gazette*'s coverage of many of these stories; each was frightening and depressing, but covering them was my job. Covering the synagogue massacre was different. I have always tried to open myself to those whom I write about, to walk in their shoes, as the old saying goes. But when I answered my phone that morning, and as I drove to the synagogue, my own shoes were sufficient. I never expected to be speeding to a crime scene to find out if my friends and relatives were alive. Speaking to relatives who have lost loved ones, terrified witnesses, or even criminals whose unfortunate circumstances in life led them down the wrong path, takes an emotional toll. I'm a reporter, and that means trying to keep my distance. Of course, reporters are human, and we have become proficient at sticking to the facts despite how we might feel. We cannot afford to become emotionally involved in a story—that can lead to bias, which can compromise the reporting. Sometimes, though, emotions can still overwhelm.

Although I did not directly experience the shooting, and while my family and friends were safe, the massacre was emotionally jarring. I knew some of the victims. I knew the synagogue. I knew the neighborhood and the community and the city. And because of that sense of belonging, I felt as though I were under attack. I was horrified and distraught. How was I supposed to write about this without fear or favor? I stayed outside the synagogue for a few hours that morning, conducting interviews and getting updates from the police department. After I returned home to prepare for what was going to be a long day, I received a call from David Shribman, then the executive editor of the *Post-Gazette*, who lived on Murray Hill Avenue, just a couple of blocks from Tree of Life. He asked me if I was okay; I lied and said I was. He said that this was going to be difficult, but the community was going to rely on us, and we had a responsibility to do our best work. He was right.

I am often in awe of my colleagues at the *Post-Gazette*, but I was never more appreciative of them than I was that morning. Photo editor Jim Mendenhall called me to ask if I was all right. I was relieved to see Kris Mamula, a business reporter, as well as photographers Pam Panchak and Alexandra Wimley. Even Sean Gentille, a sportswriter for the *Post-Gazette* at the time, came to the scene with a notebook and asked me if there was anything he could do. Having some familiar faces there that morning comforted me and made me realize I wasn't alone as I spoke with neighbors and concerned citizens who arrived at the scene. There was Chuck Diamond, the former Tree of Life–Or L'Simcha rabbi, who speculated that the attack was based in antisemitism. There was Jeff Finkelstein, the CEO of the Jewish Federation of Greater Pittsburgh, who spoke calmly but whose face gave away his worry. I talked to a man who was hysterical because he thought he had family members inside the synagogue, and who directed some of his anger at the media. It was upsetting, but it was not the first time someone had become upset at journalists asking questions and photographing a crime scene. I told him that we were all trying to figure out what was happening, we were all going to get through this together. I saw him a day or two later and asked him about his family members. He said they were all right.

After the shooting stopped and the bloodshed ended, the shock was just beginning to set in. For most of the day I stayed outside the synagogue, searching for people to talk to and trying to make sense of what had occurred. That evening, as people started to leave and the media frenzy outside calmed, I called the newsroom to ask if there was anything else I could do before the day was over. The editor who answered the phone, Lillian Thomas, who had coordinated much of the *Post-Gazette*'s efforts that day and over the course of the next few weeks, told me that I could go home. As I milled around the synagogue, getting ready to leave, I realized I had nowhere to go. I was in Squirrel Hill. I was already home. What was I going to do, drive five minutes away and wait for the next morning?

Word spread that there was going to be a vigil at the corner of Forbes and Murray Avenues. The Allderdice students who had organized the event felt that people needed somewhere to go that night— and they were right. I decided to go. I stood on the edge of the lawn outside the Sixth Presbyterian Church, overlooking the intersection filled with thousands of mourners feeling the same way. There were short speeches and prayers; many people held signs. I saw colleagues, friends, and family members, including my aunt, uncle, and cousins who belonged to Tree of Life. It was comforting to be there, surrounded by the community, sharing our grief. And yet it was so strange to be in a place so familiar with so many strangers all feeling the same way.

A light rain fell. As I looked out into the crowd I noticed a sign among the umbrellas that read *Love Thy Neighbor*. The sign appeared like a beacon amid the otherwise dreary scene. While I was waiting for the vigil to begin, I overheard the people standing next to me point out landmarks in the surrounding area that were important to them. They were not from Squirrel Hill, but their experiences were similar to my own. They went to the neighborhood's branch of the Carnegie Library of Pittsburgh, as I had. They drank at the Squirrel Hill Café, a dive bar known locally as the "Squirrel Cage," as I had. Although I was from Squirrel Hill and they were not, we shared this neighborhood.

The week that followed was a great challenge to my journalistic professionalism. While I was not working during the vigil on the night of October 27 and was able to become part of the crowd, I had to do my job during many of the emotional gatherings over the next several days after the massacre. Reporting and writing helped to get me through them. Having a goal to accomplish—trying to make sense of it all for our readers and myself—was therapeutic. The difficulty, however, was that while my job required me to be an impartial observer, I also wanted to participate in the commemorations as a member of the Squirrel Hill Jewish community. Even in small moments, emotions become overwhelming. The morning after the shooting, I was in the newsroom when the Allegheny County medical examiner's office released the identities of the victims. I sat with reporter Ashley Murray, and I read and spelled out the names of the eleven deceased victims as she typed them. Already troubled, I became more so as I recognized some of the names on the list.

Later that day, as I walked along Murray Avenue, I saw a sign on the door of Pinsker's that read *Closed Because of Yesterday*.

On Tuesday, October 30, President Donald Trump came to Pittsburgh to pay his respects at the synagogue. I was assigned to cover a rally and march protesting his presence. As the crowd began forming, I spotted a friend I had not seen since high school. His family had belonged to Tree of Life. I tried to talk to him, but he was too upset to speak. I asked him if he knew some of the victims, and he nodded. As the rally began, the leaders began singing "Olam Chesed Yibaneh." The song, which alternates Hebrew and English, is about building a world with love, words from Psalm 89:3. As the group began marching slowly from Beechwood Boulevard to Forbes Avenue and then to Shady Avenue, the song became seared into my mind. I don't know if it was the song or the moment, but reality finally set in. The tears flowed uncontrollably, and I don't think I was alone, even among the media. I tried to call into the newsroom with some information from the rally, but I was unable to get words out of my mouth.

I did not have another experience as intense as that in the rest of that first week after the shooting, but there were other moments that left me breathless. On Thursday, November 1, I was standing next to the desk of my editor, Tom Birdsong, when he pulled up an early rendering of the front page of the Friday edition of the *Post-Gazette*. That was the first time I saw the headline that would be seen worldwide: the mourner's Kaddish, in Hebrew letters across the top of the front page of the newspaper. My jaw dropped when I saw it, and I couldn't wait to see it in print the next day. More than anything, that headline is what people ask me about when I talk about the *Post-Gazette*'s coverage of the massacre. David Shribman was responsible for it, and he wrote a small piece to explain what it meant. He also told readers that when you cannot find the right words to express the enormity of a situation, perhaps you have to think in a different language.

The same day that edition of the paper came out, Friday, came the first Shabbat services after the shooting. I was assigned to the large community service at Rodef Shalom, while my colleague, *Post-Gazette* religion editor Peter Smith, went to the private Tree of Life service held in another chapel in the same building. Our editors decided that we should wrap all of our material into one story. When the service ended, I went back to the newsroom to begin to write my portion. Peter sent his information to me, and I began putting everything together. Part of the way through, I once again became overwhelmed with grief. I walked over to editor Liz Gray, who told me to just breathe, and assured me I would get it done. And so I did.

Over the course of the next year I covered many stories relating to the shooting in one way or another. Some were more hopeful. I wrote about the windscreens covered by student artwork that were placed over the fence surrounding the Tree of Life building, bringing some light back to what had become a dark corner. Others were more stressful. Exactly six months to the day from the massacre, a gunman opened fire at the Chabad of Poway, near San Diego. I happened to be working that day, and out of nowhere the horror rushed back to me as I followed the coverage on the newsroom televisions and on social media. I went to a vigil that night outside Tree of Life, attended by several survivors of the Pittsburgh shooting, including Rabbi Jeffrey Myers. The sadness was palpable. It was dark and raining lightly when the vigil began. Rabbi Myers and Mayor Bill Peduto both spoke briefly, rebuking intolerance and gun violence. The vigil, however, felt absent of any real hope that the madness would stop.

As October 2019 approached, the *Post-Gazette* prepared to mark the one-year commemoration of the shooting. I was assigned several stories that required me to interview many of the people who were closely involved in the massacre, some of whom I had already met or spoken to at various times throughout the year. But there was still so much of the story that hadn't been told. These people had experienced a trauma most people never will, and never should. Yet they were all regular people, with jobs and families, who never brought any attention to themselves until they were thrust into something totally out of their control that made them well known overnight. One of the survivors I interviewed told me about how the media had hounded him for months after the massacre, when he was in no condition or mood to participate. I felt bad because I, in fact, had asked this man to speak with me on multiple occasions in the months prior to him granting an interview at his home. I had been feeling badly for months, wondering if I had gone too far with him and others I tried to interview. Journalists are used to tracking down and seeking interviews with people who are going through hardships, because those people are able to provide a perspective into the harsh realities of the world that few others can. Still, it is easy for reporters to feel guilty after speaking with a vulnerable person and publishing their emotions and thoughts for the world to see. I know I have felt that way. I told the man I was interviewing that I hoped he did not feel like I was a part of the media that had been bothering him. He said no, and it was as though a great weight was lifted off my shoulders.

Despite the unwanted attention, the belief in Judaism and in community that brought these people to the synagogue on October 27, 2018, remains, and their conviction for warning the world about intolerance and remembering the friends they lost struck me as a noble endeavor. Still, it was easy to see the toll it had taken on them. What happened at Tree of Life changed everyone it touched. Some of the people who survived the shooting were left with physical wounds that will affect them for the rest of their lives. Everyone who was there lost friends. People who were in the synagogue and countless people in the extended community suffer from mental health issues related to the shooting. But for me, as well as others, it also created a stronger sense of community and a desire to serve, through volunteering, charity, or simply trying to be a nicer person in daily life.

One of the articles I wrote as we approached the one-year mark since the shooting was about the many opinions on what should be done with the Tree of Life building. People have many different ideas, and the emotions around this subject are strong. What concerns me is that whatever is decided will not make everyone happy. No matter what happens, I hope the outcome does not drive the community apart. Another story was about Dor Hadash and its members' actions for social justice. One of these, a service called "Refugee Shabbat," in partnership with Hebrew Immigrant Aid Society, an immigrant and refugee advocacy group, had likely prompted the racist, antisemitic gunman to seek out the congregation. The members of Dor Hadash wanted to be informed on refugee issues and learn how they might help those in need. The gunman, rabid in his hate, wanted to stop them from doing that work. But he couldn't stop the members of Dor Hadash. Their bravery in the face of evil has been inspirational to me. They did not give in to fear. They are now stronger than ever in their conviction for social justice. The gunman's brutality only brought more attention to the efforts he attempted to destroy. The only thing that should be remembered about the gunman was that he ultimately failed in his mission.

On a Saturday morning in early 2005, I went to the Tree of Life synagogue to attend the bar mitzvah ceremony of Zachary Weiss, a friend from middle school who remains a close friend to this day. One of the topics of his ceremony that stood out to me was *l'dor v'dor*, Hebrew for "from generation to generation." The expression represents the responsibility that Jewish people have to pass our religion and heritage on to future generations. Jewish history is full of beautiful tradition and astounding people worth remembering. But it's also important to take away more difficult lessons from the past. The push to remember the Holocaust remains strong seventy-five years after Auschwitz was liberated. It is necessary to remember the Holocaust, but it is also vital to remember the years of bigotry against the Jewish people of Europe, which created the environment allowing it to occur. I often think about how important it is to remember what happened here in Pittsburgh and the reasons, however senseless, that it happened. Antisemitic bigotry still exists in dark and light places alike. Since the massacre at Tree of Life, the United States has experienced a rash of antisemitic violence. There was, of course, the shooting at Chabad of Poway. There was also a shooting that targeted a kosher store in Jersey City, and a stabbing spree at a rabbi's house outside of New York City on the seventh night of Hanukkah in 2019, not to mention countless assaults and slurs directed at Jewish people—particularly those in the Orthodox community—that have been reported over the past year. Europe may have an even bigger antisemitism problem than the United States. If we do not learn from the past, we might be forced to repeat it. In Squirrel Hill, we now have seen what antisemitism and racial intolerance can do when it is unleashed. Just as the Holocaust survivors once warned my generation, those of us who saw what happened at Tree of Life must tell those who come next.

One of the survivors of the massacre asked me if I thought people would remember what happened at Tree of Life. I still believe what I told him: some people will remember. As a reporter, I will do my best to make sure more people remember. I don't know what opportunities there will be in the future for me to do that, but I will take advantage of the ones I can. That is now my responsibility. That is now my job.

I READ SOMEWHERE THAT PITTSBURGH IS STRONGER THAN HATE

Tony Norman

ALL HATE CRIMES THAT END in a massacre are alike; each hate crime is an unspeakable event in its own way. Readers of Leo Tolstoy will recognize the appropriation of the first line of *Anna Karenina* to make a point: even though mass shootings are initially shocking because they're unexpected, they always feel familiar when they're happening. It's the same numbness that overwhelms us when we see raw footage of a high school under siege by a young gunman who couldn't let go of his adolescent rage, so he returns to the scene of his humiliation with the family gun.

It's a tragically portable feeling of déjà vu. We felt it at a Charleston church in 2015 when nine congregants were murdered after welcoming their killer, a neo-Nazi, to an evening Bible study. It also felt familiar—but different when the death toll reached 58 with 869 injured, 413 of those injuries by gunfire—at the Route 91 Harvest Music Festival in Las Vegas in 2017. And, of course, there are always nightclub shootings, workplace killings, and school massacres of various sizes in between. The only universal constant is the shooter's assumption that he (and it is almost always a he) must have the element of surprise and that none of his victims be in a position to defend themselves.

So this feeling of impotence we experience as we watch the news of the latest massacre unfold is always with us, even as the killings happen in different contexts. Each spasmodic act of violence has its own unique cultural signature that is initially baffling until we impose order on the tragedy once the terror passes.

The shootings at the Tree of Life synagogue in Squirrel Hill on October 27, 2018, are no exception to this pattern. Like everyone in Pittsburgh that day, I obsessively followed the events unfolding a few neighborhoods over from where I live, in Swisshelm Park. I caught glimpses of my *Pittsburgh Post-Gazette* colleagues in wide shots talking to cops and ordinary citizens. The following year, their relentless canvassing of the neighborhood would earn them a Pulitzer Prize for their coverage of the shooting.

As a columnist, my job is to take in events, synthesize what I can and write something that would give us all some perspective about what is happening. I gave it an early stab that afternoon with a Facebook post that was widely shared:

> The shooting this morning at the Tree of Life Synagogue in Squirrel Hill is just another brutal reminder of how thin the line between carnage and civilization really is in a culture awash in high-powered weapons. It doesn't surprise anyone that the gunman, Robert Bowers, was ranting antisemitic conspiracy theories while shooting as many people as he could shoot. It's not even surprising that Bowers was taken alive after being injured in an exchange with officers. These gun-toting cowards are always more interested in "making statements" than dying for whatever cause has compelled them to shoot unarmed people. The content of his social media posts indicate he is yet another QAnon-spouting loser who blames shadowy conspiracies, diversity, Jews, and menacing ghosts for his (and America's) problems. It's too early to speculate about his politics or motives, but it's obvious that his hatred for Jews qualifies what he did as an unambiguous hate crime. Hate crimes seem to be the rage these days, unfortunately. As a society, we're going to have to face the fact that the forces of hatred feel more emboldened today than they ever have. The intersection of easy access to guns and perceived "permission" to be as evil as one wants to be, along with lack of access to mental health resources, has put our entire society in the crosshairs. As horrific as this is, we know in our hearts that

it is only the beginning. These massacres will continue to happen until we resolve (as a society) to take seriously the rantings of the demons among us instead of merely tolerating them until the next tragedy.

As a former Squirrel Hill resident, I recognized each landmark as the local news affiliates incessantly cycled through the same images because police barriers kept them three blocks from the action. I watched the news conferences in which the mayor and the police commissioner tried to explain how an event of such hateful magnitude could happen in Pittsburgh's Squirrel Hill neighborhood, of all places, as if the neighborhood was until that morning uniquely immune to danger.

I understood the sentiment the city's leaders were trying to express. I sympathized with their attempt to highlight what was special about the neighborhood, especially with the whole world tuning in to watch the aftermath of the biggest loss of Jewish life by domestic terrorism in American history. But as the week progressed, the pronouncements by the city's leaders began to feel like a Chamber of Commerce hard sell about an idyllic neighborhood inexplicably visited by violence. The result was a recasting of a fine neighborhood with a unique set of problems and idiosyncrasies into a mythic place where the ghost of Mr. Rogers still dwells.

The emerging narrative, ahistorical and grossly sentimental, failed to take into consideration the fact that Squirrel Hill is part of a much larger community and not some Xanadu on the East End. Anyone who actually lives in this town knows that Pittsburgh is more than familiar with the kind of hatred expressed by the gunman. The violence he used to actualize that hatred is not unprecedented in this town. It was bred here. To act as if any of the city's neighborhoods was somehow walled off from the problem of festering intolerance that afflicts the entire community encourages a naïve exceptionalism.

Although Neal Rosenblum, an Orthodox Jew, was murdered in Squirrel Hill in 1986, a year before I moved to Pittsburgh, the notoriety of that crime hung in the air for years, including the years I lived in the neighborhood with my wife and three young sons. Rosenblum, a twenty-four-year-old student, was murdered by a self-proclaimed Nazi who singled him out on a Squirrel Hill street after services one evening because he was wearing the distinctive garb of an Orthodox believer. Thanks to a prison informant, the killer, a man named Steven Tielsch, was tracked down and convicted years later. He served fifteen years of a twenty-year third-degree murder sentence and was released from prison in 2017.

But I wasn't thinking about the murder of Neal Rosenblum while watching the news on the morning and afternoon of October 27, 2018. I was thinking about other local massacres from years past that were similar—but different—from what was happening in Squirrel Hill that day. I was experiencing the most surreal kind of déjà vu. Nine years earlier, on April 4, 2009—another overcast Saturday morning—Richard Poplawski, yet another member of this region's legion of neo-Nazis, used an AK-47 to mow down three Pittsburgh police officers answering a domestic disturbance call at his mother's home in Stanton Heights. Poplawski's killing of the three officers was a spontaneous display of rage aimed at all of civil society. Those officers were stand-ins for the rest of us because Pittsburgh was his ultimate target. We all understood that.

Miraculously, Poplawski was taken alive despite having killed three officers in quick succession. The professionalism of the Pittsburgh police, which was often questioned because of brutality complaints that weren't taken seriously by the departmental brass, was on full display. I remember thinking that if they could keep their cool while under fire from a Nazi, then there should never be another incident of police brutality or excessive force against an unarmed Black person in Pittsburgh ever again.

During the week that followed, Stanton Heights, a perfectly fine residential neighborhood, was neither lionized nor pilloried by politicians or police. It just happened to be the neighborhood where a rage-filled, chronically unemployed and unemployable Nazi lived with his mother. There wasn't the same level of spontaneous outpouring of emotion and vigils citywide for the officers that ordinary citizens would express years later over Tree of Life, though the officers' funerals were attended by hundreds of grieving citizens. The officers also received a tribute at Soldiers and Sailors Memorial Hall. It was a very big deal, but it did not attract a visit by President Obama to mourn with the city. The officers received the honor procession they deserved from officers from across the nation as well as the appreciation of the public, but there was not a welling up of emotion that insisted that such a terrible thing should never be allowed to happen again.

But for all of the surface differences, for me both incidents triggered the same numbness of spirit and inchoate rage. How is it that alienated white men who openly revere Nazi ideology can legally own as many guns as they can afford? How is this able to happen repeatedly?

To be a Black newspaper columnist in Pittsburgh is to be well acquainted with hate in this region. There is a lot of it and it isn't acknowledged nearly enough. It is not an abstraction to me. It comes to me before dawn in the form of calls to my office phone at the PG—usually a string of racial epithets let loose on the world like a scabrous jazz solo. There are also dedicated letter writers, both emailers and snail mailers, who have written to me for decades. They never cease reminding me that I'm Black, useless, an "affirmative action hire," and a bad writer compared to my white colleagues. They have no idea that I put their emails on auto-delete years ago. And as soon as I see the familiar arthritic scrawl of the racist letter writers (who always include their actual address) I pitch the letter unopened into the nearest wastebasket. I like the fact that the insults they continue to take the time to compose are never seen or read. They never ask themselves why I don't reply, but they're committed to making their hatred of Blacks known to me for however long it takes.

A couple of times a year I go to the auto-delete file just to see if the string of racist invective has continued. Yep, the dentist from Monroeville still addresses me with the *N*-word within the first two lines of his minimalist diatribes. Yep, the retired engineer (or so he claims) still has a detailed critique of columns that deal explicitly with white racism. Then there is the angry white woman who writes occasionally to repeat that all Black men are rapists and should be locked up "like animals." Here is an April 12 note from "Bill," a longtime hater who contributes to the delete file several times a month: "Molignane [*sic*] took 14 days off. Now back to shooting each other. What they do best." Though cryptic (this note refers to the Italian slur for Blacks, though misspelled), it is relatively tame compared to others I get. Most is illiterate or unprintable. I get enough of it not to have any illusions about the level of bigotry in Western Pennsylvania.

If you really want to be depressed, check out the comments under the columns and news stories at practically every paper in the region, including the PG. Because of the public nature of the space, the trolls rarely engage in blatant racial epithets, but there are all sorts of code they resort to. For instance, former president Obama will often be referred to as "Buckwheat Obama." When the commenter, who usually uses a pseudonym, is called on it, he'll claim he's using it affectionately, as a reference to his favorite *Little Rascals* character. This is the level of intellectual dishonesty we're dealing with. But as bad as posted comments, letters, and early morning calls are, they don't represent the work of people like Bowers or Poplawski—hardcore haters willing to take their neo-Nazi convictions to the next level.

It is also important to remember that the Pittsburgh region has experienced several high-profile mass shootings over the last two decades that were triggered by either racism, misogyny, or petty street vengeance. Ronald Taylor, an African American who "heard voices," shot five white men at an apartment building and at two fast food restaurants in Wilkinsburg on March 1, 2000. Three of his victims died. Taylor ranted antiwhite conspiracy theories as he stalked his victims. That incident of racist horror was followed on April 28 by a killing spree by Richard Baumhammers, who murdered a Jewish neighbor, two Asian Americans, a South Asian Indian, and a Black man during a seventy-two-minute rampage that ranged from Mount Lebanon to Beaver County. Another South Asian man who was injured and paralyzed that day died in 2007, bringing the shooter's death count to six. Baumhammers was a vocal and active antisemite who spewed his hatred of non-Aryans in online chat rooms and message boards. He also demonstrated his hatred of Jews by shooting up two synagogues and spray-painting swastikas, so there would be no doubt about his political and racial sympathies. He, too, was taken alive and currently sits on Pennsylvania's death row.

There were also mass shootings by men who weren't explicitly motivated by racial hatred. One thinks of George Sodini, the sexually frustrated man who killed three women at an L.A. Fitness in Collier Township and injured nine before killing himself in 2009. He claimed to hate all women because he hadn't had a date or been sexually intimate with a woman since the '90s. In death, Sodini has become the patron saint of the so-called Incel (involuntarily celibate) movement, which overlaps with the white power movement.

We know that there's hate in Pittsburgh. It metastasizes online and is accessible with only a few strokes of a keyboard. These haters rant openly about their genocidal intentions for Jews, Blacks, immigrants, and those they consider threatening to their notions of racial purity.

But as the Tree of Life massacre showed, there is also considerable community pushback to evil. While much of the nation was still in shock, the seeds of an extraordinary response took root in a city often divided by race and class. Squirrel Hill was its epicenter.

I can't think of another local tragedy in the three decades I've lived here that has prompted people of all races, religions, and socioeconomic levels here to come together to mourn a great loss and to renew itself as a community committed to changing for the better. It was gratifying to see stately old churches and mosques open their doors for ecumenical and interfaith services. There was plenty of singing, whether psalms or gospel songs or secular folk anthems. It was a cross-generational celebration of life, perhaps unprecedented in the city's history. When the Steelers win a Super Bowl or the Penguins win a Stanley Cup, there is general pandemonium and far bigger crowds, but it translates into: *Look at what our home team did for us.*

What made the vigils for the Tree of Life so important and inspiring was the way those who stood on the sidewalks singing in the chilly rain were willing to integrate such heartbreaking loss into a positive vision of the future. Paradoxically, I don't think I've ever seen people who were clearly mourning generate such a positive outlook despite the lack of a systematic program to get them to where they wanted to be.

Going to the shops and cafes of Squirrel Hill during that period revealed a community that had decided to overcome a great trauma by embracing neighborliness and civic decency that went above and beyond the call of duty. There was a courtliness and patience on the streets of Squirrel Hill and even at the supermarkets long notorious for short-fused shoppers that certainly wasn't present when I lived there decades ago.

Pittsburgh is still healing from the events of the overcast October morning in 2018. In many ways, it will be impossible to put that event behind us—and nor should we. It was a direct assault on not only a historically persecuted community but the larger civil society as well. Squirrel Hill was never immune from the violence that is much more prevalent in other neighborhoods and nothing is to be gained by pretending it was. What's important and truly impressive about Squirrel Hill is how it has chosen to deal with a crisis that began with the ruthless shedding of innocent blood. My hope is that every community in the city will begin a serious dialogue about how to deal with the haters who live among us and who have been normalized by our indifference. They carry a contagion called hate. I read somewhere that Pittsburgh is stronger than hate.

THE NEWS
NEXT DOOR

On Covering a Neighborhood
Terror Attack

Ann Belser

ON OCTOBER 27, 2018, AT 9:50 A.M., I was walking my family's
Corgi puppy.

I know this fact now, and forever, because that was when I heard
the first five gunshots fired inside the Tree of Life synagogue. The dog
heard them, too. He tried to run away, pulling me from the synagogue.
I thought heavy boxes had fallen inside the UPS truck that had just
turned the corner behind us.

On October 27 I had a busy day planned: Calvary Episcopal
Church in Shadyside had a bazaar that day from 10:00 a.m. to 2:00
p.m. to raise money for poor families; a thirteen-year-old had started
her own business with her mother's help, selling sweatshirts for dogs
with sayings on them. I was out walking the dog before heading out
to the church to take photos of the bazaar for the hyperlocal weekly
newspaper I had started in 2015. But when the puppy and I made it
home, my ex-wife was outside to say there was a man in my house who
had run from the synagogue.

As the shooting occurred, my ex and our fifteen-year-old son were
driving past the synagogue, and between the synagogue and my house
they had seen the man running. When they parked, he asked for a
phone. He did not have his because he had gone to the synagogue. "I
think there was a shooter in the synagogue," he said.

"I will go check," I said, and I grabbed my camera.

"I'm pretty sure," he said.

"I'll see," I replied, and I headed out the door and started to run back the way he had just come. It is four hundred feet to the synagogue from my house. In the days after the shooting I checked that distance using a mapping app for runners. Four hundred feet. We can see the building from our first-floor bathroom window.

Police officers searching an alley spotted me and told me to get back.

The first time I covered a murder I was about twenty-three years old, which would have been around 1986. I was living in Chelsea, Massachusetts. Chelsea had a small daily newspaper, in a news group with three weekly newspapers. I worked for its Winthrop paper, the *Winthrop Sun-Transcript*. I was doing laundry when Pat, who ran the laundromat, said, "Ann, did you know there was a murder upstairs?"

"When?" I asked, thinking it was a trivia question about years gone by.

"About ten minutes ago," she said.

"Can I borrow your phone?" I asked.

I called the office, a long block away, and told them to send Carl the photographer and an extra notebook. I remember the conversation, and the body being carried down the stairs. And I remember that I folded laundry as I waited for the detectives, while a television crew waited outside. One journalist who had been dispatched to the scene asked me if I always brought my laundry to crime scenes. I don't remember if it was spring or fall. I don't remember the details of the murder, though I believe it was a man who had been stabbed. I don't know his name. It was not released from the scene, and the daily newspaper staff took over the coverage as soon as I typed up my notes. But I was reminded of the crime every time I did my laundry for the next four years. Pat and I eventually stopped talking about it every week, but it was a struggle.

In the mid-1990s I was the night police reporter for the *Pittsburgh Post-Gazette*. The job meant going to the worst scenes when they were still "in progress." Often, on homicides, the bodies were still there. At the scene of a double homicide one snowy night, I wound up stepping around the body of the second victim as I walked from my car to the front of the building, alerting the police to his presence.

In June 1995 the police scanner went off about a drive-by shooting in the Northview Heights neighborhood, a public housing project that pretty much had one way in and out. In 1993 it gained notoriety for a killing in which two men were shot, one fatally, on a ball field in front of a couple of hundred people. A third man was beaten to death on the pitcher's mound by men wielding baseball bats. Two years later, on the day of the sentencing of one of the ballfield killers, Joseph Davis IV, age eighteen, was standing next to his car in that same neighborhood when a group of kids affiliated with one of the gangs drove past, shooting. Joseph was hit, ran to his mother's apartment, and died in the entryway as she answered the door. I arrived shortly after his death and the neighbors were upset that a young man who had nothing to do with the gangs had been slain. There was a lot of yelling and running while police were trying to contain a potentially violent situation.

The next night, realizing how much the neighbors cared about the young man who had been killed, I went back and knocked on his mother's door. Victoria Davis was all alone. When she answered the door, she looked at me and said, "Oh, it's you." I did not know how she knew me, but she explained that we had met a couple of years earlier, when I had been working in the courthouse for another newspaper and she was looking for the clerk's office as part of her coursework to be a paralegal. I had offered to show her around if she wanted to tag along on my daily rounds. She did. Then two years later, there I was again. I sat with her and talked about her son. Sadly, fifteen years later, she too was murdered. Joseph Davis III stabbed her to death while their second son, born six years after the murder of his brother, watched.

When I covered homicides, I was always able to distance myself. None were in my neighborhood. In fact, when I first looked for a house, while working as a police reporter, my criterion was to look only in neighborhoods where I had not been sent to cover a crime. I had gone to Squirrel Hill for work one night. Lightning had struck a chimney. I gave that a pass.

In 1995 I bought a house in Squirrel Hill that had been built in 1914. I knew we were a lesbian couple moving to a Jewish neighborhood. My family was Jewish, but I had a secular upbringing. We were, we joked, Jew-ish. My father, who had been raised in an Orthodox household and was drafted into the US Army during World War II, asked why I would live in a Jewish neighborhood. "They will know where to find you," he said of the antisemites.

Squirrel Hill is surrounded by an eruv. In reality, it is a wire that stretches around the neighborhood. The purpose is to delineate the neighborhood as a home on the Sabbath. By expanding the boundary of their homes, Orthodox Jews can carry items, such as keys, and push baby carriages on the Sabbath, which they are not supposed to do when they are "outside."

I learned about the eruv in 2008 through an exhibit at the American Jewish Museum at the Jewish Community Center. Ben Schachter, the museum's artist-in-residence, had asked members of the community for words to define what their community meant to them. He then stitched those words, along with rough sketches of houses and trees, onto strips of Tyvek house wrap, which he hung around the top of the JCC. I bought one of the pieces and had it framed. My house, the last one inside the eruv that ends at Wilkins Avenue, has a representation of the eruv that says *Identity*.

On October 27, 2018, after running from the shooting, the man who had been in the synagogue is in my living room, staring out the window toward Tree of Life.

Outside, an older woman parks across the street. She starts to head up Wilkins, walking. I stop her. "Please, don't go that way," I say.

"I am just trying to get to the synagogue," she says.

"There's been a shooting there, you can't go." She stares at me. "You are welcome to come into my house," I say. "You can collect yourself if you need to."

"I am just going to go home," she says, and gets back into her car.

I go back into the house and look at the man we now know as Marty. I offer him tea, but he shakes his head and keeps looking out the window. My son has downloaded a police scanner app and is listening to the transmissions. Commander Jason Lando is speaking. I have known Jason for years and immediately feel the situation will be under control.

I go back outside. The media are gathering three blocks away. I run over. The mayor is just arriving; he does not know anything. Members of the police SWAT team are driving there in their own personal vehicles, getting their gear on and running toward the synagogue. I run back home and stand on the corner of the block, watching. A reporter friend is there with me. We used to work together.

The sound of huge bursts of gunfire comes out of the building. A door on the third floor opens to the roof and we can see it. If the shooter runs out and the police follow him, shooting, I am right in the line of fire. I duck behind an embankment on my neighbor's yard as an officer screams at us to get back.

My daughter calls neighbors and they come get her. She tells them she does not want to be alone. We have a house full of people. Our neighbors run over and my daughter comes out. They hug on the street and I get a photo—so does the *New York Times*, and it is sent worldwide.

There's another press conference. The shooter is in custody. Eleven people are dead. Names are not released.

Around 1:00 I head over to the church bazaar, the event I had planned to attend before the shooting. It is less than a mile from Tree of Life; both houses of worship are on Shady Avenue. The news of the shooting has subdued the bazaar. The Rev. Jonathan Jensen tells me he has had the same conversation again and again. The women who put together the bazaar to help others tell me there is an added urgency to their work in a time of crisis.

Back at home, more media show up. Tents are put up where local news stations, CNN, and MSNBC are all broadcasting in the intersection next to my house. I realize, as the media is all sitting there, that I cut about three feet off my hedges on Friday and had every intention to bag up the debris on Sunday, but the branches are all over my lawn. Crime scene tape is tied to the corner of bare hedges.

My daughter, Cody, is with her friend and neighbor Marina at the Starbucks in Squirrel Hill. A neighbor, Sara Mayo, hears them planning a vigil for that night. Cody and Marina have decided that no one in Squirrel Hill should be alone, so they use Snapchat to pull together a group of high school kids who previously organized an antigun rally after the shooting at a high school in Parkland, Florida. Sara sits with them, giving some guidance, but lets them work it out themselves. Marina's mother, Amanda Godley, talks to a friend in the city, who contacts the public safety department. The center of Squirrel Hill is shut down for the vigil even though the Jewish Federation of Greater Pittsburgh has decided not to hold a vigil until tomorrow night.

It is all happening on the Sabbath. The sun has not gone down, and all of this is within the eruv. It is, figuratively, inside our house.

None of us can go outside without being interviewed by a member of the media. My dog is on local television because he heard the shots. I am asked how it will change our neighborhood and I am resolute that Squirrel Hill is a special place; we will be fine. As one veteran of mass shooting coverage explains to me, the media arrives in order of the distance traveled. News crews from DC, four hours away, arrive faster than reporters from New York City, seven hours away.

The vigil is held at 7:00 p.m., after sunset. We all know by now that eleven people have died in a mass shooting. But we do not know their names—they will not be released until the next day. Cody is the main speaker at the vigil. Sara leads the gathering in song. People hold candles. A young man shouts from the crowd, "We're still Squirrel Hill." The crowd picks up the chant, followed by another: "Vote! Vote! Vote!" I crouch in front of a makeshift stage taking pictures of my daughter and her friends.

At the end I go up on a hillside across the street, making my way around the crowd, and I look out. People are still crowded in, unwilling to leave. The national news interviews my daughter. As I look out at the crowd from above I realize the enormity of the gathering. There are more than two thousand people filling the streets and the intersection of Murray and Forbes Avenues, the heart of Squirrel Hill. It, too, is inside the eruv.

The activity does not slow down. Reporters from China and Japan who have now made it to Pittsburgh from New York are interviewing my wife and our sons. Our puppy becomes a media favorite. That night the crews are still outside, still making noise, slamming van doors and leaving their generators running. At 4:00 a.m. I go outside and start yelling at them to quiet down.

The next morning is the press conference where the police release the names. I am in the room with about fifty journalists. I don't recognize the names. But over time I realize that I did know some of the victims. I knew Cecil and David Rosenthal from the JCC. Nearly a year later I will realize that Rose Mallinger was one of the women who used to hang out with Bicky Goldzer, our late Democratic Committeewoman. I will realize this when I get to know her daughter, Andrea Wedner, who was injured in the shooting, at events memorializing the victims.

In the hours and days after the shooting our house turns into an odd staging area for the reaction to the tragedy. My wife, Jan, becomes friends with a man who is offering soup to the media and first responders. She brings him in so he can use our microwave to warm the soup.

I write in my den, looking out at the rest of the media in their festival-style tents. I let a few know they can use my bathroom, and it becomes a communal restroom.

When the police finally allow people to walk in front of the synagogue, the memorial starts to grow. Flowers and cards are placed there.

And community activism is suddenly directed at protesting a visit to the site by President Donald Trump. I am at Sara and Jonathan Mayo's house as they plan to protest a president whose rhetoric has raised the level of hatred in the country.

More than a thousand protesters march toward the synagogue singing a song based on Psalm 89: "Olam chesed yibaneh. We will build this world from love."

There is so much for me to write. There is so much the outside media does not know, because they do not know our community. They don't live inside the eruv.

I watch over the next two weeks as the pile of landscaping stones slowly diminishes from next to my neighbor's driveway. People are coming to pay their respects and realize that the Jewish tradition is for mourners to leave a stone. My neighbor's stones are taken eleven at a time.

For weeks the memorials keep growing. The day after the shooting, Greg Zanis from Illinois shows up with white crosses onto which he tacks white Stars of David. They become an iconic portion of the memorial and are later placed inside the doors of the synagogue.

Signs go up all over Squirrel Hill that say *Stronger than Hate*. Tim Hindes of South Park comes up with a logo, a Star of David incorporated into the Steelers logo. And then T-shirts appear. In a uniquely American response, at least six different T-shirts come out of the tragedy. Jeanne Clark, the chairman of the Shadyside Democratic Committee, places the logo on an "I voted" sticker that is distributed at the polls just days after the shooting. Across the street from my polling place, someone has hung on their hedges eleven T-shirts that say *Now is exactly the right time to talk about gun control.*

As the media thins, moving on to the next mass shooting at a bar in California (near my high school classmate's house), the mourners keep coming. For weeks the parking on our street is filled as people arrive with flowers, cards, and mementos. They walk to the synagogue with grim faces and come back to their cars in tears. I hug people I have never seen before because they just seem to need it.

After a couple of weeks the crowds are heavy only on weekends. Still, I realize what it must be like to live in Lower Manhattan near Ground Zero. Our neighborhood has become the Jewish Ground Zero.

What I don't realize is what is happening outside of the eruv. Jews across the country and across the world are also absorbing this shock. Three weeks after the shooting, thousands of knitted or crocheted Stars of David, each with a small heart on it, are hung all over our neighborhood, in trees and phone poles, on the fence around the Tree of Life, and in the park on Murray Avenue. By this time it has been three weeks of a constant outpouring of grief. It is days before our streets reopen. A full two weeks before the last satellite truck is gone.

The Stars of David with the hearts were meant as a way to wrap Squirrel Hill with love, like a hand-crocheted afghan from a beloved grandmother. But for those first weeks or months they were up, it felt like another assault: a reminder that we had all been victims, in one way or another, of this act of hate. For a moment, walking the streets, my mind might wander away from the mass shooting that was consuming our lives. Then I would see one of those little woolen Stars of David, hanging from a tree or a utility pole. I rejected that act of love because I didn't want us to need it. I just wanted our house to be left alone.

I cleared my yard of the hedge debris a few weeks after the shooting, but in the months afterward I realized there was still police tape tied on a branch in the middle of the hedge. I did not pull it out immediately. It was like the torn strip of black cloth that mourners wear after losing a loved one.

The knitted Stars of David have lasted more than a year and a half now. There were two hanging from a telephone pole that was marked for replacement, so I rescued them in the middle of the night. We are cleaning them and letting them dry while the phone company replaces the equipment on the new pole. When they are done, I will hang the stars up again because they have become, for me, what they were all along: a sign of love, sent to Squirrel Hill from all over the world.

A great loss happened here. It happened inside the eruv, inside our house, but ultimately, we're still Squirrel Hill.

WIRE
AND
STRING

Kevin Haworth

WHEN I WAS GROWING UP in rural New York, I understood that there were places that were not safe for Jews. One of those places was Eastern Europe. The other was Israel.

Eastern Europe was obvious. The evidence was all around me, even here in America. Our rabbi, a tiny bearded man with features directly out of a Talmud story, had survived Auschwitz. So had his wife. The numbers on his arm, sea-green and blurred with age, would peek out when he reached for a book or held up a loaf of challah for a blessing. His wife always wore sleeves that reached her wrists but there were rumors from the girls in my Hebrew school class that someone had seen her numbers while she washed her hands in the women's bathroom. From this, as Hebrew school kids, we knew to stay away from Europe—the eastern part, anyway. That was a place where people killed Jews. If your parents wanted to take you on vacation to Europe, you should go to Paris, where some bad things happened to Jews but it was somehow different. Nobody's parents were going to take them on vacation to Poland. One does not go on vacation to a cemetery.

Israel was different. Israel was dangerous—that was one of its defining facts. It shaped the way everyone spoke about it. Hebrew schools of the 1980s were not known for their nuanced discussion of the Israeli-Palestinian conflict, and my Orthodox synagogue in rural

New York was no exception. We learned that after the Holocaust, Jews needed to make their own country. When Arabs tried to kill Jews in this place, we fought back. And fought back again. And again and again. We would keep doing so until the world learned that Jews could not be slaughtered anymore. That Jews were still slaughtered—in Munich, or on a hijacked cruise ship or airplane, or in some remote part of Israel itself—only reinforced the narrative.

When I went to live in Israel after college, the danger was part of the point. I was twenty-one years old and I wanted adventure. I understood that if I were to be murdered in Israel, it would be for being Jewish. It was okay to be killed in Israel for being Jewish. There, it was the right story. The story of Israel was that there, Jews fought so that the place could be Jewish, really Jewish. Not like Europe, where people allowed Jews to live (until they didn't). The difference, as I understood it, was that in Israel there was no expectation of safety. To live in that space was to take on the historical burden of the Jewish people as endangered bodies, to wear those bodies in solidarity with our history.

This was almost thirty years ago. That is a long time in some ways and not a long time also, and we haven't continued to talk about the Holocaust or Israel that way. We know better now. But a lot of things have changed since I was in Hebrew school and since I was twenty-one. It's hard to look at our own past and not see it as a strange time.

In 2015 my children and I moved from a small town in Appalachian Ohio to Pittsburgh. Specifically, we moved to Squirrel Hill, a neighborhood known both for its sizable Jewish population and for the diversity of that population—a neighborhood of many synagogues, of Jewish schools, of secular Jews and identifiably religious Jews and Jews like myself, who fall in some idiosyncratic and yet deeply felt place in between. We purchased a house that had been built by a branch of a locally famous Jewish family. It was the first time in America that I moved into a house where I didn't have to hang a mezuzah myself, where I found one already waiting for us in our new home. The mezuzot in the entranceways had been painted over multiple times, but they were still clearly visible and raised to the touch.

We were also moving inside the Pittsburgh eruv, the ritual enclosure that makes, from the standpoint of Jewish law, everything inside it a kind of private, shared space. For those who observe Shabbat, the eruv is transformative. Practically, it allows people to transfer—that is, carry belongings—from one house to another, from inside to outside, from home to synagogue, which in turn makes possible any number of outdoor activities or even simple tasks like pushing a baby stroller. Philosophically, it creates a shared Jewish space. The original Pittsburgh eruv encompassed the core Jewish neighborhoods of Squirrel Hill and Greenfield as well as much of neighboring Frick Park to allow for children to play and families to walk. Later it was extended to the college neighborhood of Oakland, where it then turns north and grows narrower, just far enough to embrace Children's Hospital. Most days I travel from my house to the nearby university and back without ever leaving the eruv.

The eruv is a combination of natural barriers and existing fences, with fishing line or wire strung between otherwise open spaces to create one contiguous, definable area. It is unnoticeable unless you are looking for it, and even then hard to see. It is also impermanent: fences can come loose, string can break, wires can fall. It must be inspected every week to ensure its validity. This is done by a rabbi with eyes for the barely visible; someone is trained to see a wall where others just see string. I thought a lot about this eruv as we prepared to move. Being inside it made me feel safe.

I arrived in Israel in 1992, shortly after the first Gulf War ended, and when I reached my kibbutz near the northern city of Haifa, I saw what life had been like there the year before. I became close with a kibbutz family and they told me how they had taped their windows shut in case Saddam's missiles carried poisonous sarin, and how they slept with gas masks next to their beds. The residue from the tape was still visible around the edges of the glass.

Here was a story that felt comfortable. When we took trips from the kibbutz—hikes in the beautiful Galilee hills, or visits to a nearby village, one or two of the kibbutzniks carried military rifles, just in case. This was personal danger as national power. The man I worked for in the avocado fields carried a pistol in his waistband because we were all by ourselves, far from the kibbutz center, and "you never know." The father from my kibbutz family carried a pistol in his waistband when we gathered for Shabbat dinner because we were all together in a large group, and "you never know." When the teenagers came home from army service for those same Shabbat dinners, they walked onto the kibbutz carrying their army-issued automatic weapons, which they hurriedly stashed so that we could get in a quick pickup game of basketball or soccer before dinner, them still in their green or tan uniforms and combat boots. All these weapons gave physical form to something we all knew: to be Jewish was to not be safe, not entirely, not ever.

I returned to Israel several times over the next twenty years. I worked for a landscaper on another kibbutz, so close to Lebanon that we could see the fence. I lived in Jerusalem, where I struggled to finish a book and stared at the walls of the Old City from my desk window. I had seen the Oslo Accords give way to a new Intifada, the new tension when riding buses, the intense security checks at the entry to every mall, concert venue, public event. As always in Israel, to be alone was to be vulnerable; to be together was to invite threat. During those visits I traveled freely, on buses nearly every day, and on trains, and in taxis. I sat in cafes and read the books I had to read and wrote the stories and essays I was trying to write. These were not inherently safe places—by definition they were targets. A suicide bomber could kill many people by stepping on a bus or into a cafe. They did so many times. But to say no to the buses, to the cafes, to the public markets—it felt wrong. A person could be in danger anywhere. But to be in danger here, as a Jew in a country full of other Jews, felt right. It was an unexpected kind of belonging.

By 2011 I returned to Israel as the faculty director for a program at Tel Aviv University. This time I was responsible for college students who had traveled with me to study. And I was with my children. The university I worked for in Ohio was nervous about the program. Parents were nervous, too. Israel, after all, was known to be dangerous. (One student's parents yanked her from the trip just a few weeks before we were to leave. She cried all the way to my office to tell me, and all the way back.) To soothe these nervous parents, I would say that in terms of crime, Tel Aviv was less dangerous than many American cities. I would say, "If I were nervous about going, would I take my children with me?"

This is the difference between actual safety and the stories that we tell ourselves to feel safe. Actual safety is a matter of statistics, of likelihoods and unlikelihoods, a measurable data set. It can be rendered in numbers. But we still need stories to guide our response to those numbers.

In Talmudic thinking, there is the *rashut harabim*, the public domain, and the *rashut hayachid*, the private domain. Through its metaphorical power, the eruv collapses the two into a single private domain, so that the normal strictures of carrying items from one domain to another no longer apply. The Talmud first illustrates this distinction in tractate Shabbat (2a). A poor person is standing outside a house—maybe on the other side of the property line, or a small fence. The homeowner is inside the fence, in his private domain. The poor person hands something to the homeowner. The object is not specified, but it is often understood to be an empty basket. The homeowner then returns the basket, with food in it. In the Talmud, this story distinguishes the public space from the private space, and uses the handing of the basket as an example of carrying objects from one area to another. But many commentators note that within this legal discussion hides a story—of neighborliness and sharing, of kindness.

In the summer of 2014, my children's fifth summer in Tel Aviv, Israel and Gaza went to war with each other. Hamas fired missiles by the hundreds from Gaza, first at nearby towns in southern Israel, then east toward Jerusalem, north to Tel Aviv, and farther up the coast toward the summer camp where my children were staying for two weeks. Several times a day sirens told us to run to nearby shelters, in public places like underground parking lots, or the basements of apartment houses. The sirens could go off at any moment. At cafes and falafel stands some people chatted about the war and some people didn't.

One afternoon, after I finished teaching, I found myself walking down Nordau Street. This was one of my favorite routes—a wide pedestrian walkway and bicycle path bisecting the car lanes, what Israelis call a *midrechov*, with kiosks and cafes and falafel shops and even small playgrounds right in the middle of the street. All over Tel Aviv are such streets, like Rothschild or Chen, walking parks that carry you from one part of the city to another.

As I was walking, a boy of about eleven—my own son's age—fell in next to me. As soon as I looked at him I thought of my boy, an hour away to the north. There had been no sirens yet that day but it was only a matter of time. We were walking next to each other—not together in any official sense, just two people whose pace happened to match, a temporary alliance of walkers. Suddenly he turned to me and said, in Hebrew, "If a missile came right now, what would we do?"

I don't know where he was going. Maybe to the beach to look at the waves. Maybe to the convenience store a block away to get a snack or pick up something for his mother. It did not surprise me to see him alone, even in the midst of a war. We live lives of constant calculation. We tell ourselves what is okay and what isn't. We don't live in bomb shelters.

I scanned the nearby apartment buildings for open doors, where we could enter and find a basement quickly. I pointed at one of them and said in my rough Hebrew, "We will run together." At the next corner we parted. He turned right on Dizengoff, onto the busy street of boutiques and restaurants, and I never saw him again. When I got home later that afternoon, a siren went off and I made my way to the basement shelter by myself.

Here in Pittsburgh, when I go for a run, I take a route that goes north on Murray Avenue, past the Judaica shop, past the kosher dairy restaurant, past the kosher supermarket, and past the Jewish Community Center. It also takes me by an Asian supermarket, as well as Szechuan, Taiwanese, Hong Kong, Thai, and Vietnamese restaurants, and a shop that sells Japanese ice cream. The Korean restaurant recently closed. This is the commercial stretch of Squirrel Hill. Someone else running the same route might note a different list of neighborhood landmarks, maybe focusing on the many pizza parlors and cafes, but this is what I see. I continue past the neighborhood branch of the Carnegie Library and for a couple of blocks find myself on the streets of very large and expensive houses that characterize the neighborhood north of Forbes Avenue. (There are neighborhoods within neighborhoods, always.)

My route is a three-mile loop: long enough to feel like I'm doing something. A mile in, I turn right on Wilkins Avenue. I'm starting to get tired now, so I slow down, but in truth I would slow down anyway. Because soon after I make the turn onto Wilkins, just past the large houses, I am running past Tree of Life Synagogue.

I started running this route a few months after eleven people were shot there. They were shot on a Shabbat morning in the early fall, and for a few months it felt like a well of gravity had opened up on that corner in Squirrel Hill, a singularity that pulled people toward the space and kept them standing there. The building itself was closed off and protected like an animal being allowed to heal. People brought flowers or notes or, when they got there, they saw that other people had brought flowers and notes and so they went to the stores on nearby Murray Avenue to get some and came back with their offerings. Their beautiful flowers sat on the sidewalk and got wet and frayed and no less beautiful and their handwritten notes that they pinned like ribbons to ad hoc posts or the newly erected security fence sometimes said *to Rose* or *to the brothers Cecil and David* or *to Jerry* or *to my fellow Jews* or *to Pittsburgh*.

As the months passed, the crowds dwindled. The sidewalk in front of Tree of Life became less of a site for active mourning; fewer visitors stopped by, fewer new notes replaced older ones, and the objects people left seemed to have longer lifespans. Anthropologist Katharina Schramm writes, "The memory of violence is not only embedded in peoples' bodies and minds but also inscribed onto space."[1] As people inscribed the space in front of the synagogue, it seemed to grow more stable, more permanent in what it signified, and also less sad. There is a timeline for grief and I don't fault the arc of this particular sidewalk. Even I slowed down less as I ran by.

The world's fear of our Jewish bodies makes us afraid for ourselves, our Jewish bodies. In *Between the World and Me*, Ta-Nehisi Coates begins, "Last Sunday the host of a popular news show asked me what it meant to lose my body." He is talking about his Black body, not a Jewish one. But it made me think. First, that his body, in America, has always been and is now more vulnerable than mine. It isn't a competition; we are each allowed our fears. But his fear is based on facts and a deep reckoning with America and mine must be too. Coates writes *Between the World and Me* to his teenage son. Our stories intersect here, if just for a moment, because when I also think about the safety of one's body I am thinking about Jewish bodies, which really means that I am thinking about the safety of the very specific Jewish bodies of my children.

But what is the right way to think about that, even after Tree of

---

1. Katharina Schramm, "Landscapes of Violence: Memory and Sacred Space," *History and Memory* 23, no. 1 (Spring/Summer 2011): 5–22.

Life? What is the greatest threat to their bodies? Should I be most afraid for their safety in their high schools, where the principals notify us every time there is a lockdown drill (which is often) or a real lockdown (which is often)? When my fourteen-year-old daughter goes to a concert, wearing her tall black Doc Martens and her short trying-to-be-a-teenager skirt, should I be more afraid because she's Jewish, or because she's a girl? Should I be more afraid that someone is going to burst into the bat mitzvah of one of her friends and shoot her? Or should I be afraid every time she takes the public bus downtown, because she's a fourteen-year-old girl and the world remains a desperately dangerous place for women? Now that we are in Pittsburgh and not Tel Aviv, my children do not sit in bomb shelters or stay at home. They do not ask me where they would run when something happens. They live inside *if* more than *when*.

Public domain. Private domain. Borders. Fences. Mezuzahs. Doorways. All construct a vision of inclusivity, of home, of safety. We believe fiercely in these constructs. We are surprised when they fail.

The man who murdered eleven Jews at the Tree of Life synagogue was obsessed with borders. He believed invaders were approaching the southern United States and that Jews were helping them. Where most see poor travelers, he saw a marching army. Where most see kindness and aid, he saw betrayal.

At some point, early on the morning of October 27, 2018, this man drove under a wire and was inside the Pittsburgh eruv. It had been inspected before Shabbat, as it always is, and stood intact. I am sure he did not notice the moment that he crossed it. The eruv is a border that welcomes, rather than excludes, and it welcomed him like it does everyone else. Like the idea of safety, the power of the eruv lies in what we can imagine, and what we can't. What the eruv serves to permit—a joyous Shabbat, free from negotiating the distinction of separate spaces—is part of the reason he was drawn here. So many Jews. So many targets.

Growing up in rural New York, I understood that there were places that were not safe for Jews. The story is more complicated now. I live inside an eruv, not a wall. It continues to embrace me, and my family, and all the Jews and non-Jews that live their lives inside it, to the full extent to which wire and string are capable.

IMPOSTER OR ACTIVIST

Eight Years in Squirrel Hill

Avigail S. Oren

NINETEEN DAYS AFTER THE SHOOTING at Tree of Life, I stood in front of a row of cameras at a press conference in Washington, DC. I had been invited to the District by Bend the Arc: Jewish Action—a movement of tens of thousands of progressive Jewish activists all across the United States, including myself and many fellow Pittsburghers, who are working to build a more just society. I was there to participate in a convening of organizations working together to cut funding to federal agencies that detain, incarcerate, and deport immigrants, refugees, and asylum seekers. The conveners offered me the opportunity to speak at the press conference and I nervously accepted.

"It is surreal and humbling to be standing here today," I began. "Three weeks ago I was just a Jewish historian living in Pittsburgh organizing with my local chapter of Bend the Arc: Jewish Action, alongside software engineers, lawyers, consultants, social workers, nonprofit directors, and college professors—all of us devoted to working locally to fight rising hate against vulnerable minorities and for policies that make us all safe."

As proud as I was of the carefully crafted remarks I made that day, I felt deeply uncomfortable in the role. Who was I to speak for Pittsburgh? I, who had moved to the city only seven years prior, whose family had not been part of Squirrel Hill's Jewish community for generations. I didn't belong to *any* synagogue, much less one of the three that congregated in the Tree of Life building. I went to Squirrel Hill only on Sunday mornings to teach Jewish history to teenagers at the Jewish Community Center, or on Friday nights to meet friends for Chinese food.

Yet there I stood, telling the journalists assembled before me that "on October 27, eleven members of my Jewish community were murdered in synagogue." My mouth went dry. Was I going to be called out as an imposter by Pittsburgh Jews?

The Tree of Life shooting at once upended and clarified my relationship to Pittsburgh, making me feel more rooted in the city than I ever had before, yet also painfully aware of how tenuous of a connection I had to its people. I transplanted myself here in 2011 to begin a doctoral program in history at Carnegie Mellon University—uprooting my life in New York City after a three-day visit to Pittsburgh, swayed by the kindness of other graduate students and the five-dollar pitchers of Yuengling. In one of the strangest coincidences of my life, I moved into the same apartment building that my Uncle Jimbo had lived in thirty years before. That was the extent of my connection to Pittsburgh, familial or otherwise.

Our first month here, I dragged my now-husband with me to check out the shul nearest to us. We went for Kabbalat Shabbat two or three weeks in a row but never joined, put off by the rabbi who wouldn't stop talking to us during the prayers. I also went to a few events for Jewish young adults, hoping to recreate the community I had enjoyed at Hillel during college. One nice guy that my husband and I met at a mixer texted me and asked if I wanted to go hiking; it was halfway through Frick Park that I realized he thought this was a date. At another event, a guy *twice* admonished me for saying "shit."

That ended my participation in the Jewish community for the next few years. I occasionally attended Jewish events at Carnegie Mellon, even planned a few myself, but only ventured into Squirrel Hill for High Holiday services, the occasional movie at the Manor, or to teach Jewish studies to teenagers at the JCC. As I was finishing my dissertation, Trump was elected, so I began organizing with Bend the Arc: Jewish Action Pittsburgh (BTAJAP) after its founding in January of 2017.

And so went my Jewish-adjacent life, until October 27, 2018. Those first forty-eight hours were the most *Pittsburgher* I've ever felt. Tree of Life is one mile from my home and one block from our best friends. The three congregations are the synagogues of some of my friends and colleagues and students.

As the victims' names were announced and I realized I knew none of them, a chasm opened. I was mourning the loss of our community's sense of collective safety, while almost every other Jew around me knew or had a personal connection to one (or many) of those killed or injured. I didn't know the victims because I basically knew only three types of Jews in Pittsburgh: teenagers, progressive activists, and fellow academics. I did not know the older, shul-going and shul-sustaining crowd—like my parents and their friends from the synagogue I grew up attending—because I had not joined a local synagogue. And even though I taught at the JCC, I was not a member.

And yet, all of a sudden, when I said, "I'm from Pittsburgh," it meant something—a "something" that did and did not apply to me. I *had* been through that shared experience with other Jewish Pittsburghers, with the shul-going Jews and JCC members, but I also could not claim the tragedy as my own, when so many had lost so much more. I felt affected, but I did not feel ownership.

It would take a long time for me to make peace with this.

A few months after the press conference, I enrolled in an online training course called *Don't Kvetch, Organize!* We spent a lot of time practicing that most basic of organizing skills, the one-to-one conversation, and for a few weeks I found myself staring at the pixelated faces of fellow Jews from around the country, talking about activism. These interactions began with introductions, and as I said "Pittsburgh" I noticed eyebrows rising, eyes widening, heads tilting.

One evening, I was speaking with a woman—I can no longer recall if she was from Boston, DC, or the Bay Area, but it wasn't Pittsburgh—about organizing missteps and ways to make amends. I found myself describing the days after the shooting, the frantic organization of our open letter to the president and our march of protest and mourning, the elation of exceeding our wildest expectations for attendance and press coverage, and then the difficulty afterward when the Jewish community was divided in their response to our "politicization" of the tragedy. I recalled how deflated I felt, realizing that other Jewish Pittsburghers had been angered by how we used the tragedy to criticize the president. The moment did not unite us. It highlighted divisions between us: those who lost friends and family and those who did not; those who understood the tragedy as inherently political and those who wanted politics left out of it; those who devoted themselves afterward to fighting antisemitism and those who saw the fight as part of a larger struggle against white supremacy and xenophobia.

My conversation partner listened attentively, and recognized that I was not looking for advice or an answer. So she responded with praise: "What you did in Pittsburgh was so impressive, you were so strong, what you did *moved* people." And I couldn't help but say, "Thank you. But I only did so much. I did not suffer so much."

This pattern repeated over and over. I couldn't handle the perception that people had of me when they learned my story. I *had* to tell people that I was a transplant, that I was adjacent to and not embedded in the Jewish community, and that I had not experienced the loss and trauma that many of my fellow organizers had. I was not the Pittsburgh that they had seen on the news.

If I was an imposter Pittsburgh Jew, I was not going to let myself be an imposter activist. I threw myself into the work of the Defund Hate campaign, inspired by the grassroots activists I had met at the Washington, DC, convening whose daily work was protecting their communities from the terrorism of US Immigration and Customs Enforcement (ICE) and Customs and Border Protection (CBP) officers. The goal of the campaign was to convince more members of Congress to champion the rights of immigrants and more vocally criticize the deportation and incarceration policies that separate families, detain asylum seekers, and deport vulnerable people to unsafe conditions. In Pittsburgh, we set to work trying to convince Representatives Mike Doyle and Conor Lamb and Senator Bob Casey to vote against funding for the border wall and an increase in detention beds. (Republican senator Toomey was a lost cause.)

On a frigid January afternoon in 2019, I stood behind a tableful of cookies at the corner of Murray and Forbes. Teenagers and retirees came out to join me, and we handed out free dessert and offered small flyers with information about the campaign, phone numbers for local congressional offices, and scripts with talking points as pedestrians passed by. The thirty-five-day government shutdown had ended just days earlier, and congressional funding was still at the forefront of folks' minds.

We had conversations about immigration justice with eighteen-year-olds excited to vote for the first time—including one so eager that they stood alongside our table of cookies to place their calls—and college students who wondered if they could call their representatives in their home districts (yes!), and parents coming out of the library behind us pushing strollers. The action was a success, despite universal agreement to pack up early before the frostbite set in.

Two weeks later, Congress voted on a spending package that included $1.4 billion for border wall construction and failed to restrict ICE's ability to raid other government accounts to pay for immigrant detention. Nineteen Democrats voted against the bill to protest these excesses, but neither Doyle, Lamb, nor Casey was among them.

With the funding fight for 2020's budget coming up at the year's end, BTAJAP organized house meetings to educate other Jews in the community about the importance of attacking the deportation and detention machine at its roots, the funding making it possible, if we were going to see a real systemic change. Attendees wrote Rosh Hashanah cards to Doyle, Lamb, Casey, and Toomey (yes, even Toomey) asking them to begin the Jewish New Year by speaking out against the abuses of the immigration system—and, of course, to vote against increased funding for ICE and CBP. We delivered the cards to representatives' Pittsburgh offices in beautiful baskets filled with apples and honey. "This is the Jewish New Year," we told their staff, "a time when Jews take stock of moral failings and pledge to do better in the upcoming year." And we explained, before we blew the shofar for them, that it calls us to take action, to fight injustice, and to hold ourselves—and our country—to the highest ethical standards.

On December 17, 2019, seventy-five members of Congress voted against the Department of Homeland Security funding bill in protest of its failures, once again, to significantly reform the immigrant detention system—and this time, Doyle was among them.

This year, on Martin Luther King Jr. Day 2020, I was once again at a convening—this time of core Bend the Arc: Jewish Action leaders from across the United States. We were seated in a circle so big it stretched to the walls of the large room. I sat there and told my story, of how I moved to Pittsburgh and until October 27 believed that the fight against white supremacy was the great struggle of our time and that antisemitism was just a blip on the radar, a distraction, an excuse for avoiding the hard work of social justice. And I told them about how that day had upended my entire worldview, and showed me that antisemitism is inextricably linked with racism in white nationalist ideology. And I told them about how these realizations after the shooting motivated BTAJAP to strengthen its efforts to build bridges with Pittsburgh's Black community, because the gulf between us is wide and it will take working together to uproot our enemies.

After I finished, my fellow member of BTAJAP, the only other Pittsburgher at the convening and a friend of many years, gave me a big hug. She is from a family whose roots in the city are over one hundred years old, and she lost friends at Tree of Life. And her hug told me that she did not see me as an imposter, but as an equal member of the community.

As I write this, I am at work on a new, local campaign. The Colcom Foundation is headquartered at Two Gateway Center in downtown Pittsburgh, almost exactly five miles from Tree of Life. It's from there that millions of dollars flow to anti-immigrant organizations such as the Federation for American Immigration Reform and the Center for Immigration Studies, which the Southern Poverty Law Center has designated as hate groups.[1] None of these groups are headquartered in Pittsburgh, and most of their work takes place in halls of power far away from Western Pennsylvania. But hate has a way of coming home, as we in Pittsburgh now know.

---

1. FAIR and CIS each received over $50,000 from Colcom in 2019. Colcom Foundation, "Major Grants," http://colcomfdn.org/major-grants/. Southern Poverty Law Center, https://www.splcenter.org.

And for me this city is now home. I come to this campaign as a Jewish Pittsburgher, more fully realized in that identity than ever before. At the press conference launching the campaign, I stood and held Bend the Arc: Jewish Action's banner with fellow Jews, but also union members and immigrant high school students and socialists and veterans. These Pittsburghers gave me the strength to step before the cameras once again, this time with no hesitation. "As Jews, we at Bend the Arc: Jewish Action know the danger of pointing fingers at specific groups and blaming them for global problems," I told the assembled journalists. "And as Pittsburgh Jews, we know that in addition to endangering immigrants, the funding of hate groups endangers those of us who historically and presently stand in solidarity with immigrants, refugees, and asylum seekers."

Through activism, defending each and every person's right to human dignity, I feel my Jewishness most profoundly. Through activism I have met many more people within the Jewish community, and deepened existing relationships. And, ultimately, I'm perceived as a Jewish organizer when I go about this work. So I have staked my own claim to a corner of the heterogeneous "community" and made peace with my journey from transplant to rooted Pittsburgher.

PITTSBURGH POSITIVE

Brooke Barker

IN OCTOBER 2018, I HAD A NOTE on my phone that I'd look at a few times a day. Between the note for potential dog names and the note for invention ideas (why is no one making tiny pieces of jerky you can shake into your palm and eat as a snack?) there was a note titled "The Future." My husband, Boaz, and I knew we wanted to move sometime in The Future, but we didn't know where, and the note on my phone was a list of cities. The Future kept me up at night and made my phone feel like it weighed five pounds.

We were living in Amsterdam, but we'd been flying back to America every other month for work or for family, and as much as we loved our life in the Netherlands it seemed like it might be time to move. We researched American cities with public transit, where we could afford an apartment with a laundry machine, and where we could hopefully be a part of a Jewish community. This last part was confusing to our friends in Amsterdam, almost none of whom were Jewish. We were members of a synagogue a short bike ride from our apartment, but as much as we loved listening for vocabulary words in the rabbi's talks, and even though the kiddush always included great coffee and milk chocolates, it wasn't quite the Jewish community of our dreams. There were only three other members under the age of sixty, and the Dutch Jewish community was pretty insular—it took two years to get a Shabbat invitation.

So in October 2018 we looked at the list for the last time and we chose Pittsburgh. We started looking at apartments in Squirrel Hill, and we came up with a family mantra: "Pittsburgh Positive." Becoming Pittsburgh Positive meant acting like we already lived in Pittsburgh. We had only a loose sense of Pittsburgh geography and had never heard the word "yinz," but we streamed Pittsburgh local news on our TV in Amsterdam. We read about cookie tables. We picked favorite local sports teams: Boaz chose the Penguins and I chose the Pirates. Friends learned not to get us started on Rick Sebak, libraries, Duolingo, inclines, or the beautifully designed ConnectCard. Even though we could barely spell *Pittsburgh*, it already felt like home.

So on October 27, when news of the attack in Squirrel Hill reached us and everyone else in the world, we reeled not just as people, and as Jews, but also as Pittsburghers. We mourned from six time zones away with the people we didn't know yet, and we cried for the families of the people we wouldn't get to meet. It felt almost selfish to feel as sad as we did for a city that wasn't our home yet, but we felt like Pittsburghers too.

In Amsterdam, our synagogue was guarded by two police officers and a volunteer college-age guard. There was a different guard each week, and when they discovered how bad my Dutch was they'd switch to English: "I don't think you've ever been here before. I don't recognize you." Boaz went early to services to avoid all of this, and he walked breezily into shul after greeting a man named Rol. But I don't like going early to services, and so every week I had a long conversation with the guards.

My luck had changed on my birthday, when the rabbi sent me a signed card, which I started bringing to services every week. "If I've never been here before, why do I have a birthday card signed by the rabbi?" I'd say, and the guard wouldn't ask any more questions. It rains a lot in Amsterdam and I wanted to get the birthday card laminated so that it wouldn't get damaged, but Boaz said that was weird.

On our first Shabbat in Pittsburgh, just a few months later, I worried that the city we'd felt positive about for so long might not have room for us. Would a community in the midst of mourning be ready for newcomers? But in synagogue, when the rabbi announced to the congregation that we had moved here, we got a standing ovation. That afternoon at kiddush, and that month around the neighborhood and around the city, we finally met the people we'd daydreamed about being neighbors with for so long, and they were all as friendly as we had imagined.

Now that we do live in Pittsburgh, sometimes people ask if I'm from here. If I'm feeling sneaky I can tell them I was born here. It's true, but it's misleading. My parents went to grad school at the University of Pittsburgh and Carnegie Mellon, and I lived here for a few months, before I had teeth. I can pretend to be a native, but for most of my life my relationship with Pittsburgh consisted of writing its name on forms.

I'm a Pittsburgh convert, and I'm a Jewish convert too. When I tell people I'm Jewish it feels equally misleading. I can't play Jewish geography and don't have a good answer for what my parents are doing for Rosh Hashanah. I feel as lucky to have found Judaism as I feel to have found Pittsburgh. As a shy person, being Jewish helps me turn a city into a group of neighbors and friends. As a nervous person, being Jewish is what makes me brave enough to speak up when it's important. And best of all, being Jewish makes me feel like me—it feels like something I was meant to be all along.

As a Pittsburgh Jew who hasn't always been a Pittsburgher or Jewish, it feels like my life has finally settled in the way it was always supposed to be. Sure, I may still picture a bird every time someone mentions the local grocery store, Giant Eagle. I may never pronounce "Monongahela" with confidence. But the Pittsburgh Jewish community is my community, and Squirrel Hill is full of my squirrels. Every week at synagogue I listen as we read the names of the people murdered on October 27. I'll never get a chance to spend time with these eleven Pittsburgh Jews, but since moving here I have heard so many warm memories from those who did know them.

Last October we attended a memorial at Soldiers and Sailors Memorial Hall with people who now really are our neighbors. We cried again for our friends and for the families of the neighbors we will never get to meet. In a bizarre turn of events, a photo slideshow that played as we walked in showed half a dozen photos of the dog we adopted when we moved here, which we named Kip. The photos had been taken that morning, as we biked with other volunteers to deliver cookies to first responders, and our dog tagged along comfortably in a backpack. We'll never get to know Pittsburgh exactly as it was before we moved here, but I'm honored to be a part of its future.

SHARING
THEIR STORIES

Reciprocating the Compassionate
Response to the Tree of Life Massacre

Laura Zittrain Eisenberg

MOST HISTORIANS HAVE AN ORIGIN STORY about how they chose
their field of expertise. I have such a story about how I came to study
Middle East history. Sometimes, however, a subject reaches out and
seizes you by the throat, demanding your attention and consuming your
thoughts. The terrible massacre at the Tree of Life synagogue building
on October 27, 2018, occasioned such a moment for me. My family
and I are third-generation members of Tree of Life Congregation; my
husband is the immediate past president and was moments away from
arriving at services on the day of the shooting. We live two blocks away.
The attack shocked me, as a congregant and community member, but
the fact that this was the worst attack on American Jewry in US history
resonated with my sensibilities as a historian. I gravitated toward the
sprawling sidewalk memorial that sprang up outside the synagogue
building within hours, a spontaneous outpouring of anguish, love, and
flowers from the immediate community and beyond. I wanted to make
sure that the historical record would reflect the heartfelt response of our
neighbors as well as the heart-sickening story of the attack.[1]

---

1. Eisenberg, "Memorializing the Memorial to the Tree of Life Shooting," Association
for Political and Legal Anthropology, PoLARS series, March 23, 2019, https://politicaland
legalanthro.org/2019/03/23/memorializing-the-memorial-to-the-tree-of-life-shooting/.

Three separate congregations, Tree of Life, Dor Hadash, and New Light, shared space in the Tree of Life building and all lost members in the attack, eleven beautiful souls in all. The sidewalk memorial mourned all three congregations' victims. The mementos retrieved are temporarily on public display behind the synagogue building's bank of glass doors and are destined for eventual archival preservation. Two years later, they still provide solace, and the stories of their journeys to the corner of Wilkins and Shady now offer additional inspiration.

In the immediate aftermath of the crisis, supportive messages and beautiful objects seemed to appear, magically or miraculously, in the makeshift memorial, and were a great comfort to the three stunned and grieving congregations. Later, however, I realized that the gifts of condolence were neither magical nor miraculous but rather the hand-iwork of good people whose hearts ached for our loss. Their instincts were humanitarian: to do something tangible to let us know that we were not alone, that they mourned with us, and that together we would survive and eventually thrive again. As proclaimed by the signs appearing all over the neighborhood—ubiquitous even today—we are "Stronger Together" and "Stronger than Hate."

Shortly after the shooting, my husband and I spoke at the Smithfield United Church of Christ in downtown Pittsburgh. I noticed, but only in passing, how many parishioners wanted to tell us *their* October 27 stories: how they learned of the shooting, where they were, how they felt, who they turned to, how they talked to their children about it, what actions they took in response. Talking about the memorial objects had been an outlet for processing my own distress, but eventually I remembered that the tragedy had made a deep impression on many people, Jewish and non-Jewish, and that they also needed and wanted to tell their tales. Our listening is one way to begin reciprocating their kindness.

Over time, those of us who had assumed responsibility for preserving the makeshift memorial had discovered backstories to some of the anonymous contributions, and in every case, already touching items became even more poignant. As we recover, we are able to think more about others than ourselves, and we are interested in knowing what moved individuals to leave artifacts among the flowers. What were their intended messages; what did the act of choosing or creating their gift and leaving it at the sidewalk mean to them; how did it make them feel? Some objects have obvious messages and relevance, whereas others are intriguing precisely because their intent is less clear. Thus was born the stories collection project. We reexamined items, looking for clues to their donors. Some we tracked down; others had left gifts anonymously, so we reached out to the public via social media and the press, directing people to a webpage where they could upload their stories. Almost fifty moving narratives have come in, some of which I share here. Stories and quotes come from either people's submissions to the Tree of Life stories webpage or from my conversations with them.

The centerpiece of the memorial was eleven white wooden Stars of David affixed to white wooden crosses, each bearing the name of a victim, which materialized barely twenty-four hours after the shooting. They were the creation of Gregory Zanis, a carpenter from Aurora, Illinois, and the founder of Crosses for Losses, whose mission is to erect crosses in honor of victims of mass shootings.[2] Zanis's motivation was his strong Greek Orthodox Christian faith, which deeply reveres the Old Testament. He had made Stars of David for Jewish victims among those of previous massacres, but never for an attack whose victims were exclusively Jewish. In an interview, he told me that he was hesitant at first, worried about inadvertently making a cultural misstep. His wife convinced him that he must honor the Pittsburgh victims, insisting that "excluding them would itself be an 'act of hate.'"

Zanis's friend Anne Rosenberg, who had met him a year earlier at the Las Vegas shooting site, where she had brought therapy dogs, similarly argued that no one but he could honor the victims in the manner that mourners at these terrible events have come to expect. The day after the attack, Rosenberg and her colleagues from Crisis Response Canines met Zanis upon his arrival in Pittsburgh's Squirrel Hill neighborhood, where he felt conspicuously out of place in his "Crosses for Losses" truck. He parked a few blocks away from the synagogue and walked the perimeter for more than an hour, until he felt he knew where God wanted him to place the stars: behind the

---

2. After twenty years, eight hundred thousand miles, and more than twenty-seven thousand crosses, Mr. Zanis retired in December of 2019, citing the physical and emotional toll of the endeavor. He passed away on May 4, 2020. Lutheran Church Charities of Northbrook, Illinois, is continuing the Crosses for Losses project.

Photo by Brian Cohen

police tape and directly in front of the synagogue building, where some flowers and stones already lay. When he returned to his truck, confused passersby asked him, "Don't you know the victims are all Jewish?" They were overcome when he showed them the stars, and asked to help with offloading and carrying them to the site.

Zanis was relieved to have members of the local Jewish community help install the stars. As the procession moved toward the synagogue, other onlookers joined in. In a conversation I had with her, Rosenberg recalled making an effort to ensure that those who identified themselves as friends or relatives of a specific victim were able to help carry their loved one's star. Zanis carried the last one, carefully holding the cross side against his chest, so only the Star of David was visible. Talking about his contribution to the memorial, Zanis returned repeatedly to two themes. The first was that he was doing God's work and sought no personal attention; he revealed that during the twenty years of his Crosses for Losses activity, 2000–2020, every US president had requested meetings and photographs with him at one of the sites, and that he had rebuffed them all. The second was his concern that he might have unintentionally offended the Jewish community by simply showing up with the stars. He seemed relieved to hear from me that the congregations cherished his contribution, and that the horizontal bars of the crosses on which the stars were mounted created perfect shelves on which visitors could pile little stones—a traditional Jewish mourning custom.

Perhaps the second most prominent element of the memorial was the eleven tall glass-and-china flowers with copper stems and leaves. Each flower consists of a large glass or porcelain dinner plate with incrementally smaller dishes, bowls, and glasses attached concentrically. They appeared in the synagogue's garden forty-eight hours after the shooting, behind a low hedge near the row of wooden stars. Visitors marveled at their beauty, and observed that they looked so perfectly at home, they must have already been part of the garden. But the fact that there were eleven of them attested otherwise.

Their creator is Roy Penner, a local architect and artist. He told me that he had lost his wife, Barbara Cohen Penner, ten months before the shooting, after forty-one years together. When she died he created the first flower as her temporary grave marker. He made more, with the intention of giving them to Barb's family and friends for their gardens, to remind them of her. On a whim, he quickened the pace of flower production in his basement studio and created a temporary art installation at the Burning Man artistic gathering in 2018, called "REBLOOMING —An Expression of Love, Grief and the Randomness in the Order of Life." He had only recently returned with some eighty flowers, not yet unpacked, when the attack occurred. He selected eleven, looking for ones with blue and white or six-pointed shapes to echo the Star of David, and planted them at the memorial site. People became so attached to them that when bad weather necessitated the memorial's deconstruction, it was decided to keep them permanently in the garden.

A large metal angel took up a position near the glass flowers, the gift of Johnstown metal artist Lei Hennessy-Owen, whose angels of varying sizes grace many memorials, among them the three 9/11 sites and the scenes of other shootings. Lei also makes and sells ceramic paw prints, with proceeds benefiting police K-9 units. She used her contacts to reach the Zone Four police station, first to respond to the synagogue attack, and officers met her at the site to help install the heavy sculpture.

A number of objects were Holocaust-related, an apt reference at the site of an antisemitic slaughter. Katherine Kaplan-Locke made the connection by simply painting the number 6,000,011 on a stone; Janice Herzer found that the image of that stone has stayed with her, and recalled sharing a hug with the woman placing it.

Among the most mysterious artifacts were eleven tiny picture frames, each bearing a small, browning leaf and a label identifying the source as the Raoul Wallenberg Tree, in the Righteous among the Nations Walk at Yad Vashem, the Holocaust Remembrance Center, in Israel. Yad Vashem confers the honorific "Righteous among the Nations" on non-Jews who risked their lives to save Jews during the Holocaust. Wallenberg was a Swedish diplomat who saved thousands of Jews before his arrest by the Soviets in 1945 and disappearance into the gulag. Bob Bukk wrote to the story project to explain that he and his wife, Jane, who are Christians, had traveled with Jewish friends on a trip to Israel sponsored by Congregation Beth Shalom, which departed Pittsburgh on October 28, 2018, the day after the massacre.

Photo by Brian Cohen

Photos by Laurie Zittrain Eisenberg

How difficult to finally be in Israel, after months of anticipation and preparation, only to have one's thoughts focused squarely on the terrible drama unfolding back home. Bukk collected the leaves at Yad Vashem. Upon his return, he framed them and deposited them in the makeshift memorial. His impetus was to grieve with the congregations; the connection to a non-Jew who recognized Jewish pain and acted to mitigate it is perfectly fitting.

Vincent Allen worked as a bank teller while a student in the 1980s, and never forgot the patron whose outstretched arm revealed a concentration camp tattoo number. He bought flowers and laid them at Rose Mallinger's wooden star, having heard in the media that she was a Holocaust survivor. Allen wrote that despite the inaccuracy of that initial report, he was glad to have focused on Rose, even as he thought about "that man who stepped up to my teller window and how he survived evil. Together, we will also survive evil, through love and compassion."

Many respondents invoked the phrases "never forget" and "never again" in their explanations for why they felt motivated to leave flowers or items. "Never again" is a familiar expression and a welcome sentiment, but also somehow disheartening, since antisemitic acts reached "near historic levels" in 2018 and continue to surge."[3] Visitors' "identity cards" from the Holocaust Memorial Museum in Washington, DC, and a picture of Anne Frank with her quote about people being fundamentally good at heart and a wooden tulip still lack full backstories.

The Pittsburgh attack came just two weeks before the eightieth anniversary of Kristallnacht, the "night of broken glass" in which Nazi thugs and citizen mobs destroyed thousands of Jewish homes, shops and synagogues in Germany. Tree of Life rabbi Jeffrey Myers was at pains to remind people, however, that whereas the German authorities had watched the rampage from the sidelines, Pittsburgh police ran headlong into gunfire to rescue Jewish worshippers, and

---

3. "Anti-Semitic Incidents Remained at Near-Historic Levels in 2018; Assaults against Jews More than Doubled," Anti-Defamation League press release, April 30, 2019, https://www.adl.org/news/press-releases/anti-semitic-incidents-remained-at-near-historic-levels-in-2018-assaults.

public officials and their constituents immediately rushed to the Jewish community's side.

Many visitors returned repeatedly to view the constantly evolving collection of flowers, signs, and keepsakes, and everyone had their favorites, which spoke most deeply to them. A partial list of objects includes flags, candles, stuffed animals, religious icons, a guitar, and an array of artwork, comprising fabric arts, sculpture, sketches, paintings, and drawings by children and experienced artists, variously rolled into Ziploc bags, laminated, framed or simply laid in the garden. Most numerous were the masses of flowers, numbering in the thousands. Several bouquets comprised eleven blooms. One bunch had a sticker with a victim's name on each stem; a storyteller who wishes to remain unnamed attached a rosary to each of eleven roses, placed one at each of the eleven wooden stars, and recited eleven decades of the rosary. In all, we recovered several dozen rosaries.

Many people left stones, as Jews do at gravesites: thousands of ordinary stones made sacred by their placement, and hundreds of painted stones. Barbara Sims painted stones blue and adorned each with a white Star of David, with a heart in the center. Debbie Gregor had already been painting cheerful stones and leaving them around the neighborhood for delighted residents to find. Her designs specific to the shooting featured roses, doves, teardrops, and butterflies. Other stone artists included students from Saint Edmund's Academy. Janice Rizzo and Tracey Kniess contributed an etched stone reading *Scatter seeds of kindness and find peace*. It had taken Sara Henry, an employee of the Charles Morris Rehabilitation Center, a long thirty minutes to learn that none of the center's residents were at the Tree of Life building at the time of the attack; she and her aunt brought shiny blue and white stones to the memorial. The profusion of stones in the traditionally Jewish colors showed they were not alone. Julie and Jimmy Wallace delivered eleven little bottles from the United Church of Christ in Kent, Ohio, each containing a blue rose from the church's altar and a small stone. When Julie learned that the congregations had saved the bottles, she broke down in tears.

Jessica Zozom "grew up" in the Tree of Life Congregation and building; the Zozoms placed eleven stones they found on their walk to the site on the far end of the memorial, along Shady Avenue. The crowd was so thick around the wooden stars that they could not get close enough to lay a stone at each one. The Sikov family left clear blue stones, which had been part of Tyler's centerpieces at his bar mitzvah at Tree of Life. Also documenting their connection to Tree of Life, David and Fran Fall left pictures of each of their four grandchildren in front of the Tree of Life building on their bar and bat mitzvah days. Michal Gray-Schaffer, who had been a student cantor at Tree of Life from 2005 to 2007, had spent the morning of the attack weeping and sheltering in place at the Coffee Tree Roasters. The owner asked her to come back two days later to speak to the distressed employees, who knew some of the victims as regular customers. She did, and then together they walked to the memorial to lay yellow roses and notes at each wooden star.

Offerings from Jewish institutions came from near and far. The Ner Yisrael Congregation in London sent a large white shadow box, with hundreds of good wishes written on small discs strung within it. The sixth-graders of Park Avenue Synagogue in New York wrote their own prayers and placed them in plastic sleeves in a binder labeled "READ ME" for visitors to peruse. Eleven New York state flags, each tagged with a victim's name, came from Magen David Yeshivah in Brooklyn.

Candles proliferated, many in tall glass cylinders adorned with either Hebrew prayers and Jewish symbols or images of Jesus and various saints. Marc and Pat Liebman toured Israel with a group from Saint Boniface Church and brought back a memorial candle to contribute. Mark Abramowitz had kept an unburned yahrzeit candle on a closet shelf since his father's passing in 1997; some twenty years later, wick met match at Wilkins and Shady Avenues. There were many tea lights, often in groups of eleven. Eagle-eyed young Tree of Life congregant Thomas Levine noticed that a candle had started a small fire as his family drove by and they pulled over so his mother could stomp out the flames. Cautious mourners left LED candles at the site. Student Kerry Jo Green attended the Squirrel Hill prayer vigil the night of the shooting and recognized the slim white tapers someone handed her as Advent candles, familiar from her Catholic youth, which reminded her of "how interfaith our grief and love are." She left one candle stub at the memorial and kept one for herself.

One week after the shooting, Sarah Davies found herself in New York, suiting up for the city's marathon. She impulsively bought some markers and inked a message of hope on the back of her jersey, identifying herself as a Jewish Pittsburgher. People called out to her encouragingly along the route, and upon returning home, she left her jersey and her finisher's medal at the memorial. Davies believes in "the power of loss to intensify determination and will" for both runners and communities.

Lillian Wolff brought two American flags, pained by the fact that an American citizen had committed this abomination, but seeing in the flags the goodness of the country, nonetheless. Dawn O'Brien left a white rubber bracelet bearing the name of Ethan Song, a family friend who died in an accidental shooting with an unsecured gun at a friend's home; the Songstrong Foundation works to reduce gun violence, among other community projects. A luggage tag featuring words of encouragement exhorts viewers to "live like Devon," a civic-minded young man who drowned at twenty-seven and whose mother works to lift up fellow travelers on unexpected journeys of grief. She notes that Devon, "a good Catholic boy," was the recipient of his high school's Anne Frank Humanitarian Award for his efforts to better the lives of others. Kathryn Feeney scattered eleven "love" bottle openers among the flowers, leftover wedding favors. Descendants of Italian immigrants in Squirrel Hill, one of whom did landscaping for Tree of Life Congregation many years ago, left a large scalloped seashell with their family names and a Jewish star. Sue Link left a white dove ornament that "spoke" to her.

Stars, Jewish and otherwise, and hearts were everywhere. Two years later, many still hang on railings and bushes throughout Squirrel Hill. Some were decorated and delivered from afar by members of national organizations established to bring hope to communities struck by tragedy. The Barbara and Randy Grossman family of Pittsburgh established the #ShareAHeartPGH initiative to make and place handmade hearts in public places as reminders of the power of kindness. To date they have displayed 5,500 hearts, and Barb continues to place them as she walks through Pittsburgh and Squirrel Hill. Amy Raslevich crocheted and felted hearts for each victim's memorial wooden star; other locals crafted similar hearts and stars and hung them at the site and around the neighborhood. Emily Presacreta took her three-year-old son Gavin to pick out two heart-shaped balloons to contribute.

Messages appeared on everything from small notes tucked inside the cellophane wrap on bouquets to hotel stationery, signs of every size and material, large banners, jerseys, a jack-o'-lantern, and framed certificates. The most frequent sentiments were sorrow, love, support, and resistance in the face of hate. Numerous items sported the Steelers logo, modified to include a Star of David. Many objects bore multiple signatures of members of teams, schools, houses of worship, fraternities, organizations, or other groups.

At the end of the long, emotional day on which we disassembled the memorial and moved the objects indoors, a woman appeared at the synagogue and handed me a tiny wooden cross. As I recall, she explained that she was a nurse and had worked for many years with one of the victims, Dr. Jerry Rabinowitz. The cross belonged to a patient she had nursed, and when he eventually passed away, his family gave it to her. She wanted us to have it. I thanked her, but looking at the hundreds of objects piled around me, urged her to keep it. She was insistent. Physically and mentally exhausted, I let her leave without getting her name. The cross is safe, but I wish we had her name and the details of her story properly recorded.

Obviously, messages and gifts came from well-wishers of many religions, ethnicities, and races, a majority, perhaps, emphasizing in their messages and stories that they are Christians. Everyone's sentiments were uniformly loving and supportive—the only off-key note came from a messianic Jews-for-Jesus chapter, which left pamphlets and a hand-annotated New Testament in a package addressed to "a very special rabbi."

Many of the storytellers mentioned an initial sense of helplessness and then an overwhelming urge to *do something*. For many that meant leaving flowers, physical objects or notes, but others performed acts of lovingkindness intended to honor the victims and comfort the people mourning them. At different times, violinists played on the sidewalk; Devin Arrington chose the theme from *Schindler's List* and Monique Mead fastened a poster to her music stand quoting Leonard Bernstein: "This will be our response to violence: to make music more intensely, more beautifully, more devotedly than ever before." In separate stories, Devin and Monique both described their musical offerings as their "bouquets." Following services the day after the Saturday shooting, the Saint Bede choir impulsively walked from the church to the synagogue building, slowing down to accommodate several members using walkers. There they sang "Let There Be Peace on Earth." Raymond Werner recalled that most of the people who happened to be at the corner joined in, and "a chill went up our spines. That hymn was never sung more beautifully, ever."

Janet DiPaolo brought her therapy dog to the memorial several times, where there was no shortage of visitors grateful for a moment or two with the calm and soothing Elsa. Richard Yeomans, a former law enforcement chaplain, flew in from California to leave a large pile of "Understanding Trauma" pamphlets on the edge of the memorial, courtesy of Emergency Ministry Services. Karen Seibert left a self-authored book about her son's successful recovery from addiction, hoping that someone in need would take it. The pamphlets were gone within a day or two, and Seibert's book was not among the items found in the mountains of flowers, so hopefully both went home with people who could benefit from them. Haley Grenesko and her Girl Scout troop baked cookies and delivered them to the Zone Four station house and the operation center across from the synagogue site.

A set of camp chairs was both a tangible gift and a loving act in honor of the victims. Retired Long Island firefighter Tommy Maher founded the Honor Network after the Las Vegas concert shooting in 2017. Network members visit communities struck by mass gun violence to make random gestures of benevolence to honor each victim. At the Tree of Life corner, Maher asked people, if there were something needed at the site, what would it be? Several suggested that it would be comforting if visitors could sit in contemplation among the heaps of flowers. The team went directly to the local Target and purchased the collapsible chairs, to which they attached small cards with the names and pictures of the victims. Among the eleven acts of lovingkindness they performed, Honor Network members visited several restaurants in Squirrel Hill and left as much as $300 with startled cashiers, asking them to cover the bills of other customers and give them the cards with the victims' images and names. The goal is not simply to remember those lost but to actively honor them in ways that affect others and, hopefully, inspire the beneficiaries to pay it forward.

The Zittrain Gardens at Tree of Life also deserve mention, for serving as the backdrop to the sidewalk memorial. They were the gift many years ago of my parents, Ruth and Lester Zittrain, avid gardeners who intended them as a beautiful setting for members' wedding and bar and bat mitzvah pictures, synagogue events, and as a pretty burst of color in the neighborhood. They could not have imagined, but would have found comfort in, the gardens' role hosting the post-massacre bouquets and artifacts, and offering visitors a quiet place of reflection, even after the memorial's dismantlement. Flowers, painted stones, decorative hearts, and small wooden stars still appear there regularly.

The backstory of one the most intriguing items, a pair of glittery gold high-top basketball shoes, remains a mystery. On the white rubber toe of the right shoe is written "Shalom Aleichem, Salaam Aleikum," loosely translated as "peace be upon you" in Hebrew and Arabic. The left toe reads "Shalom Aleichem, Love and Light." Whatever inspired the donor to leave messages on such an incongruous, inexplicable object? They are the artifact that I most frequently return to in my thoughts, and perhaps therein lies the answer. Like the tomb of an unknown soldier, the sparkly footwear stands in for all of the beautiful people whose anonymous gestures bear evidence of the goodness in so many hearts. But I wouldn't mind knowing the full story.

The Pittsburgh Jewish community observed the one-year anniversary of the shooting with a campaign designed to reciprocate the love it had received over the past twelve months, organizing blood drives and more than thirty community service activities at libraries, food pantries, and social service organizations across the city, under the slogan "Remember. Repair. Together." The streets of Squirrel Hill, in particular, buzzed with energy and life that day. October 27, 2019, also saw members from Tree of Life, New Light, and Dor Hadash take up positions at Zittrain Gardens, where they greeted and thanked people coming to pay respects. Many visitors left fresh flowers and new signs along the hedge in front of the glass flowers and welcomed the opportunity to speak directly to congregants.

Violinist Monique Mead performed at a private gathering of the victims' families on the eve of the one-year mark, and again the next

Photo by Laurie Zittrain Eisenberg

day on the synagogue sidewalk where she had made her impromptu performance a year earlier. Children from the Islamic Center of Pittsburgh Sunday school, accompanied by teachers and parents, walked up Wilkins Avenue bearing bright handmade posters decorated with words and pictures of peace and encouragement, which they leaned against the hedge. The corner witnessed a new burst of hearts and stars, among them Taylor Bushroe's two homemade wooden hearts reading *Love will always win* and *You matter, you are so loved*, which he had driven in from Fort Wayne, Indiana, to deliver.

Michelle Lubetsky wrote a poem, in which she both posed and answered the question of how to talk about the anniversary of the attack to children:

> What do you say to a three-year-old when the world comes tumbling down;
>
> When eleven neighbors are heinously murdered in your backyard;
>
> When it feels like the world stopped spinning and all sense of normalcy is gone?
>
> What do you say to a three-year-old to acknowledge the passing year, when evil overcame good, when every fiber of your being was diminished by sorrow and grief?
>
> You say to that innocent, delightful toddler, come with Mimi and we'll create something new! You lead him to the porch that overlooks a somber Tree of Life, our workplace for healing. You show him the bright colors of life, the ribbons of hope, and glue of binding love. You guide him to create a palette of loving kindness to promote goodness and compassion.

Lubetsky explained to her three-year-old grandson Liam that people were using art to make sad people feel better at the synagogue behind her house, and a few hours later, she and Liam hung his string of paper heart panels on the low fence in front of the hedge.

Fourteen-year-old artist Ashley LaRocque was "crushed" when she heard about the attack and immediately began a painting depicting a pair of strong hands cradling the city of Pittsburgh. Visitors to the synagogue site on the one-year commemoration of the shooting could see Ashley's painting—along with one hundred others—on colorful windscreens covering the perimeter fence running the length of the property along Wilkins. The congregations had noticed how frequently people turned to art to express their deepest feelings and conceived of "Hearts Together: The Art of Rebuilding," a public art project intended to thank the community for its support by replacing the dingy blue fence tarps with a vivid sidewalk gallery of inspirational artwork by young people, printed on windscreens. In transforming the site of the tragedy into one of beauty, the congregations sought to project outward the strength and positivity that the neighborhood, the city, and the world shared with them during their darkest days. They received over 200 submissions, 108 of which came from students at Marjory Stoneman Douglas High School in Parkland, Florida, which had suffered a terrible shooting only eight months prior to the assault in Pittsburgh. The healing and uplifting works of art aimed to reflect and honor the loving, joyful lives of the eleven victims and to bring light and beauty back to the corner of Wilkins and Shady. There was room for only 101 pieces of artwork on the fence wind-screens, but all 224 appear on the "Hearts Together" webpage at https://www.treeoflifepgh.org/heartstogether.

Similar space constraints prohibit me from sharing all of the memorial objects' stories and all of the storytellers' names. I have focused on items left at the memorial site, although the three congregations also deeply cherish the many items mailed or delivered to the Tree of Life's temporary office, off-site. Some donors may find meaning in anonymity; being one in a swell of thousands may be more comfortable than singling themselves out to tell their stories. We thank our unnamed contributors and want them to know we feel the love. But for readers who want to share their stories of items left or acts of lovingkindness performed at the sidewalk memorial, or of gifts otherwise presented to the congregations, the portal for uploading stories and pictures remains open at https://www.treeoflifepgh.org/stories.

Two years in, we can appreciate that the stories of the objects we recovered began not with our finding them but with the impulse of other people to give them to us. Together, the giving and the receiving bind us one to the other and make us a potentially powerful, positive force working to confront those who hate and would do harm. Eventually, edited versions of all the stories will be viewable on the Tree of Life website, where we believe people will draw strength and inspiration from them. We hope the storytellers also find fulfillment in telling their tales. We are listening.

PROCESSING

Eric Lidji

THE ATTACK ON OCTOBER 27, 2018, lasted 83 minutes from the moment the gunman entered the synagogue until the moment the police apprehended him. In the 18 months since that Saturday morning, I have collected 189 boxes of things documenting the impact of those 83 minutes on the Jewish population of Western Pennsylvania. "Things" in this case means things you can touch—flyers, programs, signs, speeches, sermons, posters, and the many letters and gifts sent as gestures of consolation. They currently occupy a section of metal shelves in a back corner of the archive where I work, down one long row and halfway down the next. Seeing all these things together in one place is overwhelming. They are the manifestation of a collective emotional response to one tragedy. In the archives of other communities are the responses to other tragedies. If you multiply our shelves by those tragedies, and imagine standing before all of it, you can appreciate the enduring relevance of the Talmudic dictum by Abba Binyamin: "If the eye were given permission to see them, no creature would be able to withstand the demons surrounding us" (Tractate Berakhot 6a). Grief is a class of demon. If we could see it, its ubiquity would be unbearable.

I was briefly given permission the morning after the attack, as I drove into Squirrel Hill. I had gone to sleep heartbroken and woken a few hours later in a state I had never experienced before and could not diagnose. My limbs were limp as thread. A patch of numbness buzzed behind each of my ears, and at the pulse points in my wrists. I sobbed in the shower until I was gasping for air, and again in the car, listening to the news. Over and over in those initial weeks, I fell apart anytime my friends were on the news, being interviewed or, worse, standing in the background of a photograph. The news is usually so distant. The people being interviewed are strangers, and the people in the background are anonymous.

The morning was damp and gray. I took Beechwood Boulevard into Squirrel Hill to avoid the police barricades along Shady Avenue blocking the approach to the crime scene. Beechwood and Shady run parallel for several blocks, and at each intersection I glanced to my right, not to rubberneck but to reestablish my personal connection to a street corner I have passed a thousand times without consequence. Peering down one of those side streets, I saw the neon streak of an ambulance zipping through the intersection, up Shady, toward the synagogue.

All at once I was overcome. My head started swimming, and my skin broke out in dull dime-sized tingles. *I'm going to pass out*, I thought. I pulled the car over, dropped my face into my hands, and sobbed while the sensation coursed through my body. It expanded across my midsection, spread down my arms and legs, and spilled into my fingers and toes. After about a minute, it subsided. The way it passed unfiltered through my body reminded me of an earthquake I had experienced in Alaska, how the tremor had slipped along its fault line like an invisible train barreling down invisible tracks, the force gradually strengthening as it approached, briefly overwhelming on arrival, and fading as it departed. As I sat there in the car that morning, wondering what had just happened, I had an epiphany, almost too big to handle. It was this: *Someone is always feeling what I just felt.* Grief is always striking somewhere. And just as the reverberations diminish in one place, grief strikes anew somewhere else. Grief is one of the constant undertones of human existence. Until that morning, I had been largely unaware.

All over the world, thousands of people were also overcome by the attack and were subsequently compelled to channel their feelings into flyers, programs, signs, speeches, sermons, posters, letters, and gifts.

They sent those things to people throughout the region. In time, as the aftershocks lessened, those people lent those things to me. Then the processing began.

Processing is a sequence of tasks intended to make records easier to use. An archivist appraises the records, transfers them to acid-free folders and boxes, arranges them, describes them, and eventually catalogs them, at which point they become available to any researcher who wants to see them for any reason. A well-processed collection is like a city with good roads. It makes getting anywhere easier, even if you don't quite know where to go or how to get there.

Outside of the archival world, "processing" has also become a common term for the psychological task of reckoning with an emotionally intense experience. It involves thinking through the experience until you can live with the feelings it provokes. You turn everything over in your head. You crouch down to examine the details. You step back to view it from a distance. You talk about it. You dream about it. You search for connections in the experiences of other people, or in art. You try to find a place for it within your general understanding of how the world works. Only that's not it—not exactly—because thinking through an experience can change your understanding of how the world works. Emotional processing is the interplay between a mind and its memories, each working on the other until equilibrium is restored. People call that equilibrium "coming to terms" with an event, or they call it "acceptance." It is distinct from finding "meaning" or "purpose." Those are what processing allows you to acquire.

Archival processing is the same activity, only with paper instead of emotions. A collection of records arrives at an archive without any definitive explanation of its reason for being. It is a code without a key. Archivists learn as much as they can about the creator of the records and about the circumstances surrounding the creation of the records. They review the records over and over in search of connections, themes, and groupings. They eventually come to understand the essential nature of the records—why they were made, and what they do. At that point they can write a finding aid, which is an abstract, a table of contents, and an index, all in one. It describes the contents and the context of a collection in simple language, allowing researchers to navigate the records. A tenacious researcher can muscle through an unprocessed collection of records and find what they want to find, just as a tenacious person can charge through life without processing any anger or pain. But in both cases, processing is based on the premise that making sense of complexity gives you a better chance of benefiting from it.

An important step in archival processing is measuring a collection. The 189 boxes of things stacked neatly on the shelves at the Jewish archives are impressive to behold because they occupy so much physical space. But they are insignificant compared to the things that take up almost no physical space at all. We have collected 18.45 gigabytes of digital photographs, flyers, videos, and audio recordings, and an additional 146.9 gigabytes of online materials: websites, news articles, social media posts. Beyond that are other records, things we know exist and hope to someday collect, things too sensitive to be entrusted into our care just yet. Beyond the records we know about are the records we don't know about, but would want if we did. (Imagine, in a drawer somewhere, an eloquent diary chronicling the aftermath.) And each of these categories—the physical and the digital, the known and the unknown—is constantly accumulating things, day by day by day, as the reverberations of the attack continue to shake the ground beneath our feet.

For survivors of the attack, for families of the victims, for the three attacked congregations, for the Jewish community in this region, and for its allies around the city and across the world, each new day expands the experience of being so close to such horror. And that expansion generates things. Mourners send gifts of consolation. Writers tell stories. Artists make art. Activists act. Lawyers write briefs. Each similar attack somewhere else generates comparisons to the attack in Pittsburgh, and often a response from groups in Pittsburgh, which in turn generates more flyers and more programs and more posters and more speeches.

The Jewish calendar continually encourages reflection—the week of shiva, the month of *shloshim*, the first Hanukkah and the first Purim with their twin archetypes of antisemitism, the first Passover with its first somber yizkor to recall the dead, the first Yom Hashoah connecting our attack to the worst attack perpetrated against our people, the first Tisha b'Av with its echoes of Jewish tragedy throughout the ages, the first High Holidays, the first unveiling of grave markers, the first yahrzeit of the attack on the Gregorian calendar and on the Hebrew calendar, and then the second Hanukkah, and the second Purim, and so on, until daily life itself becomes a response to the attack, as the ongoing act of recovery silently infuses every sermon, every lecture, every exhibit, every article, every flyer, every conversation, without ever needing to make the reference explicit. A community produces a lot of documentation as it collectively processes its pain. Try to imagine a room large enough to contain all the things that would not exist if those 83 minutes had not occurred. That is the impossible ideal the archive is chasing.

The first item added to this collection was a program. It was handed out at a large vigil at Soldiers and Sailors Memorial Hall, the day after the attack. It is a single sheet of paper, with a statement on one side and a song sheet on the other, including the lyrics to Irving Berlin's "God Bless America." Over the months that followed, I rushed to vigils, classes, lectures, conversations, and symposia, collecting whatever documentation I could find. Having a defined role initially eased my private sorrow. Being out in the world—observing, listening, collecting—opened my heart wide. The emotions of any given moment crashed over me with full force, but when they receded, they seemed to leave no residue. It thought I had found instant processing.

But it was nothing more than experiencing too much too quickly, and inevitably it caught up with me. The city limped back to its routines, and I was still picking through the remnants of other people's grief. The emotions kept crashing over me and crashing over me, and after they had receded, bits clung to me for days. A few months after the attack, I began recording oral histories. The interviews were personal and intense, each revealing a hidden world of pain. Hearing other people talk through their grief was enlightening. But it was also exhausting. Every oral history started with the same question: "What were you doing on the morning of October 27, 2018?" I returned to that morning again and again and again, living those awful hours alongside one person and then alongside another person, and another. I eventually lost the desire to record interviews. I found I was increasingly unable to stare into the eyes of someone articulating pain.

In the spring of 2019, I started a database tracking local media coverage of the attack and its aftermath. I went day by day through every publication in the city. I logged breaking news reports from the crime scene, followed by accounts of the funerals, the financial distributions, the court case, and the community service projects, until I arrived at the present. The present was always a welcome respite: it was proof we had survived this far. But then I would start on the next publication, and return to the shock of that morning, and I would sink into confusion and heartache again. The present always yielded to the past. Healing always reverted to harm. I came to dread that cycle of emotions. And so I procrastinated, and the database fell behind, because the aftermath was still happening. It is still happening, now. The articles keep coming.

Between the oral histories and the articles, I returned to that morning perhaps 70 times, and many more if you count all the casual conversations with other people in the community who were going through the same cycle, in their own way. Bit by bit, my prevailing emotional state became a brittle form of tedium vulcanized by a mutating, electric sorrow. I remember how meaningful it had been, back in mid-November 2018, to dismantle the spontaneous memorial growing outside the synagogue. A small group of us tended to each offering of consolation and heartbreak as though we were cradling the very heart of the person who had added the thing to the memorial. And I remember the jittery frustration I felt just a few months later, at the end of January 2019, standing on the front steps of Tree of Life, removing the dozens of yellow Post-it notes that visitors had been taping to the red marble wall outside the shuttered doors. I was trying to peel them loose without ripping them. The day was freezing and blustery, and the marble was like a slab of ice. I didn't have gloves. My fingertips turned white and waxy with frostnip as I picked at the tape. Every few minutes, I sought shelter inside the lobby, among all the memorial objects we had collected months earlier. I paced through the piles of heartbreak with my hands jammed in my pockets, impatiently waiting for the feeling to return to my fingertips, all while thinking, *Enough already! Enough! No more things!* And then, once I had recovered my reverence for the work, I went back outside to drag my fingernails across the frozen tape corners.

A psychiatrist told me, "Remember, it's not *your* pain." I believe him, and yet it has been so hard to yank my heart away from the pain of other people. On quiet days, I still duck into the archive, pull a box from the shelves, and sit on the cold tile floor, reading through the letters of consolation. Every time I do, I discover some new facet of the collective grief. Some word choice makes everything real and immediate again. Pressure rises up my neck and floods my cheeks, a minor recurrence of the incapacitation I first felt in the car. The inner life of other people, set down on paper, is so much more sharply defined than the muddle I feel when I reckon with my own response to the attack. Their pain has become an artifact, and mine is just pain.

In an early strategic conversation, a colleague warned me against trying to collect everything. Find the emblematic pieces, she said, the things that represent bigger facets of the story. She proposed the shears of the florist who had prepared bouquets for the funerals. I disagreed. We had to get everything, or as close to everything as we could get. That was the only way to do justice to the experience. No single object could possibly stand in opposition to the magnitude of the horror committed that morning. Only all of it, filling shelf after shelf in the archives, row after row in the databases, file after file on the hard drives, could convey the extent of the pain caused by this one person. Each object was another piece of evidence against him.

Like so many other people, I marveled at the work of our local *chevra kadisha*s in those ugly early days. The honor they showed to the dead was the perfect response to the crime and its disrespect for life. A basic tenet of any chevra kadisha is to collect everything. No drop of blood or gram of flesh is left in plain view, to be dishonored by our disgust. Everything must be returned to the earth, even if that means burying carpet and wood and cloth. I was inspired by that dedication, and I wanted the archive to operate on the same principle. Our work was not to collect parts of the body but imprints of the soul , emotions as they had become preserved in physical objects and digital files. I am fascinated by the stories behind the most distinctive of these items, but I continue to be most drawn to the piles of anonymous things—the thousands of small blank stones left at the memorial, the dozens of spent aluminum tea lights, the plastic sheathing that once held bouquets. These common things would be meaningless if not for the circumstances.

How do you process the records of an ongoing event? One piece at a time. We photograph each object from every angle, and then we describe it a dozen different ways. Who made it? What is it made of? What condition is it in? And most importantly, what is it about?

Over the past two years, any time I have attended any event associated with the attack, I have collected whatever documentation I could find—a flyer, a program, a poster, any remarks, anything tangible. Back at the archive, I placed these in a box on my desk, to deal with later. In early November 2019, during the three-week yahrzeit season between the Gregorian and Hebrew dates of the attack, I began processing this subset of the larger collection. By then it had grown to fill a little more than two boxes. I went through these boxes sheet by sheet, bringing the sheets together into folders by event, and gathering the folders by organization, and arranging the organizations alphabetically, starting with the Reform congregation Adat Shalom in the suburban North Hills and ending with the Hasidic high school Yeshiva Schools in urban Squirrel Hill.

I created a spreadsheet, and I went through the boxes organization by organization, listing every event hosted by each organization and inventorying all the items I had collected from that event. I searched online for associated websites or images. I followed up with the organizations to see if I had missed any of their events or any of the other endeavors they had undertaken as a response to the attack. I tried to find something from every Jewish organization in the region, something reflecting every age group and every approach to Jewish life. Eventually, these folders will be added to the records of each organization that are already housed in the archives, records stretching back 150 years, documenting all the mundane and transcendent aspects of Jewish communal life. Someday, these new records will also be 150 years old. The aftermath will no longer fill the air as it does now, and these things will be asked to speak on our behalf.

The work remains perpetually ongoing. New demands are always pushing it aside. But whenever I am able to turn my attention to it, it provides me the only sustained comfort I have felt since the attack aside from the idyll of daily prayer. I have no special insight into why this attack happened, or why it happened here. I don't know what would have prevented it from happening here or what would prevent it from happening again somewhere else. I don't understand the depth of my sorrow or the vast sorrow of others. All I know is this: there are 189 boxes of things stacked neatly on our shelves, plus 18.45 gigabytes of digital materials and another 146.9 gigabytes of online materials stored on servers and hard drives. In due time, with persistence, I can know just the tiniest bit more. I can know each thing individually. I will be able to describe it, and I will be able to situate it among all the other things in the archive, so that nothing is ever lost or overlooked, so that others can someday make meaning from it all.

"Any act of description is, to some extent, an act of praise," John Updike once said, defending his verbosity, "so that even when the event is unpleasant or horrifying or spiritually stunning, the very attempt to describe it is, in some way, part of that Old Testament injunction to give praise."[1] Since my epiphany in the car that gray October morning, I have spent some part of every day trying to reckon with the murkiness of my grief by describing the grief of other people, as it exists in the thousands of things they created. But every day adds to this collection, contributing to the ongoing story of recovery, and so I will never be any further along than when I started. It will consume as much of my life as I choose to give to it, and then it will consume just as much of the life of whoever follows me, and whoever follows that person, as well.

The work is not therapy, and it cannot take the place of a private reckoning. It is simply an act of praise, a way to dignify a communal experience. Like any act of praise, it is uplifting, but only temporarily. Praise redirects the tremendous energy given to self-regard. Anytime I look outside myself, and I marvel at what I see, I always feel a little better. When I return to myself and to my tired thoughts, I am changed. And until that feeling wears off, I can breathe again.

---

1. Thomas Fensch, ed., *Conversations with John Updike* (University Press of Mississippi, 1994).

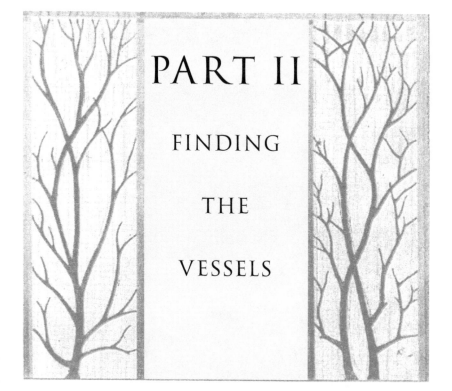

PART II

FINDING

THE

VESSELS

HONEY FROM
THE CARCASS

Beth Kissileff

THE STORY STARTS with being unable to tell the story. It ends with a riddle.

For me, it began when the words of my husband reached my ears, though what they ultimately meant was unclear to both of us. "There's been a shooting at the shul."

In the moments leading up to my hearing those words, I was eating breakfast, reading the Saturday *New York Times* and feeling relief that the man mailing bombs to prominent Jews like Debbie Wasserman Schultz and George Soros had been apprehended. Sitting at the table, reading the news of the outside world, lingering before getting dressed to join my husband at the synagogue, I was thinking about things to keep in mind for a three-week writing residency at the Collegeville Institute in Minnesota; I was due there in a few days to write an essay about memory in the Biblical book of Exodus for an anthology I was editing. Grasping the newspaper upright, I had my entire field of vision occupied. As I turned a page, I thought I heard the door open, which didn't make sense since my rabbi husband had left an hour before and wasn't supposed to be back for another two hours, when his Sabbath morning service concluded.

The door shut. I put the paper down. I heard the words; I couldn't understand them.

When he said "at the shul," my first thought was that a person had come and shot *at* the building—broke the glass doors, or shot at the walls to create havoc and devastation. It didn't occur to me that the shooter's goal was, rather, the destruction of the lives of those praying there. I asked my husband if we should go to a different synagogue then, if we could not go to his. It was a terrible idea, but it was my first thought—*okay, let's find somewhere else to go.*

He recounted what had happened as best he could: he heard a noise, and, though he had never heard live gunfire in his life, intuited what the noise was and knew that he and the other three people at the front of the room must quickly run and hide. A door from our basement-level sanctuary led into a pitch-dark electrical storage room, which he ushered them into. Each of them found a spot to hide in. My husband felt his way around the walls and found a passage out, up a flight of stairs to a door that led outside. When he came out of the building, a hysterical policeman screamed at him, to "Get the fuck out of here, go home," so in a neighborhood on strict lockdown orders, my fortunate husband was the only one able to walk home, following the same path he had taken an hour earlier.

I'm not sure of the order of events—did I give him tea or a glass of water? Did he tell me when he came in, from the door, or did he sit on the couch while I went to sit beside him? How much time elapsed until I woke up our fourteen-year-old daughter from her sound sleep? I first said, "Abba is okay," and then, "There has been a shooting at the shul."

"What?" she asked, confused by this nonsensical thing to hear upon awakening. I repeated myself and she said, "I hope people won't be afraid to go to shul. Will Abba lose his job now?" I hadn't even thought about the possibility, but she was right to worry. If no one wanted to come to our small shul anymore, if they were afraid, what would happen?

The three of us tried to pray together in our living room once the calls to our immediate family had been placed, but the doorbell kept ringing with people wanting to see if we were okay. What would have been if my husband had not been safely home? It would have been horrible to repeat his absence, had he been missing. Throughout the day, we kept hearing updates from others who were using electronics on the Sabbath: four killed, six killed, eight killed, four bodies in the basement. Our hearts sank when we heard that. We did not know an exact number until we went to the Jewish Community Center in the evening, after the Sabbath ended.

As a writer, my natural impulse would have been to try to comprehend the event in writing. However, the first thing I could put down—the only thing I could write for a long time—was based in part on what I thought about in the middle of the night and then spoke of at a Sunday morning gathering that my daughter's classmates organized at their former Jewish middle school, which has a Shoah (Holocaust) memorial containing six million soda can tabs, harvested by students over years to visually represent the numbers of those lost. The gathering was a chance for the students to come together and process the fact that people they knew—the students had prayed weekly at Tree of Life in seventh and eighth grades and knew many congregants—had been slaughtered by someone who hated Jews just as surely as those who had taken European Jewish lives in the past. An event we had all thought consigned to history was now very much present; it had happened in a synagogue they had all been to and to people they knew. My daughter and I both spoke about our three dead congregants; we all recited mourner's prayers, sang, and embraced.[1] In the first of many acts of kindness we received, the mother of one of her classmates asked if she could bring us dinner that night. It hadn't really occurred to me, but I shrugged and said sure.

When they came, they brought us not just enough for dinner but also breakfast and my daughter's favorite yogurt for her lunches. They also gave us a generous donation, but we were embarrassed by the gift and weren't even sure at the time what the money would be for, so we let weeks go by before cashing the check. It was the kindness, and the fact that they came so quickly, anticipating our needs without making us think about what they might be, that helped our healing.

The next afternoon, a woman whose son had been in my daughter's class, but whom I did not know well, showed up unexpectedly at my door with a tray of food from the kosher restaurant. She asked if she could do anything and I asked her to answer the phone so that I could

---

1. This was covered by Emma Green in "A Broken Jewish Community," *Atlantic*, October 28, 2018. https://www.theatlantic.com/politics/archive/2018/10/broken-jewish-community/574216/.

eat. I had eaten nothing at all that day, constantly disrupted and not at all hungry. Later, we ate the food she had brought for dinner, also I drove my husband to the home of the first family who had lost a loved one in the shooting. The last time I had driven him anywhere was twenty-six years earlier, when he was nervous about performing correctly at the very first wedding he was officiating. When we returned, friends had come over to do our dishes and help our kids clean up, as well as try to cheer them up.

What I wrote that Sunday afternoon, sitting at my kitchen table, phone ringing, my husband organizing his thoughts for his speech at the vigil, was for the 929 English website that encourages people to read one of the 929 chapters of the Bible a day over three and a half years.[2] When I could not sleep the previous night, I came downstairs at 2:00 a.m. and read that week's Torah portion, Chayei Sarah, Genesis 23:1–18, and immediately knew what I needed to say. The first words of the *parsha* are about Sarah—who she was and how she lived, not her death and when and how it happened. In remembering the martyrs of the Shoah, I had always believed it is much more important to remember who they were and what they stood for, what kind of lives they led, rather than focusing on the details of their deaths. I never thought I would be writing about those who died "al Kiddush Hashem," sanctifying God's name, people I knew and worshipped with, but I knew, guided by the verses about Sarah being remembered for her life, that I wanted to write about them in terms of their lives.

> All three of these men were dream congregants, the kind every rabbi wants, those willing to go above and beyond the call of duty.
>
> Melvin Wax was always the first in the synagogue for each service. He was devoted and caring, a pure soul. He often led parts of the service and read *haftarah* regularly. I hope his daughter, son-in-law, grandson, and family find comfort among the mourners of Zion and Jerusalem.

---

2. I first encountered the site in writing an article about it, "Secular Bible Study, for the Internet Age," *Tower*, June 2015, http://www.thetower.org/article/secular-bible-study-for-the-internet -age/. Its founder, Rabbi Benny Lau, claims that his goal is to return the Bible to being "the property of all Israel."

Rich Gottfried broke both his knees on the ice last winter. He was not expected to make a quick or full recovery, but due to his determination he was back at shul, reading haftarah as he did many weeks with his leg braces. He was due to retire soon and wanted to spend more time strengthening himself and the shul. He will never get the chance to do that. I hope his widow and his three sisters, including his twin, find comfort among the mourners of Zion and Jerusalem.

Dan Stein just became a grandfather seven months ago. I wish his grandson could have gotten to know him. Dan always had a word of cheer and a fist bump for everyone at shul. He read his bar mitzvah haftarah each year, annotated with the date. I hope his son will continue. May his widow, son and daughter-in-law, daughter, grandson, and family find comfort among the mourners of Zion and Jerusalem.

Rashi says about Genesis 23:1 that "the word *years* is repeated and without a number to indicate that they were all equally good." All the years of the lives of Daniel Stein, Richard Gottfried, and Melvin Wax were filled with goodness and devotion to Judaism. May their memories be for a blessing and may the occasion of their tragic deaths help us all, in the words of Abraham Lincoln's Gettysburg address, "increase devotion" so their deaths shall not have been in vain.

Please do not be afraid to gather in multitudes in synagogues, to sanctify God's name among the multitudes.

Please do all you can to advance the cause of gun control so that no more of these senseless tragedies occur.

Please acknowledge all those around you as being created "in the image of God," *b'tzelem elokim*, with a spark of divinity within them. We need to treat each human with kindness and respect as our tradition teaches, and anyone fomenting hate must be stopped.

As I have now learned, trauma disarrays the brain and makes the normal arrangement of organizing ideas in prose problematic. If an event itself makes no sense, and seems itself an impossibility—How did this thing happen? Could it really have happened or is this all a bad dream?—the story one will narrate about it too is disordered, nonsensical, impossible. As trauma researcher Bessel van der Kolk writes, "The nature of trauma is that you have no recollection of it as a story. The nature of traumatic experience is that the brain doesn't allow a story to be created."

I am a person who constantly thinks about how to write about experiences that I have had. Since I was in fourth grade I have kept a diary. If I don't have a notebook and a pen, I am lost, as I need to constantly record and process my reality. When I could not sleep in the middle of the night for that first week after the shooting, I went to the bathroom to put the light on so I wouldn't disturb my husband (if he was actually sleeping, which was not often). I closed the door so the light wouldn't spread to the darkened bedroom, sat on the floor, and started to write. After a sentence or two I would get another thought, my mind would race, and after that sentence I would again turn the page to get the next thought out and the next. I wanted to finish each idea but there were just too many thoughts, racing too quickly. They were all important and meaningful and good ideas, but I was unable to complete any of them.

My manic state of racing ideas and chaotic thoughts came to a head on Thursday morning, five days after the shooting, and the day of Rich Gottfried's funeral, the last of the three for New Light congregants. The night before, October 31, we had gone to a prayer service at Rodman Street Missionary Baptist Church, where, in April 2018, we had heard a man who had memorized the speeches of Dr. Martin Luther King and performed them on the fiftieth anniversary of King's death.[3] I wrote about the event and felt moved by the coincidence that the date of King's death fell during Passover, and that his view of liberation was even more meaningful during the Passover holiday, the time Jews celebrate liberation.[4] But, being at Rodman, I was very conscious that King was shot by an assailant who hated him for being someone who spoke out for civil rights and freedom for his people.

3. Shira Hanau, "Church, Synagogue Pray Together for Healing and Reconciliation," *New York Jewish Week*, November 2, 2018, https://jewishweek.timesofisrael.com/church-synagogue-pray-together-for-healing-and-reconciliation/.

4. Kissileff, "MLK's Message: Unity Is Way Out of Slavery," *New York Jewish Week*, April 5, 2018, https://jewishweek.timesofisrael.com/mlks-message-unity-is-way-out-of-slavery/.

Now, as my husband and I left our house Thursday morning, I saw a white object on our lawn. I asked my husband to please call the police to inspect it—what if some antisemite decided that, as King's home had been subject to bomb attempts, our home should be targeted too, that they might harm those who survived the synagogue attack? My husband made the call as we drove. When I got home, police were there investigating.[5] The object turned out to be a lightbulb, probably one that fell from our outdoor light, but I was not pacified. Neighbors and friends were there to see the commotion, as I screamed about the thing on my lawn. Soon there was a gaggle of people around my dining room table. I just remember speaking and screaming at them to record what I was saying because it was important. I have no clue now if they did, but they held their phones as though they were. I am embarrassed now to have people remember the incident and think of me in a manic state that day, so I've never asked any of them whether they actually recorded me, though I do want to know what I said.

I just needed a way to talk, to express myself, to be heard. I was talking about my fear that someone was going to bomb my house—maybe exaggerated, but maybe not—after all, who would have thought someone would shoot at my synagogue? I was also talking about my distress over learning how many teachers at my high school had harmed so many students by sexually molesting them over the years.[6] I am not sure what the connection was—I guess the proximity to evil. My friend Lorraine, a tough and logical lawyer who once prosecuted Nazi war criminals in her first job at the Justice Department

---

5. Editing this piece in June 2020, while the country is in the midst of Black Lives Matter protests against police brutality that took the life of George Floyd and takes the life of over one thousand Americans each year (according to Mapping Police Violence, accessed June 22, 2020, https://mappingpoliceviolence.org/). I want to acknowledge that my comfort in calling the police is part of my white privilege, though at the same time I can be a target of white supremacist brutality as a Jew. In contrast to our experience in Pittsburgh, the emergency response to the shooting at the Mother Emanuel Church in Charleston on June 17, 2015, was not as rapid as it might have been, as discussed by Jennifer Berry Hawes in her *Grace Will Lead Us Home: The Charleston Church Massacre and the Hard, Inspiring Journey to Forgiveness* (New York: Macmillan, 2019).

6. As documented in Amos Kamil, *Great is the Truth: Secrecy, Scandal, and the Quest for Justice at the Horace Mann School, with Sean Elder* (New York: Farrar, Straus and Giroux, 2015).

in Washington, has told me she saw some logic in my rant. Another friend, a psychologist, suggested that I speak with a group of trauma therapists she had brought to the house at some point. But, having finally gotten my thoughts out and, I hoped, recorded, I decided that the best thing was to seek the help of a massage therapist. Now that I felt I had been listened to I was able finally to let some of the tension out of my body, and I drifted into a nap on the massage table. Rich's funeral was not till 4:00 that day, I guess to fit in the others. I still have no idea how Schugar's Funeral Home managed to plan and coordinate eleven funerals in four days with the least amount of overlap possible.

It was scary for me and the people around me—fortunately our kids encouraged me to talk to our psychiatrist friend Holly, who told me why I needed to take over-the-counter sleep aids to regain some stability—and I still can't think of the shooting without thinking of this manic episode and the days when I was unable to write or think clearly. My whole being was unmoored by violence that I had not even experienced directly, only through my spouse. It felt overwhelming and invasive to have a group of people in my house, ostensibly to help me, but I didn't know all of them. Did some of them come to gawk at me, to see how the trauma had affected even someone who had not been present? I suspect that what happened that morning, speaking manically and refusing to talk to the trauma experts I did not ask for, was that I had to learn to make decisions about what I wanted to do, what I felt, and how I was going to experience and communicate.

"You have to call the shots," my friend, artist Aimee Orkin, advised me. Many years ago, she lost her young husband to an aneurysm he suffered at the shiva for his own father, buried earlier that day. For months afterward people would approach her gingerly, both wanting to talk about her huge loss and not wanting to; sometimes she herself wanted to speak about it, sometimes she did not. She gradually realized that she had to tell people what she wanted, that she had to be in control of letting others know how to approach her. For me, learning to take control over how to talk about what happened was a way of defying the person who wanted so much to cause me harm.

Here is evil, I do not deny it, and I will not conceal it with fruitless casuistry. I am, however, interested in it from a halakhic [Jewish legal] point of view; and as a person who wants to know what action to take. I ask a single question: What should the sufferer do to live with his suffering? . . . The halakhic answer to this question is very simple. Suffering comes to elevate man, to purify his spirit and sanctify him, to cleanse his mind and purify it from the chaff of superficiality and the dross of crudeness; to sensitize his soul and expand his horizons. In general, the purpose of suffering is to repair the imperfection in man's persona. The halakhah teaches us that an afflicted person commits a criminal act if he allows his pain to go for naught and to remain without meaning or purpose. Suffering appears in the world in order to contribute something to man, in order to atone for him, in order to redeem him from moral impurity, from crudeness and lowliness of spirit.

These are the words of Rabbi Joseph Soloveitchik from his book *Kol Dodi Dofek*. If, as he writes, suffering comes to elevate man and purify his spirit, how can this possibly be accomplished? How will *I* do this?

Being able to talk about what happened is part of the way to heal from a tragedy. It is the tragedy itself, the enormity, and shock and horror of what occurred, that makes discussion of it so difficult, so troubling that I experienced a fit of mania because I was unable to process and respond to all the stimuli and experiences I was having. One of the things that most helped our family was an envelope full of letters we received shortly after the event—the postmark tells me it was sent November 7, 2018. They were from people who had lost family members to terrorism around the world. The young woman who sent them, Mijal Tennenbaum, lost her own father in the AMIA (equivalent to Jewish Community Center) bombing in Argentina in 1994. She wrote to us, in part, "I hope you know how much we love and support your congregation and how much we care about your healing and rebuilding. May your future be bright and may we never forget the ones we lost." Carly Gordenstein, who lost her mother on 9/11, when she was three, wrote, "The best and essentially only way to move on from terrorism is to not respond with the fear they desire, but rather with a calculated resignation to fight that hate with love and understanding." Francesca Picerno, who lost her father on 9/11, when she was nine, wrote about how much difficulty she had faced and how alone she had felt at times. She concluded, "I've learned in this life that no matter how much negativity there may seem to be, positivity exists too. Yes. . . . sometimes it's nearly IMPOSSIBLE to live on the brighter side of things and that's OKAY." The honesty expressed by these young people we did not know was so meaningful to us, and we felt honored to have been recipients of the letters though we ourselves had not lost family members. We asked them to send letters to the teenaged grandson of one of the victims, as well as the infant grandson of another.

All of the three New Light congregants killed were active in the ritual life of the synagogue, leading prayers, chanting the prophetic portion, rolling the Torah to the correct section, and giving out the parts to those coming up to make a blessing over the Torah. In hearing people speak about them, one theme emerged consistently: participating and creating communal prayer and study was important to them, and they all excelled at enabling others to find their Jewish voices, be it helping someone to put on tefillin, to take a part in the service, or to say the blessings over the Torah.

I learned things about all three of them after their death, though. Dan Stein had helped my daughter with a paper about local history. He took her to the Homestead neighborhood, where he grew up, and showed her the synagogue that his family helped found, and the Jewish cemetery there. At his shiva, my daughter told his widow how he had also edited her fifteen-page paper. After arriving home from Israel, my daughter came directly from the airport to see his widow, without doing anything else first. I was stunned by the care and consideration Dan took in following through with that extra step of editing, after also giving the tour and the interview. That was characteristic of him; I wish his infant grandson could have been the recipient of all that care and attention as well. It saddens me no end to think about that, as well as how he is missed by other members of his family.

Mel Wax was a retired accountant and would do people's taxes for free. He was meticulous in his gentleness and concern for others. For example, he never parked in the synagogue lot because others who did not walk as well needed to park there more than he did. This small gesture says everything you need to know about a person who also organized voter registration drives and collected supplies in his senior citizen apartment building to donate to victims of Hurricane Florence in the Carolinas to be sent with a truck that Rodman Street Baptist Church invited us to contribute to. At his funeral, I learned that he and his grandson loved to play games and that he hated being in the military but said he would do it again if he could spare his brother a tour of duty. Mel led the prayers in his steady voice, showing up first, always with a jacket and tie out of respect for the Sabbath. One of those who survived comes every week now, without fail, Friday and Saturday, and always with a jacket and tie, which he did not wear before, in Mel's honor. It is a beautiful tribute.

Rich Gottfried was a dentist on the verge of retirement, looking forward to enjoying his golden years with his wife and dental partner, and having more time to continue being active at the synagogue. He volunteered his time at a clinic giving free dental care and he and his wife counseled other Jews and Catholics who were marrying each other, advising them on how to create relationships of mutual respect for one another's traditions, as they had. Rich was such a determined person that after he broke his knees in winter 2018 he defied all his doctor's predictions about the speed of his recovery and hastened it greatly because of his diligence with physical therapy. I had never known the date of the birthday he shared with his twin sister; I found out at his shiva that it was the same as my own. For the past two years I have been his twin's "birthday buddy," and we have gone on outings to Phipps Conservatory to celebrate.

Dan Stein's first grandchild was born in March 2018, and the baby's circumcision was held in our New Light space at Tree of Life. The mohel [ritual circumciser] was one of those in charge of the *chevra kadisha*, of cleansing the building of human remains so the deceased may receive a proper Jewish burial, holy and arduous work. That sentence should not have had to be written, nor should a person have to toggle between initiating Jews into the covenant and scouring a building of the remains of Jews killed for being part of the covenant. As a mohel, Rabbi Elisar Admon said the words from Ezekiel 16:6, *B'dmaiyech hayeich*, "in your blood you shall live." After the shooting, Admon, whose name means "red one" in Hebrew, has continued to serve as both mohel and member of the *chevra kadisha*. To live by the commandments, not die by them—that too is yet another riddle of Jewish existence that needs to be parsed.

As I write, it is Passover and we have just read over the Haggadah, twice. The telling of this text is the primary way Jews address their history of being enslaved and overcoming it. As we read this year, I was struck by the section that says, "It is this that has stood by our ancestors and us; for not only one has risen up against us to destroy us but in all generations they rise up against us to destroy us. But the Holy Blessed One saves us from their hands." This seems to be the source of Jewish resilience and adaptability, the knowledge that as difficult as it has been to encounter this attempt to destroy our community, as Jews, we have experienced this before. And most importantly, we have overcome it, painful as the process is. In addition, the order represented by the very word "seder" enables us to present our story, to ourselves and to others in a precise way that resembles, as one writer of a Haggadah commentary has said, the exact precision of a Japanese tea ceremony.[7]

Nevertheless, I do feel the unfairness and the randomness: why is my family still intact, when my husband was in the Tree of Life building and yet survived? I do know that it is our responsibility to honor the lives of those who died and commit to the values they were committed to, to emulate them by doing good deeds both in and out of the synagogue as they did. I've worked hard over the past eighteen months to train two new haftarah readers, giving them lessons every week, and have begun lessons with a third. For the first year after the shooting, I wrote a commentary on the Torah portion of the week for 929 English, never missing a week. I am currently participating in *daf yomi*, the cycle of reading a page of the Babylonian Talmud a day. I've planned programs at the synagogue, planned and led a trip to Charleston on Martin Luther King weekend in 2019, to learn from the experiences of the congregation and the survivors and families of victims there, and hosted families of the victims and guests from out of town for Sabbath

7. Marc-Alain Ouaknin in his *Haggadah* (New York: Assouline, 2001).

meals.[8] I have participated in many interfaith events and written for many different publications, for Jews and non-Jews alike. None of it helps me answer the riddle of why my family was spared when others were not.

The murders of October 27, 2018, are an awful, horrific thing. Eleven souls are gone, plucked from their roles in life and from their loved ones and the joy and compassion they brought to others. Nine families will always be bereft of those who had been part of their lives. The impact is felt by the families, the synagogues, the Pittsburgh Jewish community, the American Jewish community—none of these have been left untouched. And yet Passover teaches us that this has happened in the past and that there is an order in how we tell the story, how we speak about it.

Although, as I have said, the trauma of the shooting made it difficult for me to write or speak coherently at first, one Biblical metaphor helped clarify things: the riddle that Samson tells after he is first aware of the superhuman strength God has given him. The story, in short, recounts how Samson kills a lion, not realizing before he does so that he has this capability.[9] Some time later, on a return journey, he passes the same area. The carcass of the lion he has killed remains in position, and yet something has changed. As the Bible tells it, "behold, there was a swarm of bees in the lion's carcass, and honey" (Judges 14:8). Samson scrapes out the honey and eats it, and gives some to

---

8. I wrote about the experience of going to Charleston; see "Healing Comes from Healing: Searching for an Antidote to Hate after the Tree of Life Tragedy," *Pittsburgh Post-Gazette*, February 3, 2019, https://www.post-gazette.com/opinion/Op-Ed/2019/02/03/Searching-for-an-antidote-to-hate-after-the-Tree-of-Life-tragedy-Beth-Kissileff-Next-Page/stories/201902030081; and "Fighting hate, from Tree of Life Synagogue to Charleston's Mother Emanuel Church," *Religion News Service*, January 29, 2019, https://religionnews.com/2019/01/29/fighting-hate-from-tree-of-life-synagogue-to-charlestons-mother-emanuel-church/. It was covered in Jennifer Berry Hawes, "Pittsburgh Synagogue Shooting Survivors Join Emanuel AME Church in Shared Sorrow," *Post and Courier*, January 20, 2019, https://www.postandcourier.com/church_shooting/pittsburgh-synagogue-shooting-survivors-join-emanuel-ame-church-in-shared-sorrow/article_7f397986-1b4b-11e9-862a-b701f14f5630.html.
9. "The spirit of the Lord seized him, and he tore it as one would tear a kid goat, with nothing in his hand and he did not tell his father and his mother what he had done" (Judges 14: 6). The phrasing here is adapted from Robert Alter's *The Hebrew Bible: A Translation with Commentary* (New York: W. W. Norton, 2018).

his parents, without telling them where it is from. Samson turns the episode into a riddle that he posits to the Philistines, the first of his many challenges to them: "From the eater came forth eats, and from the strong came forth sweet" (Judges 14:14).

There are times when only a riddle can make things clear, even if there is no expectation that it can be solved rationally. Samson's power was not just physical but verbal. It is not enough for Samson to scoop the honey, eat it, and feed it to his parents. To create meaning from his actions, he needs to describe them, to convey to others what this moment is to him, how it is truly the moment of his becoming. David Grossman, an Israeli novelist, wrote of this idea in his book about the story of Samson, *Lion's Honey*, written before Grossman himself became a bereaved father upon the death of his son Uri in the Israeli Army in 2006.[10] I hope Grossman's deep knowledge of Samson's story provided him the comfort it has brought me.

The first Sabbath that New Light was closed for the COVID-19 quarantine, we tried an experiment, holding our Friday Kabbalat Shabbat prayers over Zoom before sunset. Our kids made sure that the table was set and that they were dressed for Shabbat. My husband began to sing and our children joined in with him; my laptop, the very machine I am now using to compose these words, became a vehicle of community, transmitting the faces and voices and images of all the worshippers. My husband and our other two survivors were present on Zoom, as was the widow of one of those killed, and the sister of another. All of us—or, I should speak for myself—craving a sense of normalcy, that there was still a stability to the world, a rhythm for the week. The Sabbath had arrived and we were going to greet it. We would not be deterred by the inability to physically gather but would affirm with our assembled voices that our beliefs and way of life are eternal. Not unchanging, certainly, for even a few weeks ago we would never have imagined that we would need to come together on a screen and worship.

---

10. *Lion's Honey: The Myth of Samson* (New York: Knopf, 2005); Grossman's son Uri was killed August 12, 2006, in Lebanon.

On October 27, 2018, my daughter's first thought, after her concern that her father was okay, was to say, "I don't want people to stop coming to shul because they are afraid." There is a certain satisfaction in knowing that, even when we can't gather physically we will not be deterred from creating community, in whatever form it must take.

I see both the honey and the carcass. The lesson for me is that even if the carcass does not change, what it is able to contain does. New memories can be made. In another odd coincidence, or sign of divine kindness, the bar mitzvah haftarah of one of our New Light martyrs, the first portion of Exodus, turned out to be the same one that was assigned to one of my students, as it was the closest to her Hebrew birthday. Rich's sister had read it in December 2018, though teary and emotional, in her brother's stead just weeks after his murder. Now, when my adult student read for the first time, Rich's sister was so pleased that this date marked not just sadness that her brother was not there to read it but the possibility of new memories, a chance for the congregation together to rejoice at a milestone for one of our own, who had increased her commitment and knowledge by spending a year practicing this new skill. Though the carcass will never alter—the haftarah will always be Rich Gottfried's—now it is Julie Harris's as well, the sweetness of her accomplishment and devotion our new addition. What that date contains can be transfigured over time; sweetness can coexist with grief, just as honey was created inside the carcass.

Our task now, as individuals and as a congregation, is to be ourselves the bees, to find the ways to create that honey, to hold and support new memories, ideas, and endeavors. We can't bring any of the eleven dead back, but we can honor their memories by valuing what they valued and continuing our paths as Jews, as a congregation, and as a community.

The riddle is that these things coexist, and finally I am able to write about them and to create a story that coheres, and elicit the stories of others.

"What then is sweeter than honey and what then is stronger than a lion?" (Judges 14:18).

LISA'S TANGO
SURVIVAL
STRATEGY

Lisa D. Brush

WHAT CAN ONE DO when the world suddenly feels shattered? How can one be calm, collected, and connected in the face of disruption, uncertainty, and trauma? Where can one turn for support when the Jewish community is reeling? I answer these questions with some insights from the ways my practice and friends in the Pittsburgh Argentine tango community gathered me in during the hours immediately following the lethal white nationalist antisemitic violence that rocked Dor Hadash, Squirrel Hill, Pittsburgh, and the broader Jewish world on October 27, 2018.

I live three blocks from the Tree of Life synagogue in Squirrel Hill. Dor Hadash, one of the three congregations that shared the building at the intersection of Shady and Wilkins, has been the cornerstone of my Jewish life for the twenty-five years that I have lived in Pittsburgh. When I moved here, to take my first professional job, I spent a long time seeking the right place to put down spiritual roots by visiting congregations and *havurot* (less formal prayer groups). Squirrel Hill attracted me as a neighborhood because of its diverse Jewish communi-

My draft readers included Akiko, Alan, Cynthia, Gabrielle, Janice, Laura, Lenore, Mehr, Rob, Sam, and Olivia, who provided crucial support for the revision.

ty. I found the recently established Jewish Women's Center, a feminist Rosh Hodesh (new moon) collective, and attended and led services and eventually helped revise the siddur (prayer book) at Bet Tikvah, the queer-friendly, unaffiliated havura that met one Friday night a month. I participated in services and met people in the various congregations that anchor the neighborhood, often starting early Shabbat morning for study and prayer with the guitar-strumming Rabbi Gibson at Temple Sinai and then later walking to New Light or the Library Minyan at Beth Shalom for a traditional Torah service. I relished weekly Torah study sessions with Dr. Ron Brauner at the Jewish Community Center, directly across the street from my first apartment in Squirrel Hill.

It's not that I was being picky, or indecisive, but I had moved to Pittsburgh from New York City, where my life as a Jewish adult had begun just the year before. While serving a postdoctoral year at the Rockefeller Foundation, I observed the High Holy Days in 1993 as a guest of Beit Simchat Torah. It was the first time that I saw an out lesbian leading a religious service; Rabbi Sharon Kleinbaum and the gay, lesbian, and bisexual Jews of CBST filled the Javits Center with song and spirit that balanced individual voices and introspection with communal support and renewal. A year later, I left to find a new home in Pittsburgh, having learned to enjoy and lead Friday night services in a feminist minyan, having discovered traditional wisdom combined with urgent care and activism in the CBST response to the AIDS epidemic, having started traditional Torah study with Hebrew flashcards, and having ritually received a Hebrew name that honored the memory of my Jewish paternal grandmother. In Pittsburgh, I wanted to learn and grow as a Jew, in a congregation that would welcome a lesbian from an interfaith marriage, whose earlier Jewish education was limited to the Hillel youth group that all my friends joined in high school and the back issues of the Jewish feminist magazine *Lilith*, lent by a friend's mother. It was a tall order.

Though never my only place in the diverse Jewish community in Squirrel Hill, Dor Hadash turned out to be a good fit. At the first service I attended, on a Friday night right after moving to Pittsburgh, I reveled in the Reconstructionist spirit (including tunes familiar from CBST), joyful approach to learning, and warm welcome. A lay-led congregation with knowledgeable members delighted to expand the pool of people contributing to the life of the community was a good place for me. For Dor Hadash, I was Jewish enough, not too feminist or too queer, and being a secular scholar with no children meant I could mentor youth and enrich adult study. Dor Hadash acknowledged my skills, fed my hunger for Jewish learning, and allowed me to participate in Torah honors despite my not having a Jewish mother or formal Jewish education and background. Over the years, I committed to congregational leadership, serving on the executive board and heading a committee as ritual vice-president. At age forty, I learned to chant Torah and celebrated being called to do so by my Hebrew name for the first time in the presence of my community and three generations of visiting family. At forty-five, I learned to blow the shofar. I spent many happy and serious and above all companionable hours studying, praying, preparing and leading services, and connecting with people through every conceivable lifecycle event, from baby naming rituals and *brit milah* (covenantal circumcision) to funerals and shiva minyan.

Three weeks after my fiftieth birthday, a second adult concussion, with symptoms that linger still, led me to pull back from Dor Hadash and many other Jewish community activities. The persistent headaches, dizziness, and fatigue were problems, but the emotional dysregulation and loss of executive function were more undermining and persistent. I resigned from my Dor Hadash leadership position as I struggled to do my day job. I stopped going to almost all Torah study sessions, especially on Shabbat, not only because work now consumed me but also because, to my chagrin, I could not keep track of my own questions without writing them down. The drop in my capacity—for learning new text and music, for remembering words, for creative thinking, for controlling my emotions, for connecting names and faces, for serving my community—overwhelmed and frightened me. Some people at work and at Dor Hadash knew, but many did not, and it hurt to be around people who knew me from "before." I felt not only different but also ashamed of who I had become—and unable to respond to even the kindest inquiries about my whereabouts and welfare, because I feared disappointing people who were eager for me to resume leadership.

That is why, on the morning of October 27, 2018, I was at Home Depot with a friend. The announcement came over the radio while we were changing light bulbs. I was not at Dor Hadash. I was not there for my friends and congregation. I was not there to fight or flee or freeze. I was not there, and it had been many months since I had been in the front room studying and davening with Jerry Rabinowitz, Dan Leger, Rabbi Doris Dyen, Deane Root, and other Saturday morning regulars. I was not there to warn them, to protect them, to share their terror, nor to witness their courage.

Most immediately, in the hours after the shooting, I needed to feel safe and held. Ordinarily I would turn to the Jewish community for comfort, but that normally safe harbor was flooded with pain and fear. Having turned on my phone and responded to frantic calls and texts from family and friends near and far, reassuring them that I was safe, I tried—desperate for shelter—to reach the people with whom I was scheduled to spend the afternoon. I walked the roundabout way (my usual route was blocked by police cars cordoning off the scene of the mass shooting—why I failed to realize what this meant, I can only attribute to shock) to the nearby Wightman School Community Center, where I was hoping to be with non-Jewish friends at a long-anticipated set of tango workshops taught by an instructor visiting from Buenos Aires. The outside door was locked. I was too stunned to associate this with the shooting; I assumed it was because I was almost half an hour late. I texted my teacher (assuming she was upstairs), saying I was sorry to be late but could someone please come down and let me in? She called me immediately and said they couldn't access the building and they had canceled the workshops at the news of the shooting and what did I need? I begged her please to reinstate the workshops. I was clearly confused but I knew one thing for sure: I desperately wanted to be with my tango friends. To her eternal credit, she came and picked me up and took me to the substitute workshop site, where she gathered a few people at my insistence: her home tango studio. I walked into the familiar room and flew into the arms of tall, solid, gently strong Tom, who held me while I wailed into his shoulder, surrounded by friends, and kept me close while I kept telling him not to let me go. I was shaken and breathless, frightened for the Dor Hadash stalwarts I imagined were in the building during the shooting, and shamelessly relieved to be safe in the arms of people I knew who were at least one step removed from violence that seemed distressingly close to me.

And then we practiced tango.

Argentine tango is a social dance. Two people come together for about twelve minutes at a time to listen, breathe, and move together. Classic Argentine tango music is straightforward popular music, steeped in nostalgia and melancholy. First intrigued by live tango music, when I started dancing I sometimes found recorded music cheesy, and certainly thought a lot of the music and dance scene was insufferably sexist and irredeemably straight. With more experience, I now hear tango music as richly layered and varied, making every beat with every partner unique. Familiarity with the rise and fall of the phrases, the contrast of the melody played on the violin and the sharp pulse from the Argentine bandoneon, and the skill dancers call "musicality" all present each dance as a space of infinite possibility—in a four-minute song that comes to a wistful or melodramatic end. The practice is solemn, deeply joyful, and literally moving. Social dance demands my complete attention to the present moment, to myself, to my partner, to the music that coordinates us, and to the smooth counterclockwise flow of couples around the dance floor.

I don't remember what we worked on that Saturday afternoon. I remember I alternated between being utterly absorbed in learning technique and having to stop and breathe as the tears and uncertainty welled up from my broken heart and ran down my cheeks. My friends gently and generously partnered with me and patiently accompanied me as my composure ebbed and flowed.

Tango helps me come alive and feel safe and connected—connected to myself in ways that are gentle, fierce, and curious, and connected to my partner and community in ways that are full of fun, care, and wonder. Tango (like yoga, moving meditation, or playing a musical instrument) is an embodied practice. It requires initially deliberate and eventually second-nature coordination of mind, body, and breath; attention to detail and surrender to flow; openness and vulnerability to receive and give care and pleasure while being responsible for my own balance and posture; and leading and protecting my partner, who is doing all the same things but backward and with eyes closed. "Befriending the body" is trauma researcher Bessel van der Kolk's phrase for simultaneously registering past pain, cultivating compassion for the wounded self, and taking in and expanding the safety and capacity for healing that come from being present with and available to another human being. As a partner dance, tango helps me find calm and comfort in the face of fear, anxiety, and loss. And beyond my own body, the cliché is totally true. All the ways that it takes two to tango help me.

The tango embrace is simple and powerful. It is basically a hug (in Spanish the word for hug and the tango embrace is the same: *abrazo*). As every child knows and every adult should relearn regularly, you cannot give a hug without receiving a hug. In tango, through the embrace, partners feel each other as we move together to the music. A tango instructor once had our class imagine our clasped hands joining the two "sides" of the embrace like a wall outlet: We have to plug in to complete the circuit. She asked us to feel our partner's feet—and show our partner our own feet—through our joined hands. That doesn't mean a tight grip, but it means extending and receiving the vibrant energy of our connection to the floor through our own center of gravity and to our partner and back.

After the shooting, I knew I needed a way to have room in myself and my life for big feelings—yes, fear and vulnerability but also the outpouring of concern and support in the form of phone calls, emails from friends and former students across the United States and Europe, memorial vigils, and eulogies. To take it all in, and offer any comfort to mourners in my community, I had to feel my own feet on the ground, the ache in my own chest, the impossible lump in my own throat. At the same time, especially in the forty-eight hours between Sunday morning, when I learned the names of the eleven martyred congregants, and Tuesday morning, when I attended the funeral for former Dor Hadash president Jerry Rabinowitz, I needed a way to stop compulsively imagining the suffering and terror of my friends in the synagogue space where we had studied, prayed, noshed, mourned, and celebrated. That was the hardest challenge for me, at first. I had to resist running the impossible, 3D, full-color, first-person horror show of my imagined version of what happened. The shared heart space of the tango embrace helped me to make myself the kind of container for big feelings that would nevertheless have no place for the corrosive, paralyzing dread to hook into me.

Tango helps me let big feelings move through me without attaching to them because the embodied practice of tango brings my emotional brain and my rational brain into balance. I have long used musical training, karate, yoga, bike racing, running, swimming, and meditation to manage the stress of researching abuse, poverty, public policy, and violence prevention. Argentine tango is both simple and technically challenging. More significantly, it is all about the connection between two people. To dance with care and fluent confidence, I have to feel intelligently and think feelingly, making myself wholeheartedly available to the moment and my partner. To tango, I have to be able to move, to feel, to be fully present and therefore able to connect with my partner without losing my own axis. I have to be comfortable and notice with respectful curiosity my partner's self and creativity. To do all that, I have to breathe, keep my own balance, attend to my partner's balance, and create the calm foundation for our cooperative improvisation. To dance, we have to listen to each other and listen together to the music, feel and share the rhythm, and be willing to go together somewhere that neither could go alone. We have to choose to connect and then give everything to each other for those three four-minute songs, that twelve-minute *tanda*. Tango is completely absorbing, so for the duration of this song, with this partner, there is no point of purchase for even the most pressing troubles and sorrow. We literally dance our woes away.

Tango helps me to move in fluent comfort and calm instead of aimlessly stumbling in traumatic fight, flight, or freeze mode. Tango reminds me that every moment and every movement counts. After the shooting, I was even more aware than usual of fragility, vulnerability, and the fact that life is uncertain and sometimes violent. Tango helps me experience each second as full and precious—the way chanting Torah requires single-minded attention to what feels like stepping into a river of sound, feeling, and history. Social dancing also reminds me that if I or my partner momentarily loses balance, it is a chance to refresh our connection and listen anew to the music. Tango viscerally teaches me that there are no mistakes, only opportunities for improvisation.

I still often feel awkward comforting someone or telling someone how I feel about the shooting. Someone simply saying, "Tell me about it," can still make me lose my breath or lose my equanimity; my heart still skips a beat, not in the good way. Sometimes the fog of loss—the way I wandered past police cars without it registering that of course tango workshops were canceled, or the way I miss the sight of Jerry trying to blow the shofar or making a point in Torah study or smiling in his bow tie—threatens to overwhelm me. My tango practice gives me a kinesthetic memo—an embodied reminder—about how to breathe, be present, and reconnect. I am so thankful for tango practice and the community that held me in an embrace that grounded me in care, gave me room to feel enormous feelings, and allowed me to receive and eventually give comfort and grace.

THE DAY
THEY
HONORED

Susan Jacobs Jablow

IT'S BECOME A GRUESOME ROUTINE. Somewhere there is a mass shooting, antisemitic attack, or another tragedy, and very quickly my email inbox and Facebook news feed fill with headlines. Jolted with horror and fear, my stomach lurches and my mind begins to race, wondering how many people were injured or killed. I try to recall who I know in the community affected, and how likely they were to be near the site of the carnage.

As details emerge, I obsessively check news websites, knowing that early information will be incomplete, but will answer some questions. This ritual helps me alleviate my fears and continue with the events of my day. It's how most of us have learned to cope with the unfathomable. As we reel at the horrors, there remains a sense of artificiality and distance that enables us to gaze from afar. We know we will soon learn about the innocent victims in tragic detail, and that we will mourn their loss, perhaps donate funds to support their families, pontificate on social media about some sort of change, and then move on with our lives.

We take comfort in knowing that, like lightning strikes and airplane crashes, these events are horrible but still far less likely to directly affect us than more pedestrian ways of dying. We stay informed but as psychologically removed as possible.

Until we can't anymore.

I never wanted to consider the possibility of a mass shooting at a synagogue, and certainly not one in my own neighborhood. And yet, there I was on the morning of October 27, 2018, walking to services with my children, less than a mile from the Tree of Life building.

Like many people who were in Squirrel Hill that day, the sounds of dozens of sirens are seared into my memory. Before then, I never paid much heed to sirens, other than to pull over to let emergency vehicles pass on the road. Since then, sirens that are too close, too loud, or too numerous reawaken my sense of dread.

Every Saturday morning, with rare exceptions, I walk to shul for Shabbos morning services. Like many Jews, despite my best intentions, I am often late.

That's what happened on October 27. I left the house around 10:00 a.m. to walk to my synagogue, Shaare Torah Congregation. Because our family strictly observes the traditional laws of Shabbos, we don't ride in a car or use electronics from shortly before sundown on Friday until after dark on Saturday, a twenty-five-hour period. Our synagogue is about a fifteen-minute walk from our house. When we left our house that day the sirens had already begun, but it was easy to dismiss the first few as routine emergencies. Perhaps someone had fallen, or there was a kitchen fire. The farther I walked, the sirens grew in number and intensity. By the time I reached Murray Avenue, vehicles with sirens blaring were streaming past me and my two children, racing to an unknown emergency. There were ambulances from suburban EMT crews, and unmarked cars with darkened windows and dashboard lights—the top brass. Something truly awful had happened.

But, because it was Shabbos, when I don't use electronics, I had no way of knowing what was going on, and no way of contacting my husband, who was already at services. People were beginning to step outside storefronts on Murray Avenue to see what was happening, simultaneously checking their phones for information. I was tempted to ask a stranger for information, but I also was afraid to know. My synagogue was my intended destination, and I felt an urgency to get there, knowing my husband would worry if I didn't make it. And I knew that in gaining a bit of information about the unfolding events, I would be distracted from focusing on Shabbos.

The concept of strictly observing Shabbos—to intentionally disconnect from the world even though we remain immersed in it—is foreign to many people, including many Jews. Unlike some religious sects, most observant Jews don't isolate themselves in rural communities or generally proscribe use of technology. Six days a week, we fully embrace technological advances and are as addicted as anyone else to our internet-connected screens. And most of us live within urban or suburban communities, closely connected to civic events and the local effects of world news. But one day a week, we cut off this contact in exchange for a sense of peace and contentment, and the opportunity to escape. We pause from the world to rest and reflect, so that we can reenter it twenty-five hours later with renewed vigor and increased insight.

In Jewish tradition, Shabbos is referred to as a "taste of the World to Come" (that is, heaven), but it is also a fragile state of being in this world. In one's home or synagogue Shabbos is a totally immersive experience that offers warmth and joy. We set aside our weekday preoccupations to sing, pray, eat, rest, and engage with time in a more fluid way. There are no appointments, meetings, or sports practices to quicken our pace. However, to maintain this atmosphere of holiness requires effort. Walking down a bustling commercial street or becoming involved in mundane activities can break the spell, because it's so easy to fall into the patterns of those around us who may be spending money, talking on phones, or running errands. These distractions can cause one to forget that the day is holy, a time sanctified and apart.

Stopping to ask for information about the unfolding emergency on October 27 would interrupt my observance of Shabbos while increasing my fears. In addition, the people around me didn't seem concerned for their own safety, so it didn't seem necessary for personal protection to find out what was happening. Instead, my children and I pressed on. We weren't denying the reality of what was happening around us, just recognizing our helplessness to affect it, and choosing to immerse ourselves in the spiritual comfort of Shabbos.

When I entered the synagogue, the shul president was standing in the vestibule, and I approached him to ask if he knew what was going on. "There has been an incident at Tree of Life," he said. He didn't offer more details, and because my children were present, I didn't ask for more. I wondered first if there had been a bomb or arson, not able to imagine that there had been a shooting. Then I wondered if the attack had been personal in nature. Again, I could not initially conceive of a random hate crime.

After we arrived at our synagogue safely, it became clear that it was the best place for us to be that morning. A handful of members with security training had already secured all the doors, and the non-Jewish custodian was checking local media and staying in touch with 911 dispatchers to ensure the congregation was not in danger. We had the information we needed without totally shifting our focus away from Shabbos. The custodian gave our rabbi updates throughout the service, and the rabbi made announcements to the congregation. Despite the horrific news, services continued, and the bar mitzvah boy who had trained over many months beautifully *lained* (chanted) his Torah portion.

As the news sank in, I felt myself gripped with fear. I struggled to focus on the prayers. We did not know yet that the gunman had acted alone, or that he had been contained at Tree of Life. We worried that our synagogue, packed with more than three hundred people present for the bar mitzvah, could also be a target.

Even though this heightened our feelings of vulnerability, the composure of the rabbi and other shul leaders enabled us to maintain our Shabbos routines, which provided great comfort, as did the sense of community from being together. Shocked by news of the unfathomable, we were there to process the experience together, whether through words, embraces, or silent solidarity.

I became shomer Shabbos (strictly Sabbath observant) in my late teens. From early childhood I had been raised to observe many of the traditional rituals of Shabbos, but would still ride in a car or use electricity. Through the influence of cousins and an Orthodox youth group, I learned about the laws that proscribe those activities and felt drawn to the beauty of adhering to Shabbos more strictly. I saw that the parameters of these laws, while demanding, created a warm, joyous, and peaceful atmosphere. Since then, I have not generally found them to be that difficult to follow. Once I disconnect before candle-lighting on Friday afternoon before sunset, I put the burdens of the outside world on hold, and feel a sense of relief to focus on family, comfort foods, Torah study, and rest for twenty-five hours. However, there are notable times when this disconnection has been unnerving.

When I was nine months pregnant with each of my children, I knew that if I went into labor on Shabbos, we could "break Shabbos" to call a cab to get to the hospital. In medical emergencies and other critical circumstances, the Shabbos laws are superseded. But those needs don't extend to calling family members to tell them about a birth or to seek reassurance while one is in labor. (In the end, both of my children were born on Fridays.) Similarly, when family members are ill or far away on Shabbos, we can't simply pick up the phone to check on them. At times like these, unable to make the connections we make effortlessly on other days, Shabbos can feel interminable.

On October 27 I knew that family members all over the world would hear about what had happened and would worry about us. It felt awful not to be able to reach out to them. My sister, who is not shomer Shabbos and also lives in Squirrel Hill, came to our shul that morning to check on us, and without discussing it, I knew she would let other family members know that we were okay. This provided a measure of relief, as I was imagining the panic our parents would feel when they heard about a shooting at a Pittsburgh synagogue. On the other hand, I also had some feelings of conflict, knowing that we were benefiting from others breaking the laws of Shabbos.

After leaving the synagogue, we walked home with another family we had invited that week for Shabbos lunch. During the meal we avoided talking about the shooting, and tried generally to maintain an upbeat atmosphere for the children. Our friends were a positive distraction, but they left quickly after lunch to get back to their own home. It was the first time we had invited them over, and we understood that they wanted to take their kids home where they could be most candid and process what had happened together.

During that long afternoon, when the neighborhood became eerily quiet, we stayed at home, feeling we were safest there. However, being removed from our friends and neighbors in the community heightened our feelings of unease. We were reassured not to hear more sirens, but there was a deep sense of foreboding in the neighborhood, a natural symptom of that morning's tragedy, and there was no way to allay our fears. Far from the peacefulness and respite of a normal Shabbos, our withdrawal from technology felt like a liability rather than an asset.

However, just as we had done during the final weeks of my pregnancies and other times of uncertainty, we persisted. In strictly following the laws of Shabbos, we relied upon our beliefs in the importance of adhering to halakah (Jewish law), and demonstrated to our children that our laws and practices have depth and heft that cannot easily be displaced. We follow laws that are deeply embedded with great wisdom, and their application confers benefits even when we find it difficult to keep them. For example, keeping Shabbos that day meant we didn't have the reassurance of hearing the voices of close family members or learning about further developments in the news.

These restrictions come directly from the Torah. Exodus 34:21 commands us, "Six days you may work, and on the seventh day you shall rest." The traditional commentaries see in this verse not just permission to work on weekdays but an injunction to do so. Shabbos is special because the withdrawal from work that it requires is distinct from other days in which we *should* work. And work itself is broadly defined. In halakah there are thirty-nine categories of creative work, called *melacha*, encompassing a range of endeavors, including use of electronics.

There are many benefits to being digitally connected to the world around us. Access to information gives us knowledge and power to make decisions in our best interests. However, this same access can also increase our anxiety, and give us an illusion of knowing and understanding events that are beyond our grasp. Very often, our extreme focus on the news throws us into emotional tailspins. Sometimes it is healthier to wait for a fuller report of news to emerge, rather than to fixate on each snippet of information as it is reported in real time. But it's difficult to do this when our society expects us to always be connected, and when we fear that by unplugging we will be missing out.

On October 27, I sat with my children, and talked to them about the information we then had, and how it made us feel. I was able to listen to them, with their many questions about how such a thing could happen. My daughter, who was nine, kept asking why the gunman had gone into a synagogue to kill people, and why he had chosen that particular synagogue. I had no answers to these questions, but I was able to sit with my children, verbalize my own inability to understand what had happened, and show them that our life had not been irretrievably shaken. It was still Shabbos, and we were still observing it as we always did. Despite the upheaval in our community, this was a bit of stability to cling to.

Keeping Shabbos, and maintaining its rituals for our family, was the most psychologically healthy decision we could have made that day. We were fortunate not to be directly affected, and we were not in a position to assist those who were. Like most members of our community, we were on the periphery, feeling the shock and fear, even though we had not been in the Tree of Life building.

As I thought about it later, I realized that our determined observance of Shabbos was also an act of defiance. The gunman, like other violent antisemites throughout the ages, had been bent on not just killing us but attacking a house of worship and desecrating our religion. That morning, eleven holy souls had been deprived of their ability to celebrate Shabbos. In keeping the holy day, I was carrying on their legacy, ensuring that the day they honored would not itself become a casualty of violence.

One of the biggest challenges of keeping Shabbos is letting go of the control, or the illusion of control, that we feel the rest of the week. When we step back from the tasks that define us through our work, we lose a bit of our power and are left to just be ourselves, vulnerable to forces beyond our control, and fully aware of our vulnerability. However, in an age in which we are increasingly tethered to our electronic devices, Shabbos is an opportunity to restore a different sort of power—the power to filter our experiences and limit the images and sounds that intrude into our homes. The power to choose holiness and insight, and to realize that we can survive without constant information and entertainment.

On October 27 I was scared and shaken, sad and anxious, but I was not powerless. The structure of Shabbos provided guidance in how to proceed with the rest of that day. We walked home from services, we ate lunch with friends, we read books, and we tried to address our children's questions. Our job that day was to not let terror take away the gift of Shabbos, and though the day was unforgettably long, it was still undeniably Shabbos. That day we kept Shabbos, and in doing so, felt that we were reclaiming the sanctity and peace that had been taken from our community that morning.

COVERING
THE
UNPRECEDENTED

Peter Smith

IN THE DAYS AFTER OCTOBER 27, I would stop by the corner of Shady and Wilkins to observe the ever-growing, spontaneous memorial there. I watched as the people arrived individually or in groups: the stunned, the determined, the grieving, the disbelieving. Some stopped in solemn meditation, others paced slowly along the sidewalk by the memorial, shaking their heads. Some added to the scores of bouquets already there—roses, sunflowers, carnations, daisies, their soft, primary-colored blossoms mingled with the brittle, muted autumn leaves that had fallen from the neighboring trees. Other people left stuffed animals, votive candles, artwork, or photos. A child had left a hand-made card with awkward letters and a flock of owl stickers. Others had laid memorial pebbles on the eleven Star of David markers, which bore them like epaulettes. As the shocking last days of October transitioned into the first Tuesday in November, visitors left "I Voted" stickers and pins, an implicit reference to the belief that elections matter, and that they mattered right here.

One man from the South Hills came to see the site at his wife's urging, sixty-one years after they'd been married at Tree of Life. But the visit was stirring memories older than that, and he didn't want to linger. "I'm a survivor of the Holocaust to begin with," he said. "I saw enough death. It's enough."

Some came alone, to bear solitary tribute, others in groups, still others seeking communion with others. There was the barista whose customers had been reeling from grief, and who needed to quietly express some of her own. There were the school bus drivers, watching solemnly as they waited to pick up students across the street at the Children's Institute. There were the Jewish schoolgirls, visiting from their New York yeshiva. There were the canine handlers from New England who brought their therapy dogs. There were the musicians and other artists who formed an impromptu community, gathering each night across Shady Avenue, mingling stories and music, saxophone and guitar. They took on the name Tree of Life Arts Healing. One participant said that on the night of the shootings he showed up with his guitar, began singing hymns, and looked up to see about fifty people around him. "I realized this was where I was supposed to be," he said.

And there were the African immigrants who gathered one dark, drizzly November evening to play what they called their talking drums and sing Bob Marley's "One Love" and other songs. "The sky is crying right now," one Nigerian woman said as a light drizzle began. "We are all crying." But, she said, "With this, we're not trying to cry; we're celebrating the spirit of the dead. That's why we're playing this, to elevate their spirit, to let them know that yeah, it happened, but we celebrate you." One of them began reading off the names from each memorial star: Cecil, David, Sylvan, Bernice, Joyce, Irving, Melvin, Richard, Rose, Jerry, Daniel.

The Africans had made Tree of Life their destination that night because they knew why the killer had made it his on that recent Shabbat. He had targeted the address because he hated Jews and he hated immigrants, and he hated Jews who showed love to immigrants, and really, he just hated. "We want to stand by the Jewish community, who have been our longstanding allies to integrate the African community," a Nigerian immigrant told me. "We want to stand with them, to say no to hatred." A Congolese native was still processing the enormity of the crime: "This is not the America I came for. We forgot what made America so great." It was not financial or military might, he said, but the way America "respected human beings," he said. "I was like, 'This cannot happen here.'"

This cannot happen here.
We forgot what made America great.
The sky is crying right now.

I was in my basement that Saturday morning when my editor called. A gunman had invaded the Tree of Life synagogue in Squirrel Hill and killed several people. "It's bad."

I've done my share of breaking-news coverage of deadly events over the years—a natural gas explosion that killed six at a restaurant, a tornado that killed dozens along the Ohio Valley, a highway collision that wiped out a Mennonite family bound for a wedding, a flash flood that swept an Amish buggy away, taking four children to their deaths. After the 2006 Comair crash that killed forty-nine in Kentucky, I spoke at length with anguished, surviving loved ones around the country.

But this Squirrel Hill massacre was different in kind. Saturday brought something new in the land, a one-man antisemitic pogrom of unprecedented carnage. Some of my colleagues had raced to the scene in Squirrel Hill, capturing those first frantic moments in unforgettable words and images. Others were covering the news conferences with the mayor and law enforcement officials. Still others came to the newsroom and began plumbing the conspiratorial warrens of the internet, following the digital trail left by the suspect and finding, as we always find in these shootings, pathetic crumbs of hateful banality.

As the religion writer with the *Post-Gazette*, my task was to reach into Pittsburgh's Jewish community and cover the reverberations there, and to cover the wider response of the city's faith communities. I knew that long hours and long days of work lay ahead. So before I headed to Squirrel Hill that morning, I went for a quick jog in my South Hills neighborhood, so incongruously quiet, as I tried to work off some of the shock and collect a torrent of thoughts.

I've been covering religion news for close to twenty-five years now. Before that, I'd worked as a small-town reporter and editor, mostly grinding out stories on local government and crime, moving on to the next day's news before there was time to make sense of the previous day's. Eventually I decided that if I were going to make a career in journalism, I should write about something I'm passionately interested in. I learned about journalists who were covering religion, not as a freak show or an inherent scandal nor, conversely, as something benign and benevolent to be kid-gloved, but as a source from which people draw their deepest meaning, aspire to their noblest ideals, and justify their darkest deeds. People tend to do as they believe and believe as they do, and they form bonds with those who believe and do as they do. Any sort of meaning making, whether spiritual or secular—and any community building based on that—tells us much about who we are and who our neighbors are. Once you start reporting on that, little else seems as important.

I began working as a freelancer for Religion News Service, covering religion throughout North America and Europe, before working as the religion writer for the *Courier-Journal* in the Bible Belt crossroads of Louisville and Kentucky, and then coming to Pittsburgh in 2013 to cover religion for the *Post-Gazette*. Through it all, I learned that there are moments when religion journalists get to cover the extraordinary, and to find the extraordinary in the ordinary. To cover the sacred. That happened at a summer camp in rural Poland for Jews rediscovering their heritage after the traumas of the Holocaust and communist persecution. That happened at an Indiana temple after a summer squall, when the Dalai Lama spoke in his native tongue to the rain-soaked Tibetan and Mongolian immigrants who had crowded into every available space. That happened at a mosque in Pittsburgh during midnight prayers in Ramadan, at a Kentucky warehouse that echoed with the mournful harmonies of a Mennonite congregation that had lost ten of its members in a tragic crash, at a tiny storefront church in Pittsburgh's Hill District, where a baptismal service brought together an Eastern Orthodox priest recovering from postwar trauma and a convert recovering from alcoholism.

Too often, though, religion reporting can be more troubling than transcendent. I had spent much of 2018 covering one of Pennsylvania's biggest religious scandals in recent memory: The statewide grand jury report into sexual abuse in the Diocese of Pittsburgh and five other dioceses. I was working closely with reporters who cover law enforcement and politics, and so we were already operating as a team by October 27, when we needed to be. If there is a common thread between what we covered before and on October 27, it is the communitywide impact of unspeakable assaults in sacred settings.

This cannot happen here.

But really, didn't we know better, after Oak Creek, after Charleston, after Quebec City? After Parkland, after Las Vegas, after Newtown? After Charlottesville? As one rabbi told me, Pittsburgh learned to stop saying it couldn't happen here in 2000, with the antisemitic and racist murder spree of Richard Baumhammers. Since at least that time, as Middle East tensions rose with the Second Intifada and 9/11, synagogues across the country had been increasing security measures.

And the last Saturday of October 2018 was the capstone to an especially bad week. On Wednesday, October 24, about seventy people were gathered for a midday service at First Baptist Church in Jeffersontown, Kentucky, a church founded by antebellum slaves. Most had left, but several people were still in the building by the time the armed white man arrived. Surveillance video showed him unsuccessfully trying to open the locked door, which had been unlocked just a short time before. He left and went to a nearby Kroger supermarket, where he shot two Black shoppers dead; as of this writing he is awaiting trial on hate crimes and other charges. If he had come earlier, or if someone hadn't locked the church door, it could easily have been another Charleston.

On Friday, October 26, authorities in Florida arrested a man on charges that he sent explosive packages to Democrats and media figures he considered enemies of President Trump. No one was hurt, but the proliferation of these packages had caused days of alarming news.

We forgot what made America great.

So what happened on October 27 wasn't unthinkable, but it was unprecedented. How does one cover the unprecedented? All I knew to do was to show up. Show up and start reporting.

My first stop was at Chabad of the South Hills, for no other reason than that it was in my own neighborhood and on my route into town. Of course, the Orthodox restrict their use of phones on the Sabbath, but word reached them. Someone had answered the phone before arriving at shul and received the news in a roundabout way from someone in Israel who had heard that there was a shooting in Pittsburgh. As word of the attack spread through the congregation, the rabbi offered prayers for the strength they'd need in the days ahead.

When I got to Squirrel Hill, Orthodox men in dark suits and women in long dresses were leaving Shaare Torah Congregation on Murray Avenue. As I parked and made my way to the synagogue, another driver slowed down and shouted words of encouragement out the car window to the group. Like all the synagogues in Squirrel Hill, this one had immediately gone into lockdown. The rabbi, Daniel Wasserman, told me he had told the congregants, "'We are in the middle of prayers, so let's pray.' If I had some real information, I shared it." Eventually the worshippers got the all clear, and proceeded with a bar mitzvah. By the time I got there, hundreds of people were still there for the celebratory meal that followed, complete with balloons and Steeler-themed yarmulkes. Going through with the bar mitzvah was a small act of resilience. "It reminds us that happy occasions are fleeting. Sometimes we have to focus on them," Wasserman said.

I then went over to the Jewish Community Center. It was already closed to normal activities for the day as it became an all-purpose command post. FBI, local police, the coroner—everyone set up to work there. Counselors from around the corner at Jewish Family and Community Services were there to comfort the bereaved. I later learned that it was there that families got word from the coroner of the deaths of their loved ones.

I did more interviews and spoke by phone to the one Tree of Life member I knew, rabbi emeritus Alvin Berkun, who was on his way to the hospital, but not for the reason everyone else was. His wife hadn't been well enough to go to shul. Rabbi Berkun himself had been just about to go to the services but checked in with her one more time. She said she'd feel reassured if he stayed home, so he did. That's why they survived that day, although the illness would take her life within the following months.

His wasn't the only near-miss. One man wasn't feeling well and didn't go to Shabbat prayers; another was delayed a few life-saving minutes. Such stories almost always emerge after mass casualty events. After the Comair crash, I interviewed a man who was one computer click away from booking the fated flight before deciding to take a later one. Usually the flip side of these stories is that for everyone who chose a later flight, there is someone who decided on a whim to catch the earlier one. On October 27, no one was in that building by happenstance at 9:30—only those who were always there for the start of services or Torah study. Under different circumstances there might have been more than twenty-two people in there, but I doubt there would have been fewer.

Late Saturday afternoon, I went to a quickly organized interfaith vigil in Sixth Presbyterian Church, across the street from the JCC. People filled the pews and were sitting in every available space on the floor. But even that did not prepare me for what was developing outside. Thousands had gathered at the rainy intersection of Murray and Forbes to mourn, to pray, to chant, "Vote! Vote! Vote!" (This was just before the midterm elections, and both bigotry and gun violence would be tacit presences on the ballot.) "I am a different Jew today than I was yesterday," said one of the Taylor Allderdice High School students who organized the outdoor gathering. "I hope that the Jew I am today will be stronger."

Memory is a quirky thing. I didn't remember until I looked back at my photos of that evening, with all the umbrellas, that it had been raining.

The next day's vigil at Soldiers and Sailors Memorial Hall, for all its planned formalities, had the feeling of something spontaneous, sacred, historic.

Scores of clergy of various faiths lined up on stage in a show of support to the rabbis representing the three congregations that were attacked.

Rabbi Jeffrey Myers chanted the El Malei Rachamim, his tenor voice soaring and at times shaking. He recited the opening line of Psalm 23, "The Lord is my shepherd. I shall not want," and saying, "Well God, I want! What I want you can't give me. You can't return these eleven beautiful souls." But, he continued, "My cup overflows with love," expressions of support from throughout the world.

Wasi Mohamed of the Islamic Center of Pittsburgh restated what he told the vigil the night before, that Muslims appreciated the Jewish community's support when their own communities faced prejudice after 9/11 and with more recent travel restrictions. "We'll be there" for you, he said.

Rabbi Cheryl Klein acknowledged that her fellow congregants at Dor Hadash would grieve "for a long time. We will pray for those who are clinging to life, and with your support, love and friendship, we will continue to do the work of our people making our community better, brighter and filled with acts of lovingkindness."

The Rev. Liddy Barlow, executive minister of the ecumenical group Christian Associates of Southwest Pennsylvania, found a way to trace the Biblical imagery of the Tree of Life from the Garden of Eden to the book of Revelation, where it bore twelve kinds of fruit, and its leaves were for the healing of nations. She was wary, she told me later, of bringing in Christian scriptures at such a moment, except for the inclusive image that followed: If one tree in the future paradise bears twelve kinds of fruit, she told the gathering, "imagine what the neighborhood looks like. I think it looks like Squirrel Hill."

Rabbi Jonathan Perlman of New Light Congregation echoed the words displayed permanently in large letters behind him from Abraham Lincoln's Gettysburg Address, infused now with new meaning, that the eleven "shall not have died in vain" in their "last full measure of devotion." The three New Light members lost in the attack, Richard Gottfried, Daniel Stein, and Melvin Wax, "cannot be replaced. But we will not be broken."

In the following week were days of funerals, attracting thousands from around the world, a mix of homage to the rich lives of the deceased and outrage at the heavily armed hatred that had taken their lives. In between I talked with all who were willing, and when people weren't, I respected their space.

I would spend the coming months attending Shabbat services and other events held by the three congregations in their new worship spaces. I'd visit members in their homes, and was particularly moved by some of the more intimate gestures, such as the eleven hydrangeas that Arlene Wolk planted in her backyard in memory of those who were lost. I covered the enduring tradition of morning minyan, the daily prayer service that lost so many regular participants but was still led on some days by survivors of the October 27 shootings. I wrote about visits by outside groups, including members of the Charleston church and the Quebec mosque who belonged to the same unwanted club of those whose houses of worship had been subject to deadly invasions.

I covered the cycle of new mourning triggers, the attempts to make Hanukkah and Passover and the High Holidays both as normal and as meaningful as possible. This led to incongruous moments and new relationships. The cavernous walls and gothic vaults of Calvary Episcopal Church in Shadyside, an architectural legacy of Pittsburgh's old WASP guard, echoed with the sonorous reveille of a shofar at the Jewish new year, part of a growing interfaith relationship between the church and Tree of Life. New Light deepened its longstanding partnership with Rodman Street Missionary Baptist Church in East Liberty and developed a new one with another historically Black church, as members visited Charleston's Mother Emanuel AME in an emotional bonding of fellow survivors. The JCC and Christian Associates pursued an interfaith discussion on the lingering effects of trauma at the Center for Victims, recognizing that while the world came to Pittsburgh to sit shiva for the eleven, there are neighborhoods in Pittsburgh where communities of color face daily onslaughts of gun violence and other traumas, and usually face them alone.

Come October 27, 2019, my colleagues and I covered all the thoughtfully planned one-year memorial tributes—the Torah study, the community service projects, and the big memorial service back at Soldiers and Sailors. As with the previous year, I found a particular hushed sacredness at the synagogue site itself, where hundreds or even thousands passed by throughout the day. The building was still closed, the spontaneous memorial had been more consolidated (with the bouquets and other perishables long since removed). But the chain link fence surrounding the building was now lined with bright, hope-filled posters drawn by students locally and by those from all-too-familiar points on our scarred psychic map: Newtown, Parkland, Columbine.

Anthony Fienberg, son of Joyce, traveled from Paris and set up a modest display table outside the synagogue, where he asked visitors to choose from one of eleven mitzvahs, such as praying onsite or committing to give blood or help refugees. He led an afternoon prayer in the garden patio outside the building. "The idea is to show the exact opposite of the intention [of the attack] is achieved," he said. "You didn't squash the Jewish community. It's vibrant. And this is still a synagogue."

More than twenty years earlier, when I was freelancing for Religion News Service, I traveled to a summer camp in the Polish countryside where participants were learning how to be Jews, an identity that many of them didn't even know they had until the end of official persecution under in the Communist era. Now, in the 1990s, Polish Judaism was being rediscovered and rekindled, and here I was able to witness it, barely fifty miles from the ruins of Auschwitz. During the week the campers did the kinds of things that religious campers do around the world, mixing scripture lessons and devotions with soccer play and squirt-gun battles. But as the evening of Shabbat approached, women put on their best dresses and men put on their suits, and they launched into song after joyful song, dancing in circles, many of them smiling broadly and raising their squinting eyes heavenward.

When the rabbi got up to speak at dinner, he reminded all of the approaching date of the 9th of Av, when Jews fasted to lament the destruction of the ancient temple by the Romans. Someone asked Rabban Yochanan ben Zakkai how their sins could now be forgiven with no temple wherein to offer sacrificial atonement. "We have a means of making atonement," he said, in the rabbi's retelling. "And what is it? It is deeds of love."[1] And so the Jewish faith was preserved, cast in a new form. The analogy to Polish Jews, rebuilding their faith after another catastrophe, was clear to all.

Recently I had a mini-reunion with some of those I met in Poland—this time in Pittsburgh. The Warsaw Jewish community sent a delegation to work on building a formal partnership with the Jewish Federation of Greater Pittsburgh. Each community has its own, very different story, but each is trauma-informed in its own way. It's been

---

1. Once when R. Johanan b. Zakkai was leaving Jerusalem, R. Joshua was walking behind him and saw the Temple in ruins. R. Joshua said, "Woe is us that this has been destroyed, the place where atonement was made for the sins of Israel." "No, my son, do you not know that we have a means of making atonement. And what is it? It is deeds of love, as it is said [Hosea 6:6]: 'For I desire kindness, and not sacrifice'" (Avot of Rabbi Nathan[1] 4, 21).

an unexpected opportunity for me to bear witness, a generation apart, to some small part of these now-braiding stories of resilience.

We learned from Elie Wiesel and other witnesses to the Holocaust to resist clouding our memory of that abomination by making it too universal. "Not all victims were Jews, but all Jews were victims," he often said. What happened on October 27 was an antisemitic act, and we should never forget that when we visit the place where the eleven died. There, their last full measure of devotion was given to the very specific acts of studying the Parshat Vayera of the Torah and praying the Kaddish d'Rabbanan.

And this is still a synagogue.

Even so, mourners of all faiths and none turned out by the countless thousands at the memorials following October 27. They saw their values to be also under attack, and some quite literally saw their own lives as under attack, like the African group, given the murderer's contempt for immigrants, refugees, and those who help them.

The corner of Shady and Wilkins may not be as busy now with pilgrims as in those early days or at the one-year mark, but people continue to visit.

Like the tree bearing twelve kinds of fruit, it has drawn pilgrims from all walks, all faiths, bringing their flowers and artworks and talking drums as they've offered their respects while hoping also to receive something from the encounter.

"I realized this was where I was supposed to be," the guitarist said. *And the leaves of the tree were for the healing of the nations.*

MEMORIALIZATION, MOURNING, SURVIVING

Reflections, Potentialities, and
Distractions from the Jewish Past

Adam Shear

IT HAPPENED IN SQUIRREL HILL, in our neighborhood, in our Jewish community. Had we been home, we might have been in synagogue—a different one, down the street. Relatives, friends, and colleagues around the country assumed we were nearby and texted, called, emailed to check in.

But we weren't there. We were out of town the day it happened. We had gone to Denver for the weekend to meet a new nephew and visit family. I heard the news first in the hotel coffee shop when alerts started going on my phone. By the time I was back upstairs in the room and waking the rest of the family, more news was coming in. In

I compiled much of the historical material here for a lecture I gave titled "Jewish Memorials of Catastrophe before Modernity," as a prelude offering context for a weekend mini-course at the University of Pittsburgh, November 2, 2019, "Memorials and the Future of the Holocaust," held in connection with an exhibition of Luigi Toscano's "Lest We Forget" photo montage on the Pitt campus. We were also mindful of the one-year anniversary of October 27, with our course falling midway between the secular and Jewish anniversaries on the calendar. I am grateful to Beth Kissileff for pushing me to connect the historical findings with a more personal reflection on the tragic event in my community and to think, even tentatively, about what the history of mourning and memorialization in Judaism might have to teach us as we move forward while continuing to look back. And I am also grateful to Beth and Eric for their editing and suggestions for improving this essay.

Denver, life was going on as normal on a sunny Saturday. In the rest of America, it was another day, another shooting: there was shock, concern, and sadness—but not direct experience. Tethered to our phones while we played with the baby and walked around, we alternated between normal and trauma.

We could understand what our neighbors went through that day in ways that others could not because it happened in our community, in our city, and to people we know. The photo of the two women and a teenage girl on a street corner, heads bowed, and reciting psalms, that was reproduced in newspapers around the world? Those were close friends of ours. But in other ways we were distant. Our stories from the day itself were not the same as those who heard the news on the streets or the houses, synagogues, cafes and shops of Squirrel Hill. We were there and we were not there: it was our holy community that was shattered; we are of the community but we did not have a common experience.

SAYING KADDISH

Of course, I didn't recite the mourner's Kaddish for the eleven. In the technical sense of halakah (Jewish law) and minhag (Jewish custom) I was not a mourner: I was not the child, the parent, the spouse, or the sibling of any of those who had been murdered. Others said Kaddish at the appropriate times in the service and I listened.

There are multiple versions of the Aramaic sanctification of God's name that goes by the name "Kaddish" in Jewish liturgy and that first appears in the *Seder Rav Amram Gaon*, a prayer book edited circa 900 CE by the leader of the most prominent yeshiva in the world, in suburban Baghdad. But it's the one recited by mourners that is best known and is so ubiquitous that "saying Kaddish" has become synonymous with mourning in popular Jewish parlance. Learned texts and popular culture both attest to the sense of the importance of this prayer.

It was in twelfth-century Germany that the first evidence of the recitation of the Kaddish by mourners—specifically, orphans—emerged. And the original "orphan's kaddish" was an expressly personal, not communal, ritual practice. The reasoning behind the practice relates to emergent Jewish ideas of the afterlife: some rabbis posited that the souls of the deceased moved into a kind of hell, a place of suffering, *gehinnom.* While some rabbis believed that this was a temporary stop before an automatic move into paradise, others believed that recitation of Kaddish, along with other good deeds by the living child of the dead, could hasten or ensure the move into paradise. There is a scholarly debate here about how much contemporary Christian conceptions of purgatory influenced the emergence of this intercessory kaddish and how much earlier rabbinic sources provided the raw material.[1]

How many Jewish mourners today believe in (or even know of) the mourner's Kaddish as an intercessory ritual that moves a soul from hell to heaven through the actions of a child? I suspect that most of us tend toward an it's-for-the-mourner-not-the-deceased outlook on most Jewish rituals of mourning, including kaddish. And we have expanded the proper scope of the mourner from the orphan to other loved ones. But what remains from the origins is the individual nature of the prayer. Although recited in a communal setting (traditionally recitation of Kaddish requires a minyan, a prayer quorum of ten adult Jews) and containing some communal responses, the prayer as a whole is not communal but individual.

In some places all are asked to rise for the Kaddish. I have heard this explained as a post-Holocaust custom: a surplus of mourning, so we must all participate somehow. In other places everyone does as they wish. That's the custom in my usual synagogue. (An old Jewish joke: A synagogue is riven by debate over whether the nonmourners should stand or sit during the Kaddish. They decide to seek out the oldest member of the congregation, someone who was there when the shul was founded. They find Mr. Goldberg in the assisted living facility and a delegation of the board goes to visit him. When they explain

---

1. The two main interlocutors here are David Shyovitz, who argued for the primary importance of the medieval Christian context in "'You Have Saved Me from the Judgment of Gehenna': The Origins of the Mourner's Kaddish in Medieval Ashkenaz," *AJS Review* 39, 1 (April 2015): 49–73; and David Brodsky, who emphasizes the Talmudic origins of the concepts in his "Mourner's Kaddish: The Prequel: The Sassanian-Persian Backstory that Gave Birth to the Medieval Prayer for the Dead," in *The Aggada of the Bavli and its Cultural World*, ed. Geoffrey Herman and Jeffrey Rubenstein (Providence, RI: Brown Judaic Studies, 2018). The debate is summarized in Kenneth Berger, *Tradition, Interpretation, and Change: Developments in the Liturgy of Medieval and Early Modern Ashkenaz* (Cincinnati: Hebrew Union College Press, 2019), 292–95.

their dilemma, he scratches his head and says, "Let me think." He goes quiet for a while. In the meantime, partisans of each position advocate for their views; the debate becomes heated. People are now shouting at each other. "Aha," says Mr. Goldberg, "I remember—this is the custom." "What? What is it? Tell us." "Yes, the custom of our shul is to argue about this and shout at each other.")

I'm a sitter. Maybe it's because I'm lazy but when I rationalize it, I think that there is something special in being a mourner. The mourner performs an obligation. I am not obligated. Jewish tradition is torn—extra piety ("supererogation" is the technical term) is welcomed by some; others look on it with some suspicion. (Another old Jewish joke: During the musaf prayer on Yom Kippur, at the moment when many lie prostrate on the ground, the cantor could be heard adding to the prayer: "Who am I, God, who am I? I am nothing, less than nothing." Then the rabbi could be heard joining: "Who am I, God? I am less than a less-than-nothing." And then from the back of the shul, the voice of the old shammas, the sexton, the beadle, "O God, I am the least of the least of the least of the nothing." "Ha," says one of the congregational leaders to his neighbor, "look who thinks he's nothing!")

On November 3, 2018, the Shabbat after October 27, when the large sanctuary of my synagogue, a few blocks away from Tree of Life, was packed with more than a thousand Jews and non-Jews, with members of the three congregations, we were all asked to stand as one for the mourner's Kaddish. This was moving to me, and not supererogatory.[2]

Many synagogues have a custom: at each daily, Sabbath, and holiday evening and morning service, when it comes time for the mourner's Kaddish, someone reads the names of those whose anniversary of their deaths are being commemorated that day on the Hebrew calendar (the yahrzeit). For a full year, many synagogues in Pittsburgh also read the names of the eleven martyrs in daily or weekly commemoration. I felt tempted to rise when I heard those names. But I didn't. Who am I to claim to be a mourner? But I marked the names; I noted the names. That is something.

---

2. Thank you to my daughter, Daniella Shear, for remembering this moment, and for her other comments and suggestions on this essay.

PRAYERS FOR THE MARTYRS

In synagogues that follow Ashkenazic traditions (which most synagogues in Pittsburgh and in North America do, regardless of whether they are Reform, Orthodox, Conservative), a special memorial service known as Yizkor is added to four holiday services throughout the year: on Yom Kippur, Shemini Atzeret, Passover, and Shavuot. Memorial prayers are recited for parents and other loved ones and for martyrs. Some congregations add a prayer for those of that community who have died in the last year. Many add a special commemoration of the Holocaust.

There is a powerful custom in the Ashkenazic tradition of leaving the service during yizkor if one's parents are alive. It is followed by many today although there is no halakic basis for it, and many rabbis oppose it. But the interplay of folk custom and normative legal reasoning has a long tradition in Judaism. Before my father died, I followed this custom. When I was very little and all four of my grandparents were alive, my parents did also. A superstitious logic seems to be at work (and most rabbis can't stand superstition): if the central part of yizkor is a prayer memorializing dead parents, would I be invoking the evil eye or tempting the angel of death to participate in such a service? But my father died when I was eighteen, so I have attended yizkor all of my adult life. I say the memorial prayer for him; I mention his name and conjure fond memories; I pledge charity in his name. And I also read other prayers, such as the one for Jewish martyrs. But perhaps because I had imbibed the folk ethos I had grown up with, perhaps because I felt my father's loss more keenly than I felt other losses, I viewed the memorial prayer for parents as central. Dad comes first, then the martyrs; we begin with personal memory and then move to communal lachrymosity.

But historically, it went the other way. The prayers we now find in the yizkor service originated in the prayers evolved in the European Middle Ages in response to communal tragedies. The yizkor for martyrs was written after the Crusade massacres of 1096, a startling outburst of anti-Jewish violence on a scale that Jewish collective memory could hardly fathom. Versions of the yizkor prayer began to be added by many Jewish communities, first in Germany and Northern France, to the Yom Kippur services.[3]

Some of the new prayers spoke of God attending to the righteous martyrs in heaven and exacting vengeance on the perpetrators. Av ha-Raḥamim was written in the same period and some communities added to it the service for the Sabbath before Shavuot (Pentecost), perhaps because the Crusade massacres had taken place in the spring: "In his great mercy, may the father of mercy who dwells on high in mercy attend to the righteous, the upright and the honest, the holy communities that gave their lives in the name of God's holiness. . . . Our God will remember them favorably among the other righteous of the world, and will avenge his servants' spilled blood."[4] Starting in the fourteenth century, other communities began to recite it on the Sabbath before the ninth of Av, the commemoration of the destruction of both the First and Second Temples, and a time when other Jewish tragedies are often marked as well. Eventually other communities (some still today) began to recite this memorial and call for vengeance every Sabbath.

By the fifteenth century, we have reports of the yizkor prayer along with Av ha-Raḥamim being recited on the last days of festivals, presaging where the yizkor service landed in modern times. Gradually, some communities added a liturgical formula to commemorate members of one's family who had died, not only as martyrs but from natural causes—the prayer I would come to know as the yizkor for my father. Printed prayer books and halakic works from the sixteenth century indicate the spread of this from Yom Kippur to other festivals in Poland. As the custom spread, it led to an early modern rabbinic discussion about whether it was even appropriate to memorialize during festivals of joy—the traditional rabbinic understanding of Shavuot, Sukkot, and Passover. The new service became even more ingrained after the

---

3. See Joel M. Hoffman, "The Traditional Yizkor Service: Translation and Commentary," in *May God Remember: Memory and Memorializing in Judaism*, ed. Lawrence Hoffman (Woodstock, VT: Jewish Lights Publishing, 2013), 133.

4. Hoffman, "The Traditional Yizkor Service," 136.

Chmielnicki massacres in the Polish-Lithuanian Commonwealth (1648–1649), another episode of mass violence against Jews that would only be surpassed in our collective memory by the pogroms of the late nineteenth and early twentieth centuries and then the Holocaust. Spanish-Portuguese congregations in Amsterdam and London added yizkor prayers for the victims of the Inquisitions.[5]

After the Chmelniecki massacres, versions of a new prayer commemorating martyrs emerged, the El Malei Raḥamim that asks God to grant "perfect peace" to the "souls we have recalled today." Different liturgical customs have developed over time—some offer distinct wordings of the prayer for martyrs, for parents, for Israeli soldiers fallen in battle. Others combine, creating an omnibus Jewish "all souls": "Exalted, compassionate God, grant perfect peace in Your sheltering presence, among the holy and the pure, whose radiance is like the heavens, to the souls of all those we have recalled today. May their memory be a blessing, and may they rest in paradise."[6] But the historical trendline is clear: commemoration and mourning for Jewish martyrs is not an add-on to the yizkor service but rather its source. Would realization of this centrality and the shock of the mass violence against Jews in America bring the nonorphans among us back into the service on yizkor? Only in Pittsburgh or across North America?

YAHRZEITS, PERSONAL & COMMUNAL

The one-year anniversary of the shooting was widely marked in the Pittsburgh community and in the broader Jewish world. It was an especially meaningful marker for my family because we were away on the event itself. My oldest daughter came home from her first year of college to be with us and with the Pittsburgh Jewish community that weekend. She was asked to speak at the Hillel on her campus, but

---

5. For much of this history, see the articles collected and reprinted by Lawrence Hoffman in the volume *May God Remember*, especially his "Introduction: Yizkor and Memorial In Jewish Tradition," Solomon Freehof, "Hazkarat N'shamot ["Memoiral of Souls"]: How It All Began," and Daniel Landes, "Remembering the Dead as Halakhic Peril."

6. Translation from *Siddur Lev Shalem* (New York: The Rabbinical Assembly, 2016), 336.

she didn't want to represent Pittsburgh elsewhere; she wanted to be here with us and with her community. Many people from Pittsburgh and beyond, Jewish and non-Jewish, wanted to commemorate as well. The massive auditorium at Soldiers and Sailors Memorial Hall was filled to capacity on October 27, 2019. Thousands also joined a virtual commemoration online. October 27, 2019, was the first secular yahrzeit for the eleven martyrs.

"Yahrzeit" is the term from Yiddish or Judeo-German used for the anniversary of a death. Children mark the anniversary of their parent's death on the Hebrew calendar by lighting a candle, giving charity, and reciting the mourner's Kaddish. They might also lead one of the prayer services that day. An observer of yahrzeit goes about his or her business normally that day, but for those moments in the prayer service joins the mourners. So there was one day during the first year after October 27 that I did stand and say the Kaddish with those mourning the martyrs; on the day of my father's yahrzeit, 13 Nisan, two days before Passover.

In the Hebrew calendar, October 27, 2018, was the eighteenth of the month of Ḥeshvan. That is now the yahrzeit for those killed at Tree of Life. In 2019, 18 Ḥeshvan fell on Saturday, November 16. Synagogues in Pittsburgh (and maybe elsewhere) marked the day. That was the last day the eleven names were read before mourner's Kaddish at my synagogue. In 2020 it will be on a Thursday, November 5. The names will be read again. And so on.

Observing the anniversary of a death of a loved one, a beloved teacher, or an important leader goes back to antiquity. The Talmud reports on fasting on the anniversary of a death. The eleventh-century commentator Rashi reports on customs of gathering at the grave to commemorate the anniversary of the death of a great teacher. The scholarly consensus pinpoints the first use of the term "yahrzeit" to refer to commemorating a parent to Isaac of Tyrnau, a fourteenth-century rabbi and author of a compendium of German Jewish customs. The custom of saying mourner's Kaddish on that day gradually took hold among Ashkenazim and gradually spread (with some reluctance) to Sephardim. The medieval Ashkenazic provenance might make one wonder whether here too the origin is in martyrology. But the more likely scenario is a cultural borrowing from Christian neighbors in a period in which anniversary masses were becoming more widespread.[7]

For catastrophes that stretched over weeks (the Crusade massacres) or years (the Holocaust), we don't know the day of death for each victim, nor can we commemorate all on the days of their deaths. Hence, we collapse multiple events into one day of collective remembrance: Yom Hashoah as a day to commemorate all the victims of the Holocaust. Perhaps this was the dynamic at work for the communities that began to say the Av ha-Raḥamim in memory of the 1096 victims on the Sabbath before Shavuot. For October 27/18 Heshvan, we have a distinct day, a yahrzeit for the families and the disciples and friends of those killed. But we also have a day for a communal yahrzeit, year by year. When the names for yahrzeit are read in my synagogue I note the names of the parents and grandparents of my friends and the names of those I knew personally (I've lived in Pittsburgh for almost two decades and I'm getting to be of a certain age). Other names float past my ears. But it's hard to imagine that I won't notice eleven particular names on 18 Heshvan if I am in synagogue on that day.

The computer database that keeps the records of the names of the deceased has its origins in a medieval book, the Ashkenazic *memorbuch*, or yizkor book. The earliest extant one dates from Nuremberg and lists the names of martyrs across Ashkenaz, from 1096 until 1349, as well as the names and dates of death of benefactors and communal leaders. Eventually some congregations began to inscribe the names and dates of death on the walls of the synagogue, giving rise in the modern synagogue to the memorial plaque with an electric bulb that is illuminated on the yahrzeit. Who belongs in the book or on the wall? Anyone the current keepers of the list deem to include; anyone whom anyone asks (or pays, in the case of the plaques) to include. If your name is on the list you are part of the community. The names of those killed on October 27 will be listed on the walls and in the databases of Tree of Life, Dor Hadash, and New Light Congregations. Will they be listed

---

7. On this, see Andreas Lehnhardt, "Christian Influences on the 'Yahrzeit Qaddish,'" in *Death in Jewish Life: Burial and Mourning Customs among Jews of Europe and Nearby Communities*, ed. S. Reif et al. (Berlin: De Gruyter, 2004), 65–78.

on the wall of other synagogues? Will synagogues outside Pittsburgh list their names and read their names as Jews in thirteenth-century Nuremberg did for Jews who died in eleventh-century Mainz?

MARTYRDOM & GOD'S VENGEANCE

Some readers might bristle at the way that many (including me here) have categorized the eleven victims of the shooting as martyrs. Martyrdom is not a familiar category of religious thinking for most contemporary Jews: would we voluntarily lay down our lives to prove our faith in God? Did those who headed to synagogue for Shabbat services on a fall day in Pittsburgh imagine that they were placing themselves in a situation in which they might be killed for being Jewish? Did the Jews of the Rhineland in the spring of 1096 imagine that the crusaders would attack them? Those in the first communities struck were shocked and surprised, as the Hebrew chronicles of the crusades suggest. After that, Jews had some warning. But nonetheless, as historian Ivan Marcus so memorably explains, the Crusade Chronicles tell us a tale of turning to martyrdom only when "normal" politics failed.[8] Key to this analysis is the realization that we don't know—we can't know—what the Jews of the Rhineland in the midst of the mass violence were actually thinking. The stories in the chronicles, the liturgical poems, the emergence of the yizkor prayers, are the retrospective sense-making of the survivors and the communities of Jews who were spared. Martyrdom is a retrospective category.

Our medieval forebears assumed that every tragedy was, at least in part, an expression of God's will, of God's providence. Had the community sinned? This logic was applied by the rabbis to the destruction of the Second Temple. It is still applied by some zealots today in the midst of a hurricane or a pandemic. But this is not the logic applied to the Crusade violence: the martyrdom proves that the community was holy, that it met the test. The slaughter of innocents is proof of the holiness of the community. If the community upheld its faith, then shouldn't God uphold his end of the bargain? As one of the Crusade chroniclers wrote:

---

8. Ivan Marcus, "From Politics to Martyrdoms: Shifting Paradigms in the Hebrew Narrative of the 1096 Crusade Rcots," *Prooftexts: A Journal of Jewish Literary History* 2 (1982): 40–52.

Who has heard or seen such a thing? Ask and see: has there ever been an *akedah* like this in all the generations since Adam? Did eleven hundred akedot take place in a single day, all of them comparable to the binding of Isaac son of Abraham[?] Yet for the one bound on Mount Moriah the world shook, as it is stated: "Behold the angels cried out and the skies darkened." What did they do now, why did the skies not darken and the stars not dim . . . when on one day . . . there were killed eleven hundred pure souls, including babes and infants . . . ? Wilt Thou remain silent for these, O Lord?[9]

Many of us in the Pittsburgh Jewish community have opposed the death penalty that federal prosecutors seek for the perpetrator of the shootings of October 27, while others view this as appropriate punishment. Perhaps some see execution as carrying out not only human but also divine justice. Others do not think Jewish tradition wants or seeks human-imposed death penalties.[10] My naturalistic, agnostic, quasi-pantheistic conception of the divine imagines something different and allows me to say these prayers: I can call on my "God" to not remain silent and to avenge the spilled blood of his pure ones, not with more blood but with something else. Perhaps the response from this understanding of God was in the outpouring of caring and love that followed the events. Perhaps vengeance on someone who hated immigrants and Jewish support for refugees will come from political victories that protect the immigrant and shelter the refugee.[11] I don't know whether this is where the ethos of the community is, or will be.

---

9. As quoted and translated by Yosef Yerushalmi in *Zakhor: Jewish History and Jewish Memory* (Seattle: University of Washington Press, 1982), 38.

10. For the view that only God can impose capital punishment, see Beth Kissileff, "The Jewish Answer on How to Punish the Pittsburgh Shooter," *Religion News Service*, February 27, 2019, https://religionnews.com/2019/02/27/the-jewish-answer-to-how-to-punish-the-pittsburgh -synagogue-shooter/.

11. Campbell Robertson of the *New York Times* opened his reporting of the anniversary events this way: "It was a scene that would have infuriated the man who set off a whole year of pain and sorrow. Men and women, Jewish, Muslim, Christian, crowded elbow to elbow around tables at the Jewish Family and Community Services building, making blankets for refugees and packing bags of crayons and coloring books for the young and undocumented." "Pittsburgh Marks a Massacre's Anniversary with Prayers and Projects," *New York Times*, October 27, 2019, https://www.nytimes.com/2019/10/27/us/tree-of-life-shooting-anniversary.html.

SPECIAL PURIMS & OTHER TALES OF DELIVERANCE

What about the survivors? What about those who were in the synagogue that day, injured or scared but not killed? We don't mourn them; we celebrate their survival while we also embrace and understand their trauma (I hope). Can we see their survival in religious terms? Do we ritually mark their survival? Jewish tradition has offered a ritual for survivors of serious illness, dangerous travel, or an emergency situation—the Birkat ha-Gomel (blessing of deliverance). In Yiddish-tinged vernacular, the survivor "benches gomel": he or she is called up (aliyah) to the Torah and, following the reading, recites a special prayer thanking God "who bestows goodness on us despite our imperfections, and who has treated me so favorably." And the congregation then responds: "May the one who has shown such favor to you continue to bestow all that is good upon you, forever."[12]

And we have communal holidays to celebrate the deliverance of the entire Jewish people from a perilous situation. But these are national holidays of survival (Purim), revolution (Hanukkah), and liberation (Passover), focused not on individuals and their survival or on local communities. Medieval and early modern Jews, however, developed an interesting custom of "local Purims" or "special Purims": these commemorated the aversion of near tragedies or tragedies that could have been worse that affected a single family or a single community: a ritual murder accusation where the authorities prevented violence against the Jews or a fire that destroyed property but did not result in loss of life.[13] The family or community would establish a day of remembrance and replicate all or some of the celebration of Purim: a fast the day before, a reading of an account of the events that took place, and a festive meal.

I thought the custom had largely died out in the twentieth century, but then I learned about the "Frimer Family Purim." In 1977, a splinter group from the Nation of Islam, the "Hanafi Movement," took over three buildings (the city hall, the Islamic Center, and the B'nai B'rith

---

12. Translations from *Siddur Lev Shalom*, 173.
13. A partial list with descriptions of these can be found in the *Jewish Encyclopedia* (1906), s.v. "special Purims," jewishencyclopedia.com.

building) in my hometown of Washington, DC, and held hostages for nearly two days. One of the hostages was Rabbi Norman Frimer. When he was released, he and his family established a special Purim, to be celebrated by the adult members of the family.[14] As far as I know, the family has kept up the tradition.

In addition to those killed on October 27, there were many in the building, hiding in closets, fleeing from the shooting. Might they and their families establish private Purims to celebrate their survival? Can the community establish a special Purim? Would such a ritual conflict with or complement the ethos of yahrzeit and yizkor for those who died? Is there a way to combine memorial commemoration with celebration of survival?

I have no tidy way to wrap this up. History teaches and can engender reflection—at least I hope so. But it doesn't dictate. Or: Jewish tradition provides a script but like all performances of the classics, we adapt and tweak to make it meaningful for us, here and now.

Erev Pesach, 5780

---

14.   Rabbi Frimer tells of his experience as a hostage and describes the Seder in his *A Jewish Quest for Religious Meaning: Collected Essays* (Ktav Publishing, 1993).

FINDING
THE
VESSELS

Rabbi Daniel Yolkut

A NOTE FROM THE EDITORS

A sermon draws power from its impulse to be eternal. Addressing the concerns of the day, it nevertheless attempts to be timeless. Delivered to a small congregation, it is still a public message. Constructed from common language, it offers a universal message.

Rabbi Daniel Yolkut has been the spiritual leader of Congregation Poale Zedeck since 2010. Poale Zedeck, or PZ, as it is colloquially known within the local Jewish community, is an Orthodox congregation in Squirrel Hill. The congregation dates to 1880, when a wave of immigration brought Austro-Hungarian Jews to Pittsburgh. The congregation is blessed with a rich sense of lived history. Some of the current children of the congregation are fifth- or even sixth-generation descendants of the founders.

Between the demands of the Sabbath and the annual Jewish holidays, the average congregational rabbi delivers between fifty and seventy-five sermons each year. A Jewish sermon, or *derash*, traditionally begins by calling attention to some curiosity from the scriptural reading of the day. By weaving together ideas from sources throughout Jewish thought, it seeks to resolve the initial question while also delivering practical spiritual guidance.

As part of his regular cycle of sermons, Rabbi Yolkut has frequently addressed the October 27, 2018, attack and its aftermath, looking for ways to provide comfort and perspective within the framework of Jewish observance, scholarship, and history. Below are two of these sermons. The first was delivered on November 3, 2018, the Sabbath following the attack, when synagogues around the world were filled with grief-stricken congregants seeking spiritual comfort. The second was delivered on Saturday, November 16, 2019, marking one year since the attack according to the Hebrew calendar. Rabbi Yolkut typically delivers his sermons extemporaneously from prepared outlines but subsequently provided written versions of these two. In the moment, Rabbi Yolkut was addressing a specific audience: religiously observant Jews who are familiar with the style, language, references, and structure of derasha.[1] We have translated the Hebrew terms but largely left his work unedited. Although the framework might be unfamiliar to some, his approach to reckoning with tragedy resonates broadly.

In a conversation with Beth Kissileff in February 2020, Yolkut noted some of the things that guided him in creating his teaching. These were how to make sense of the shooting against the backdrop of a religious worldview of covenantal history, saying, "My faith is tied into what is called the narrative of Jewish history as a whole." He said that he was trying to deal with this as "a believer in God and in Torah and the Jewish narrative" as well as "an Orthodox Jew, a religious Zionist and a descendant of survivors."[2] His father was a "big believer in the idea of the significance of our family narrative as an expression of the triumph of *mesorah*,"[3] and would speak about this at every family simcha (happy occasion). This has given Yolkut himself a sense of "living through a sense of transmission."

For Yolkut the question was "how to render where this event and the memory of these people was not just a random act of violence, has something deeper to it." He added, "My tradition from my rab-

---

1. Explication of text of Torah with a homiletic message.
2. His mother, Aline Schlesinger Yolkut, is the daughter of Margot Wind Schlesinger and Charles Chaskel Schlesinger, who were saved by Oskar Schindler and on his list.
3. The transmission of Torah study and observance through the generations.

beim [rabbis/teachers] is that we don't have tools today claiming to understand how God runs the world," which to him means that the ways of God are "a mystery that is bigger than us." His goals in his teachings were to "help to heal and regain a certain footing." He ended the conversation by saying, "Religion is not about cotton candy—not everything is pastel. There is a lot of suffering, that is part of life, and I am not denying any piece of that. But there can be meaning and that is part of something that is bigger than us in a variety of ways."

—Beth Kissileff and Eric Lidji

KEILIM
SHABBOS CHAYEI SARAH
25 HESHVAN 5779
SATURDAY, NOVEMBER 3, 2018

It is forbidden to weep on Shabbos. I told myself I wouldn't cry this morning while speaking. But the Rama teaches that there is an exception: if the only way to experience the joy of Shabbos is to cry, to release the pain in one's heart, then it is in fact permitted to weep on Shabbos.[4] So if I find myself crying, certainly this Shabbos we can rely on the Rama.

A few minutes ago, we blessed the coming month of Kislev, the month of Hanukkah.[5] And this morning, how much we all desperately need Hanukkah, those holy lights shining against the darkness, the season of wonders and consolation. It is fascinating to note that while Hanukkah is the first Yom Tov established after the closing of Tanach,[6] in a mysterious way the roots of its miracle lie centuries beforehand, in a story that we read in the *haftarah* just a week ago, not knowing yet about the carnage transpiring less than a mile away

---

4. Rabbi Moses Isserles, a leader of Polish Jewry in the sixteenth century. The source is Orach Chaim 288:2.

5. The beginning of each Hebrew month is announced in a public prayer on the Sabbath before it begins.

6. The cycle of Jewish holidays is connected to events in the Hebrew Bible, Tanach, with the exception of Hanukkah, which commemorates a later event in Jewish history.

as we were reading the words of the Navi, words that the wonderful Jews gathered in the congregations at Tree of Life would never hear.[7]

There was a widow who found herself in desperate straits, the noose of poverty and debt closing around her neck, creditors circling to take her children away. She runs and cries to the prophet Elisha, and the Navi tells her that God will save her, that she will be miraculously provided with a divine flow of olive oil, that great commodity of antiquity, that she can use to pay off her debts and support her family going forward. And yet, a strange limitation to the miracle manifests itself. When the woman fills the last *kli*, the last vessel in the home, the flow ends, the wonder is over.

So we ask ourselves why this had to be, why the *beracha* [blessing] couldn't last forever, why the need for vessels circumscribed the blessing.

I would submit that the Navi is teaching us a fundamental principle about the world that Hashem [God] put us in: while there is a constant flow of divine blessing and grace that we can access, we need to have the *keilim*, the vessels, in order to experience it.

Let me explain what I mean. We all remember last Motzei Shabbos,[8] emerging from a davening under lockdown, and the tension as rumors slowly began to concretize the details of a reality beyond our wildest nightmares, and then making Havdalah[9] and turning on our devices to encounter the crushing reality of what happened, and the calls and emails and texts from our loved ones around the world checking in to see if we were okay. So at some point that Motzei Shabbos, Anna [Yolkut's wife]—who has been my rock and strength this week, as well as being a support for so many others in our community—sat down to write down some of the conversations she had with my children on that terrible night, conversations that I am sure paralleled ones in many of our homes and families over this past week.

---

7. The Sabbath service typically includes two scriptural readings. A portion of the Torah, taken from the Five Books of Moses, is followed by a corresponding haftarah from the Prophets, known as Navi. The week of the attack, the scheduled haftarah was the famous miracle of the prophet Elisha and the widow woman, 2 Kings 4:1–37.

8. Saturday evening, following the end of the Sabbath.

9. The ceremony to ritually separate the Sabbath from the weekday.

In the Talmud and Midrash, we often encounter a practice where at significant moments our sages would stop children to ask them what texts they were learning at school, and to somehow gain insight and wisdom. Never before have I as viscerally understood the words of Tehillim,[10] "From the mouths of children / You have given us strength":

- Mommy, will we ever feel normal again?
- This was not how I thought today was going to go. I thought it would just be a regular Shabbos.
- Can we make a meal train for the families from Tree of Life and the police?
- My friends were scared so we decided to say Tehillim.[11]
- I just don't understand why this happened.
- Everything Hashem does is for a reason, right? There must be a reason . . .
- Can we please only talk about cupcakes and rainbows for a while?
- Was there anything good about the man who did this? Isn't there usually something good about everyone?
- Can you stay with me while I fall asleep tonight?
- "Today, there were worlds created and worlds destroyed, because the *Gemara* [Talmud] says that when we save a life it creates a whole world and when a life is lost a world is destroyed. Also, Hashem has a robe with the name of every person that was killed *Al Kiddush* Hashem.[12] Today His robe has eleven new names."

It was this final observation that took me most by surprise, as I strained to remember where this stunning image of the names of the *kedoshim* on Hashem's robe was from. And then I remembered: it was a midrash Tehillim that I quoted during *kinos* this past Tisha b'Av.[13]

---

10. Psalms. The quotation is from Psalm 8:2.
11. There is a long tradition within Judaism of reciting psalms for healing.
12. Literally "for the sanctification of the Name," a term for Jewish martyrdom.
13. Tisha b'Av, or the ninth day of the summer month of Av, is a day of collective Jewish mourning, commemorating a sequence of tragedies, including the destruction of the temples. It is customary to spend the day reciting dirges and elegies known as *kinos*, which have been written over many historical periods.

And that is exactly what I mean by keilim, the need for vessels. When we need Hashem's comfort most intensely, we can find it but our ability to access it depends on being able to find the right keilim, a way in which each of us, in a highly individual way, is able to capture that *shefa*, that divine flow. And watching my children use the keilim that their lives have already provided them, so as to be able to find meaning in moments of vertigo, where order seems to collapse in evil in chaos, is immeasurably inspiring.

So what are our keilim?

Chesed [kindness] is a kli. This week we have been inundated with the most profound chesed, from Jews and Gentiles, from neighbors and from people across the world who want in the worst way to find some meaningful way to give to the victims, their families, to our communities. The chesed that I have seen displayed by members of our PZ community so humbles me, that I have *zekhus* [merit] to be part of such an amazing community. On a deep level, part of this need to do chesed is the recognition that chesed is a powerful kli for meaning, for us to be able to find divine *nechama* [comfort] in this moment. My kids already know that when someone is in need, you make a meal train. Chesed is a kli.

Kevod haMeis [respect for the dead] is a kli. It's the way we stubbornly assert that when a monster turns a shul into a slaughterhouse, we can with awe and love find the *tzelem elokim* [image of God], the divine, even in the shattered vessels that once held *neshamos* [souls]. People in this room today have found such meaning in the work that they have done as part of our *chevra kadisha*, and I would just add that while for those of us in Pittsburgh, we have long known that Rabbi Wasserman is our *rebbe* in Kevod haMeis, today he is the world's rebbe in Kevod haMeis.[14]

Torah is a kli. At a time like this all the Torah we have ever learned is a receptacle for infusing meaning into our questions. When a child

---

14. Rabbi Daniel Wasserman is the spiritual leader of Shaare Torah Congregation in Pittsburgh and the president of the Gesher Hachaim Jewish Burial Society, the local Orthodox chevra kadisha. One of the many articles citing Wasserman's efforts is Emma Green, "The Jews of Pittsburgh Bury their Dead," *Atlantic*, October 30, 2018, https://www.theatlantic.com/politics/archive/2018/10/pittsburgh-jews-prepare-bury-eleven-killed-gunman/574342/. The honorific "rebbe" expresses a combination of spiritual leader and teacher.

remembers a midrash about Hashem's love for kedoshim, how their deaths have a cosmic significance that defies mortal comprehension, that kli is suddenly filled with oil that sheds light in darkness.

Tefilla [prayer] and Tehillim are a kli. Before Selichos, I shared with you the story of David Raab, a passenger on the plane hijacked by Palestinian terrorists to Jordan in September 1970:

> Every morning, I got up very early—actually I never really slept. I was usually up all night and then I slept afterward for a few hours. So around four-thirty, five o'clock I would put on my tefillin and say the "Shema" and its blessings, as well as the "Shemoneh Esreh" [the silent meditation]. I davened [prayed] as quickly as I could and then I took off my tefillin. I didn't want them to see what I was doing. I wore my yarmulke only when I ate, and I ate only when there were no guerrillas around because I didn't want them to see me wearing a yarmulke.
>
> It was the month of Elul, when we recite Psalm 27, For David: The Lord is my light, twice a day. Every time I said it, it seemed very, very appropriate. It seemed very coincidental that we had been hijacked just at the time when you say this particular chapter in Psalms. For example, one verse is, "Though a host should encamp against me, my heart shall not fear; if a war should be waged upon me, in God's succor I put my faith." Now, you can't really ask for a better verse than that. It fit the situation completely. It seemed to express my feelings. It was very reassuring; like God was telling me: Don't be afraid because in these types of situations I come through. The last sentence of the chapter seemed to have the strongest influence on me. It says, "Await the Lord; be strong, and let your heart take courage. Yes, await the Lord." It was all very comforting to me, especially since the Psalm began "For David."[15]

All week, the siddur has been such a kli, with phrases from davening feeling like they were addressed directly to me:

---

15. David Raab, *Terror in Black September: The First Eyewitness Account of the Infamous 1970 Hijackings* (New York: Palgrave MAcmillan, 2007), 79. Bracket insertions in the original.

- *Ashreinu sheanachnu mashkimim uma'arivim erev va-voker ve-omerim pa'amayim*—thinking about those precious souls, the first to come to shul in the morning.[16]
- *Kee doreish dameem otam zachar lo shachach tza-ah-kat anaveem*—that He does not forget the screams of the humble.[17]
- *Harofe lishvurei lev umchbesh l'atzvo sam* (Psalm 147:3)—that He heals the brokenhearted.

Niggun[18] is a kli. The Alter Rebbe of Lubavitch[19] taught that niggun is the quill of the *neshama*, and all week I have found such *chizuk* [strength] in niggun, from singing "Acheinu" and "Avinu Malkeinu"[20] last Motzei Shabbos with Jews who gathered outside of Tree of Life, to spending all day yesterday finding myself singing the soulful niggun of Kah Echsof, "Hashem I long for the sweetness of Shabbos."

Shabbos is an unbelievable kli. This morning I was up at 5:30, the house silent, filled with the smell of *cholent*,[21] and for the first time I had real space, uninterrupted by the incessant soul-killing ringing and beeping of devices. And, with the Rama's assent, for the first time I was really able to cry.

And Jewish history is a kli. Last Shabbos on lockdown, I almost mechanically gave the derasha I had prepared that it took days for the real significance to sink in. As sirens blared throughout the neighborhood, I recounted an experience I had earlier in that week on our shul's amazing mission to Israel, of standing on the ancient road to Yerushalayim [Jerusalem] in Gush Etzion, next to the ancient *mikvah* [ritual bath] used by our ancestors on the way to the Beis HaMikdash,[22]

---

16. "Fortunate are we that arise early and go to bed, morning and night and say twice each day."
17. Taken from Av Harachamim, a prayer for martyrs recited on the Sabbath.
18. A *niggun* is a melody, often wordless, sung at special religious occasions.
19. Rabbi Shneur Zalman of Liadi, known as the Alter Rebbe, was the founder of Chabad.
20. A pair of Jewish songs. "Acheinu," meaning "brothers," expresses Jewish solidarity. "Aveinu Malkeinu" is a beloved song of repentance usually sung during the High Holidays and on public fast days.
21. A stew prepared before the Sabbath and left to warm, allowing religiously observant families to enjoy a hot meal on Saturday afternoon, when it is forbidden to cook.
22. Temple, literally "sanctified house."

and in all probability the path used by Avraham [Abraham] and Yitzchak [Isaac] on the way to the *akedah* [the binding of Isaac]. The Ramban[23] teaches that the Talmudic comment *maaseh avos siman le-banim*, that the deeds of our fathers and mothers are a sign for the generations, is causative, that the stories in Bereishis [Genesis] laid down a template that would replay itself throughout Jewish history. So standing on the path paved by the akedah, one could see its imprint throughout Jewish history, looking in one direction to where the Maccabees took a heroic stand against the Greek elephant cavalry, in another to where the defenders of Gush Etzion died in the defense of the southern approach to Jerusalem, and in another to Yeshivat Har Etzion, where generations of boys from the Yom Kippur War until today have given their lives for Am Yisrael [the People of Israel]. Only days later did I realize that at the very moments that I was speaking, eleven *akeidos* were taken from us, and in that kli of Jewish history, the possibility of significance in the horror exists.

If I have learned one thing in this terrible and awesome week, it is that one of our core missions in life is to find and fashion keilim for ourselves out of the rich tapestry of our mesorah, so that when we need them, in calamity and catastrophe, to cope with fear and anger and anxiety, or *b'ezras* Hashem [with the help of God] in times of celebration and thanksgiving, that we can catch that divine beracha in all of these powerful vessels.

But sometimes it's not enough. What happens when we feel like we have exhausted our keilim, that try as we might we have nothing in our spiritual repertoire up to the task of illuminating the darkness? It is haunting to note that the image that the Arizal[24] used to teach about evil in the world is *sheviras he-keilim*, shattered vessels that cannot bear the divine light.

There is an obscure image in our kinos for Tisha b'Av elucidat-

---

23. Rabbi Moses ben Nahman, also known as Nachmanides, a thirteenth-century commentator. This appears in his commentary on Genesis 12:6.

24. Rabbi Isaac Luria (1534–1572), a mystical rabbi who lived in Safed, Israel.

ed by the Rav.[25] Every morning in the *mikdash* [temple], the *mishna* tell us, ninety-three vessels would be laid out for the needs of that day's *avodah*.[26] The doctors here can correct me, but I imagine that those gleaming gold and silver implements were laid out *be-kedusaha u-ve-tahara*, in pristine sanctity, much like a surgeon's precision tools for performing surgery. At the time of the Churban,[27] our great poet Rabbi Elazar HaKallir[28] describes the following scene: "Our skin crawled as the Kohen awoke, and could not find the ninety-three keilim."

What more apt metaphor for utter destruction than being stripped of all keilim?

And I'm sure that this week, many of us, at least at some point, have struggled and failed to find the keilim that we and our families need.

So the prophet Elisha has a last message for us: If you find yourself bereft of keilim, find your friends and neighbors, and borrow from them. Sometimes, we can borrow strength and experience and love from others around us when we can't find them in our own space, and like the widow in the haftarah, those borrowed keilim can be used to receive that *shemen ha-tov* ["good oil"], the strength and comfort from heaven. How many of us have found so much unexpected chizuk from those who love us as well as former strangers this week?

And that is why last Sunday, one of the first people I contacted was our speaker this morning, Dr. David Pelcovitz.[29] David has been part of our PZ family for decades, but there is perhaps no one better equipped to lend us his keilim, his finely tuned instruments to help us as people of *emunah* [faith] at this difficult moment.

---

25. Rabbi Joseph Soloveitchik (1903–1993), a founding thinker of modern Orthodoxy. Soloveitchik, *The Lord Is Righteous in All His Ways*, ed. Jacob J Schacter (Jersey City, NJ: KTAV, 2006), 165.

26. The service of priestly activities. "From the last remaining jars, a miracle, a banner around which we can rally around, was wrought for the Jewish people."

27. The destruction of the temple.

28. Hebrew poet who lived approximately 570–640 CE.

29. Pelcovitz is an Orthodox Jew and a leading figure in mental health research. His appearances in Pittsburgh immediately following the attack provided an opportunity to reckon with the interface of the soul and the psyche. "It would have been malpractice to do one without the other," Yolkut later explained.

Four weeks from tomorrow, we will gather with our families to light the first Hanukkah candle, and to sing together the secret of the prophet Elisha: from the last remaining jars, a miracle, a banner around which we can rally, was wrought for the Jewish people.

There is, though, one ultimate kli that we daven for this morning. The very last mishna in *shas* [the Talmud], after sixty-three tractates filled with wisdom and keilim—*kol ha-Torah kulah* ["all the Torah in its entirety"]—we are taught the following:

Rabbi Shimon ben Chalafta said: Hashem found no better kli to hold blessing for Israel than shalom.

Shalom means peace. Shalom means security. Shalom means peace of mind. Shalom means a restoration of our shattered wholeness. Shalom is the greatest gift we can experience all that Hashem can give us: As it says, and as this morning we daven, Hashem give strength to your nation, Hashem bless your nation with peace.

YITZCHAK'S YAHRZEIT: DERASHA ON THE FIRST YAHRZEIT OF THE KEDOSHEI PITTSBURGH
SHABBOS VAYERA
18 HESHVAN 5780
SATURDAY, NOVEMBER 16, 2019

What does one do on a yahrzeit?

Let me qualify my question. Certainly Jewish tradition provides us with a roadmap of minhagim [customs] to mark a yahrzeit: some fast while others feast, lighting candles, visiting a *kever* [grave] and studying mishna. The deeper question, which I have thought about since losing my father z'l [30] six years ago, is what do you do on a yahrzeit: what are the takeaways when the calendar once again brings you back to a visceral encounter with a time of loss and trauma?

We are all familiar with the dictum of Chazal [the sages], that the deeds and actions of our patriarchs and matriarchs laid down the models of what would happen for the descendants millennia in the fu-

---

30. *Zichrono l'vracha*, "May his memory be a blessing."

ture. In that spirit, then, let's reframe the question: What did Yitzchak Avinu [Isaac our father] do on the yahrzeit of the akedah?

I would submit that the date of the akedah represented a double yahrzeit to Yitzchak: First, in a haunting way, it marked his own yahrzeit, the date of Yitzchak's near-death experience. (And there are midrashim that even advance this notion further, that in some mysterious way Yitzchak died on the altar and returned to life.) Certainly, if a yahrzeit is an encounter with our own mortality, how much more so when it marks a day where Yitzchak's life almost ended?

Secondly, Chazal teach that as Yitzchak lay bound to the altar, life was indeed lost: on hearing of the akedah, Sarah Imenu [Sarah our mother] left the world. So beyond his own experience, in a very concrete way, the date of the akedah quite literally was a yahrzeit for Yitzchak.

There are multiple suggestions as to when the akedah took place, but this morning I would like to share with you a powerful midrash that describes the significance of the season of Pesach: "In which we were redeemed, and in which we are destined to be redeemed, in which Yitzchak was born, and in which he was bound in the akedah, and in which Yaakov received the blessings."

Accordingly, we have a snapshot of the yahrzeit hiding in plain sight: the story in Parshas Toledos of the day that Yitzchak blessed his sons.

To set the stage, Rashi[31] tells us that that particular day took place some eight decades following the akedah.

A few weeks ago, Emma Green shared a significant insight in the *Atlantic*:

> Last year's shooting at the Tree of Life synagogue was a stone dropping in water, creating concentric circles of grief. At the center were the survivors and the families of victims. Then came the first responders, and the local leaders who handled the overwhelming logistics involved in the aftermath. On and on: members of the Pittsburgh Jewish community. Pittsburghers writ large. American Jews. And, finally, the whole of the country. . . .

---

31. Rabbi Shlomo Yitzchaki, an eleventh-century French commentator.

Each of these circles has a different half-life for its grief. People in Pittsburgh's Jewish community still talk about the shooting over Shabbat dinners, but when they leave the city and strangers ask where they're from, "Pittsburgh" often no longer carries any particular meaning. . . .

Yesterday, Pittsburgh's Jewish community marked one year since the deadliest anti-Semitic attack on U.S. soil. This morning, they still woke up with their grief, while America largely continued to move on . . . [and] with each anniversary, the Pittsburgh attack will slip further into the great fog of forgetting.[32]

So I would imagine that on that Pesach, so many years later, Yitzchak too was alone in his grief. Avraham Avinu—who had shared the twin traumas of the akedah and the loss of Sarah—had long left the world, leaving Yitzchak as the sole survivor of the akedah. And while decades before, all of Chevron [Hebron] came out to mourn the matriarch and comfort the patriarch, with the passage of time, everyone else has moved on. But for Yitzchak, certainly, the significance of the day continued to reverberate.

The first thing we learn about Yitzchak's yahrzeit is his dimmed vision. Rashi shares the following midrash: "When Yitzchak was bound on the altar, and his father was about to slaughter him, the heavens opened, and the ministering angels saw and wept, and their tears fell upon Yitzchak's eyes. As a result, his eyes became dim." In other words, even many years later, elements of the trauma persisted. The tears of the *malachim* [angels] continued to glisten in his eyes, and the prism through which Yitzchak perceived reality was permanently changed, and it was in that spirit that the yahrzeit arrives.

Secondly, Yitzchak marked the yahrzeit with a profound sense of his own mortality: "And he said, 'Behold now, I have grown old; I do not know the day of my death.'"

And Rashi explains: "If a person reaches the age of [the death of] his parents, he should worry five years beforehand and five years

32. Green, "America Has Already Forgotten the Tree of Life Shooting," *Atlantic*, October 28, 2019.

afterwards, and Yitzchak was one hundred and twenty-three years old. He said, 'Perhaps I will reach the age of [the death of] my mother, and she died at one hundred and twenty-seven, and I am thus within five years of her age'; therefore, 'I do not know the day of my death.'"

On that fateful yahrzeit, as Yitzchak thought about his mother's passing and his binding—the terror he felt at the akedah and the sudden loss of Sarah Imenu—he could not shake the shadow of the fragility of his own existence, how the security (and perhaps the sweet naïveté of youth) that he felt in the stability of life was never to be recaptured.

And yet.

For all that he continued to blink through the tears of the angels, for all that he was dogged by the reality of his own mortality, there is a third element that cannot be ignored of Yitzchak's yahrzeit.

The midrash in *Pirkei d'Rebbi Eliezer*[33] describes Yitzchak's desire to bless his son on that night: The night of Pesach arrived, and Yitzchak called his son and said, "My son, on this very night, listen well, and you can hear all of the cosmos singing Hallel, and storehouses of dew"—that ancient metaphor for the deep and subtle blessings that Hashem showers on his Creation—"are open tonight!"

On that awesome and terrible day, when Yitzchak remembered the heavens parting and the angels weeping, Yitzchak could still glimpse the awesome potential of Hashem's world, where heavenly storehouses of blessing are open for the taking.

Because when Yitzchak still lay on the altar, he heard the voice of the angel: "That I will surely bless you. And through your children shall be blessed all the nations of the world because you hearkened to My voice."

And so we come to the first yahrzeit of the Kedoshei Pittsburgh, of the men and women murdered just down the road.

Like Yitzchak, this is the day the knife hovered over every Jew in every shul in Squirrel Hill. We all remember the fear on that day as the rumors continued to trickle in as we continued to daven with the doors locked and the sirens blaring through the streets.

---

33. An eighth- or ninth-century retelling of Torah stories.

Like Yitzchak, this is the day where we lost eleven Sarah Imenus—so many of those precious souls matriarchs and patriarchs for their families and for those who knew and loved them.

Like Yitzchak, as we come to the yahrzeit, do we not still need to blink through the tears of the malachim as we remember that dark week of funerals? Emma Green spoke of the concentric circles of grief—we all find ourselves plotted at various points in those circles. For some of us, do those tears not still continue to flow at unexpected moments?

Like Yitzchak, are we not aware of our vulnerability so much more keenly than we left for shul on Shabbos morning of Parshas Vayera last year? The sense of security that had been such a unique part of *Galus America*[34] was shattered that morning, and replaced by a foreboding sense of how delicate are the gossamer strands that support our community?

But like Yitzchak, today notwithstanding the tears of trauma and sense of mortality, today is also a day where we can glimpse redemption in the future, where we can continue to affirm that Hashem still has storehouses filled with the dew of blessing for *klal* Yisrael. Like Yitzchak descending from the altar, fortified by the promise of beracha and invigorated with the power to bless, the yahrzeit is an opportunity to reassert our ability to bring beracha to ourselves, our children and the world.

Last year we were confronted with horror. We faced it as children of Avraham and Sarah: with *tefilla*, with chesed, with *achdus* [unity], with Kevod haMeis. Today, we meet the yahrzeit with the *koach ha-Torah*,[35] with twenty-five hours of learning in our shuls and *batei midrash* ["houses of study"] and with a communal *siyum*[36] of the corpus of the written and oral Torahs.

Today, like Yitzchak, we continue to affirm our belief that amid all of the emotion that the yahrzeit brings in its wake, that just as the

---

34. "Exile America," a term for the diaspora experience in the United States.

35. "Strength in the Torah." To commemorate the first year since the attack, the Orthodox community of Pittsburgh organized around-the-clock Torah study throughout the entire Sabbath.

36. A celebration held upon the completion of a major course of study.

Jewish people are inexplicably called on for sacrifice, so too we are also chosen to bring blessing.

May we merit to see the fulfillment of the promise of the day: When He will swallow up death forever, erasing for all time that sense of fear and vulnerability. When Hashem will wipe away the tears from every face, even those angelic tears that dim our clarity. And the suffering of His nation He will remove from the Earth, and all of our energy and efforts will turn to the great mission of: "And through your children shall be blessed all the nations of the world."

SHOCKED,
NOT SURPRISED

Arlene Weiner

IN OCTOBER 2018, A NEW FRIEND, ROZ, said to me, "Come to services Friday—it's my birthday!" I readily went to Friday night services at our synagogue, Dor Hadash. The service on Roz's birthday was joyous. About sixty people attended, I'd guess, in the long pavilion of the Tree of Life complex in Squirrel Hill. A cheerful rabbi visiting from Oregon, "Rabbi Yitz" (Yitzhak Husbands-Hankin), played his guitar and gave a talk. A member of the congregation ended the service by calling for a blessing on all the people (pointedly including the Arab population) in Israel and the territories. And after the service there was birthday cake for the oneg Shabbat (rejoicing in the Sabbath) in the glass-walled corridor of the building.

If I had to describe Dor Hadash in one word, it would be "welcoming." Luckily, I'm allotted more than one word. Nonhierarchical. Open. Engaged. Inquiring. Dor Hadash has a DIY ethos—since its founding it has been led not by a rabbi but by lay members. Members decide on ritual, members chant from the Torah, members provide snacks. *Nonhierarchical*: once, when I was to provide food for the oneg Shabbat, the refreshments for "rejoicing in the Sabbath," the cantor realized that the attendance would be extra large, and she came early with home-baked goods and helped me set the tables. *Open*: at any given service you might see women in colorful tallits and head coverings, non-Jewish spouses and partners, same-sex couples, Jews by birth and Jews by choice, sometimes even the Kilt Man, in his neon-colored kilt and contrasting stockings. Prayers that refer to our fathers Abraham, Isaac, and Jacob also include our mothers Sarah, Rebecca, Leah, and Rachel. Dor Hadashers don't have to affirm belief; members may be "uncomfortable with G-d language." *Engaged*: the popular Social Action Group was working on two concerns that year: criminal justice, and refugees and immigrants. *Inquiring*: Dor Hadash was founded as a study group. On Saturday mornings a group convenes for study of the Torah, and the talks (we don't have sermons) are often probing and scholarly. *Welcoming*: at the High Holy Days, when many Jews who don't attend synagogue at any other time wish to attend services—and when many if not most synagogues limit attendance to paid-up members—Dor Hadash traditionally is open to all.

At about 10:20 on the morning after that joyous Friday night service, my brother called from New York. My husband answered the phone. "There's been a shooting at Tree of Life." And we were not to leave the house. "Shelter in place"—a phrase that seems routine during these days of COVID-19.

We didn't immediately know what had happened. Strangely, while I'd been at services Friday my husband had figured out how to use the TV remote, since we had received three months' free service from our cable company. That Saturday we were glued to TV for news. We knew there had been a shooting, but little more. When we knew that there had been fatalities, we waited to find out how many and who. My cousin Claudia called from California, hoping to find out whether her aunt's nephews, two men with developmental delays, were alive. "The boys" were familiar faces in our neighborhood—one broad and friendly, one thin and more skittish, anxious. They used to like to visit the fire station. They went to Tree of Life faithfully.

The news came in. Cecil and David were dead. Joyce Fienberg was dead, a friendly woman I knew because we both had worked in the same institute at the University of Pittsburgh. Jerry Rabinowitz was dead. Jerry. . . . There's a saying in Pirkei Avot, "Where there is no mensch, be a mensch."[1] "Mensch" meaning not "man" in the macho

sense, but "human being." Humane being. Jerry was that. About a
month before the shooting I was one of the congregation members
whom Jerry organized to get the once-a-year High Holiday books out
of storage, a mundane task. Big books, to be taken out of the closet,
unpacked, and put on carts. I understand that on Saturdays Jerry set
up the room for the Torah study group, filling juice cups and putting
them out. Possibly that's what he was doing on that Saturday. He was
there early for that reason. Some physicians have an elite aura—you
would never know that he was a doctor. I heard (later, later) that he
was beloved by many for having treated patients with HIV during the
peak of the AIDS crisis, holding their hands with his own ungloved
hand. Another mensch, a mainstay, one of the founders of a group
for the compassionate care of the dead, and I think the man who
invoked the blessing of peace for all the inhabitants of Israel, was
grievously wounded. A woman and six of the police who responded
were wounded. The shooter was wounded. On that Saturday morning
eleven of the congregants of three congregations were killed—killed
by a weapon of war.

The shooting tore the fabric of a beloved community. I wrote shortly afterward: "I have been feeling my emotional bones, wondering
why they are not broken. Why I am not shivering and crying. Am I
hard-hearted?" No. I'm not hard-hearted. I'm not inured to violence.
Rather, both my personal and historical memory make me conscious
of the possibility of violence and the possibility of anti-Jewish acts.
As a Jew of a certain age I have never felt completely secure. I grew
up in New York, my immediate neighborhood predominantly Irish.
On the street near my apartment house, where we played jump rope
and ball-bouncing games, I was not entirely at ease. My neighbors
all went to Catholic school and I went to public school, which made
a difference between us. But I was known and knew them. A little
further away in the neighborhood I might be bullied and taunted by
strangers. At school I was at ease. Some of my classmates were the
children of Jewish refugees from Europe. We were children; I didn't

---

1. Ethics of the Fathers, a compilation of wisdom from early rabbis. The quote is chapter
2, Mishna 6.

know what that meant, but I learned later. I'm conscious of past and present anti-Jewish feeling and actions, and I'm conscious of past and present gun violence. So when the shooting happened, I was shocked, not surprised.

Tree of Life

I marked myself *safe* on Facebook
when the alert came: active shooter
in my neighborhood.
Is *safe* a lie if you want to believe it?

I never feel safe.
When I was eight my playmate Patsy
came home from her school
and asked me *Why did you kill Christ?*
I had no answer.

Ambushed by strangers
near the synagogue,
I spilled my Hebrew-school books,
their top-heavy black letters.

At Hallowe'en I defended
my kid brother, socked with nylons
full of powdered chalk,
his jacket marked, unsafe.

I saw a movie of bulldozers
burying skeletal dead.

Shelter in place, the notice said.
My friends and neighbors text,
and I tell you: *Stay safe.*

I think I hope to harden myself against bad news by expecting it. Knowing that human life and luck are contingent—a frequent theme in my poetry. I know that there are many people who believe otherwise, that all is the Creator's plan, every sparrow's fall. Not long before the shooting, during the High Holy Days, we read, "On Rosh Hashanah it is written, and on Yom Kippur it is sealed, who shall live and who shall die, who by fire and who by water . . ." and a litany of possible fates. Who shall be torn by wild beasts. Which perhaps is what happened at Tree of Life. The beast of ignorance, the beast of rage.

In the months before the shooting, signs had bloomed in the yards of my neighborhood: *You belong here. No matter where you are from, we're glad you're our neighbor.* Many of the signs were multilingual, in English, Spanish, and Arabic, in implied contrast to the Trump Administration's actual and proposed restrictions on immigration and asylum. The man accused of the Tree of Life shooting had written posts that indicate that, in addition to his anti-Jewish feeling, he targeted Dor Hadash because we had had a refugee Shabbat—a service to remind people of the worldwide refugee crisis. He was not—explicitly not—a Trump supporter, but no doubt he had imbibed the panic being whipped up by the president about immigration and the "caravan" of likely asylum seekers. He has been quoted as saying, "All Jews must die." He shot his way into the building through the glass wall of the pavilion where we had had cake the night before.

A high school student who was one of the organizers of a massively attended vigil on the Sunday night after the massacre said she didn't think this could happen here. But it did. And I remembered that it *had* happened before, in Pittsburgh, though not on this scale. In 1986, in Squirrel Hill, a white man in a car asked Neal Rosenblum, a visibly Jewish man, for directions. Rosenblum was a young Canadian father who had just arrived in Squirrel Hill for a Passover visit. The man in the car shot him five times. Rosenblum survived long enough to speak to emergency workers, but died in the hospital. In April 2000 a racist white man, Richard Baumhammers, shot and killed his sixty-three-year-old Jewish neighbor, threw a Molotov cocktail into her house, then drove around for two hours shooting, one by one, four people of Asian descent and a Black man. He also vandalized two synagogues. He did not shoot the white man talking with the Black man. All but one of the victims died. The survivor was paralyzed and died at age thirty-two. Also in spring 2000, Ronald Taylor, a Black man who'd expressed hatred of white men, shot five white men at random in

Wilkinsburg, a town adjacent to Pittsburgh. In 2009 George Sodini targeted women at a fitness studio in Collier Township, ten miles south of Pittsburgh. Three of the women died, nine other people were injured, and Sodini committed suicide.

It's horrifying. It's horrifying when it happens at a school, it's horrifying when it happens at a church, it's horrifying when it happens at a Sikh temple, it's horrifying when it happens at a nightclub. It's horrifying when it's routine, when "only" two people are shot and it is hardly noticed. Close to the time of the Tree of Life shooting a man in Kentucky tried the doors of a Black church, found them locked, and went to a store and killed two Black people. The congregations at Tree of Life opened the doors to worshippers Saturday morning. And Death entered by shattering the glass walls.

Time and distance attenuate our attention and compassion, as I suggest in a poem I wrote after the Virginia Tech massacre in 2007. Thirty-two people were killed there and many more injured. The shooter had the advantage of semiautomatic weapons.

Nearer

> All day our brilliant screens show without letup
> hysterical screamers winning money prizes,
> a woman sneering at another's getup,
> boys doing jackass stunts in various guises,
> in aspiration to become *well known*.
> A reporter poses before a green setup
> and picturesque, a foreign ruin rises.
> A war somewhere, an earthquake. No surprises.
>
> But images now, sent from a cellphone,
> show kids you know shooting, shot, dead! Alone
> on the sofa, God sleeps through these dull affairs,
> this noise, while darling Pity watches Terror
> caper and tap dance up and down the stairs.

Not long after the Tree of Life shooting, Brad Orsini, then the director of security for the local Jewish community, a former FBI man, taught a "security training" session, very well attended, for members of

Dor Hadash. As part of the training, we saw a short film of people in an airport immediately after a gunman opened fire. One man froze, standing, a perfect target. Sometimes people run, but collect in one place, also making slaughter easy. Orsini told us that the Department of Homeland Security has worked out a simple-to-remember formula for active shooter situations, a phrase that they hope to make as familiar as "Stop, drop, and roll" in case of fire: "Run, hide, fight." Are children in school learning this now?

Security Training—Stop the Bleed

The US Department of Homeland Security advises remembering: "Run, Hide, Fight."

Run. Escape if you can.
Walk across Russia to Austria.
Get on a train to Rotterdam.
Emigrate to Cuba, which has an unfilled quota.

Hide. Shelter in place.
Shave your beard, bleach your hair.
Get a nose job.
Change your name.

Fight. As a last resort.
Look around you—everyday objects
can become weapons. Hot coffee. Pencils.
Throw accurately and with force. Strike
without apology.

Run. Hide. Fight.
Never again. Again. Again.

After the shooting there was a tremendous outpouring of ceremony and acknowledgment within Pittsburgh and from around the world. Television stations set up canopies in a literal encampment around the site. Signs saying *Hate Has No Home Here* appeared in store windows and on lawns. That I doubt (as Black people will tell you), but it's an aspiration, a hope. And the people, the wonderful people, who are a community, supporting each other, give me hope.

ELEH EZKERAH, NUSACH PITTSBURGH

Rabbi Jonathan Perlman

THE PITTSBURGH MASSACRE belongs to the ages. That is how it stands out in memory. The shooter carefully plotted to take Jewish life operating on his absurd premise that Jews were aiding and abetting Guatemalan refugees on the southwestern border of the United States and that this undermined the safety of others. Someone needed to act, the shooter felt. Given what we were told about the attacker's cache of weapons and a map of synagogues in his car, I believe that his personal war would have extended far beyond Tree of Life if not for the interception by city and county police and the daring hunt and containment by the SWAT team. That he himself was not killed in the process is still a mystery to me. All of this was followed by wailing and crying, anger and frustration, candles and songs, long hugs and whispers. The city in shock: "What the **** just happened?" Never, never in Pittsburgh.

Pittsburgh now joins the ranks of other pogroms reaching back to ancient times. Are we not told as we begin the Jewish New Year in the martyrology section of the mahzor (book of prayers for the High Holy Days) about the ten martyrs of the Hadrianic persecution of the second century? We are told in grisly detail of tortures including beheading and the burning of flesh perpetrated on saintly rabbis who led other Jews in a positive identification with Judaism. Jewish writers and poets have chronicled the violence against our people for two thousand years.

The poet Chaim Nahman Bialik wrote the heart-rending poem *City of Slaughter* in response to the 1903 pogrom in the small town of Kishinev on the western edges of Bessarabia. With lyrical skill and in Hebrew, he portrayed the Jews as defenseless, weak, and cowardly. Later scholars such as Steven Zipperstein have recently suggested that Bialik's account was exaggerated based on other chronicles of the time.[1] With desired effect, *City of Slaughter* became a great piece of propaganda in stirring fear within the Jewish soul and driving more Jews across the world to a muscular Zionism and to Palestine.

We chose to memorialize our own Pittsburgh martyrs by scribing a poem, "Eleh Ezkerah in Pittsburgh," based on the Yom Kippur liturgy and Bialik's lyrical style. This composition fits in between one of these two modes of poetry, the lyrical skill of Bialik and the liturgical poem about the ten martyrs. It also moves between Hebrew, the language of the nation, and English, the language of America. As Jews raised in America, the authors of the poem attempt to show a people's struggle with belief and unbelief at the time of the attack. Authored by three different rabbis in three different places—Pittsburgh, New York, and Israel, only one of them a witness—the poem exudes sadness and optimism. I contributed the content, while my fellow poets Rabbi Martin Cohen and Rabbi Tamar Elad-Appelbaum, whom I sought out for the lyrical and authentic feel of the poem, added verses and words.

Our poem is a commentary on the story of Akedah, relevant to the day of the Pittsburgh massacre, the Torah portion that was interrupted by death and terror. We wanted to create a theology for the inscrutability of God's presence on that remembrance day (18 Heshvan), or the yahrzeit, for the eleven victims and for Eleh Ezkerah. We acknowledge that these are painful memories in this setting. On Yom Kippur we recall martyrs who are religious models for us, the saintly rabbis of the second century who gave up their lives and inspire us to be better Jews every year. The Pittsburgh martyrs of the twenty-first century certainly belong in the same class of people.

---

1. Zipperstein, *Pogrom: Kishinev and the Tilt of History* (New York: Liveright, 2018).

"Eleh Ezkerah in Pittsburgh" opens the curtain to show things that actually happened, against the central story of the Akedah of Genesis 22, the story of Abraham and Isaac at the altar, the reading assigned by the Torah's lexicon that Tree of Life, New Light, and Dor Hadash worshippers never got to read that day. I chose this framework because the October 27 reading is the Akedah of Genesis 22, the same reading assigned to the second day of Rosh Hashanah; the story figures largely in the minds of Jewish people during the days of the beginning of the year, the High Holy Days, called *yamim nora'im*, "days of awe," in Hebrew.

Within the five services that make up the prayers for Yom Kippur is this section of martyrology, discussing ten Jewish sages killed as martyrs, which pertains to the idea of giving up of one's soul for the sake of God, which was commanded by God at the Akedah. Jews also say a blessing daily in the morning prayers that we seek to sanctify God with our lives in public. Throughout the mahzor there are mentions of Isaac and the Akedah; it is a theme that continues past the lexical reading of the High Holidays,[2] but it is repeated in the prayer language and the idea of the sacrifice of goats, another lexical reading.

The Eleh Ezkerah, or martyrology section, adds the idea that we are commanded to give our lives up for the sake of God if we are threatened physically and spiritually—a very important part of the mahzor and one of its themes, as well as much of our holiday liturgy.

ELEH EZKERAH IN PITTSBURGH

These things do I remember and my heart is grieved!
How the arrogant have devoured our people!
Who would believe that in our day there would be no intervention
For the eleven slaughtered from our holy community?

These things do I remember and my heart is grieved!: This is the traditional beginning and refrain to the poem that describes the martyrdom of the ten rabbis of the second century. Throughout our poem are

---

2. The liturgical reading from the Torah for the second day of Rosh Hashanah is Genesis 22, the Akedah.

אֵלֶּה אֶזְכְּרָה, נוסח פּיטְסְבּוּרג   Eileh Ezkarah for Pittsburgh

אֵלֶּה אֶזְכְּרָה וְנַפְשִׁי עָלַי אֶשְׁפְּכָה	These things do I remember and my heart is grieved!
כִּי בְלָעוּנוּ זֵרִים כְּעֻגָּה בְּלִי הֲפוּכָה,	How the arrogant have devoured our people!
כִּי בְיָמֵינוּ אָנוּ לֹא עָלְתָה אֲרוּכָה,	Who would believe that in our day there would be no intervention
לְאַחַד עָשָׂר הֲרוּגֵי קְהִלָּתֵינוּ הַקְּדוֹשָׁה.	For the eleven slaughtered from our holy community?

שַׁבָּת בַּבֹּקֶר כְּמִידֵי שַׁבָּת הָיְתָה	That Shabbat morning was like every Shabbat
וַיַּשְׁכִּימוּ כְּעֶשְׂרִים מִבְּנֵי הַקְּהִילָה	The twenty early-risers from the three shuls
וּבָאוּ לִקְרֹא אֶת פָּרָשַׁת וַיֵּרָא מִן הַתּוֹרָה	Came to read Parshat Vayera from the Torah
וְלֹא יָדְעוּ וְלֹא יָכְלוּ לִרְאוֹת בְּאַסְפָּקְלַרְיָה	And they did not know nor could they see in the reflection of God's mystery,
כִּי סִדְרָא תְגַלֶּה מֵאֲשֶׁר אוֹתָם יִקְרֶה	That the portion would reveal what would happen to them.

וְקָרְאוּ:	And they read:
וַיַּשְׁכֵּם אַבְרָהָם וַיִּקַּח אֶת־נְעָרָיו	Abraham rose early and brought his servant lads
אֶת בְּנוֹ יְחִידוֹ אֲשֶׁר אָהֵב	And his only son who he loved
וַיֵּלְכוּ אֶל הַר הַמּוֹרִיָּה יַחְדָּו.	They went to Mount Moriah together
יִצְחָק בְּנוֹ עַל יָדוֹ וּשְׁנֵי נְעָרָיו מֵאֲחוֹרָיו.	His son Isaac by his side and two lads behind
דֹּם הָלְכוּ שְׁלֹשֶׁת יָמִים	They walked three days in silence.
וַחֲרִישׁוֹ כִּי לֹא מָצְאוּ דָבָר	They went in hushed voices for nothing occurred to them.
וְהִנֵּה הִגִּיעוּ אֶל הָהָר	Finally they arrived at Moriah
וְשָׁם נִסָּה הָאֱלֹהִים אֶת אַבְרָהָם.	And there God tested Abraham
וַיַּנַּח אַבְרָהָם אֶת־נְעָרָיו שָׁם בְּתַחְתִּית הָהָר	And Abraham let the youths rest at the bottom of the hill.
וַיֹּאמֶר יְיָ אֶל־אַבְרָהָם עֲלֵה אֵלַי הָהָרָה כִּי אֲנַסֶּךָ.	God said to Abraham: Ascend to me on the hill and I will test you there.

וְרָאוּ:	And they saw:
וַיָּקָם אַבְרָהָם	And Abraham rose
וַיַּעַל אֶל־הַר הָאֱלֹהִים הוּא הַר הַמּוֹרִיָּה	He ascended the mountain of God, the hill of Moriah
וַיְכַס הֶעָנָן אֶת־הָהָר וַיִּקְרָא אֵלָיו יְיָ לֵאמֹר	And a cloud covered the mountain and God called to him saying:
כֹּה תֹאמַר לְבֵית יַעֲקֹב וְכֹה תַּגִּיד לִבְנֵי יִשְׂרָאֵל	Thus will you say to the house of Jacob and thus will you tell the house of Israel: You will be holy for I am holy
קְדֹשִׁים תִּהְיוּ כִּי קָדוֹשׁ אָנִי	
וְכָל הָרוֹצֶה לִכְרוֹת בְּרִיתִי וּלְבַקֵּר בְּהֵיכָלִי,	And everyone who wishes to enter my covenant and visit my Sanctuary
בְּבוֹא הָעֵת אֶת שְׁמִי הַקָּדוֹשׁ יְקַדֵּשׁ בָּרַבִּים	That time when the many will come to sanctify my Holy Name in public
כִּי אֶל אֱלֹהִים חַיִּים יִקְרָא	And to the living God they will call
וְאֶת קְדוּשַׁת הַחַיִּים וְאַהֲבָתוֹ בְּלֵב כֹּל יִטַּע	And unto the Sanctity of Life and of Love that is implanted in every heart
וַיָּשׁוּבוּ כּוּלָם אַבְרָהָם לִפְנֵיהֶם	And then the group returned, Abraham leading,
וַיֵּלְכוּ נִפְרָדִים לְבֵיתָם	And they walked separately to their homes
וַיִּדֹּמוּ כּוּלָם מִפְּנֵי הֶחָזוֹן הֶחָרֵד אֲשֶׁר רָאֲתָה עֵינָם	And they were silent all of them in reaction to the frightful vision their eyes saw.

וְכֵן שָׁמְעוּ מֵאֲחוֹרֵי הַפַּרְגּוֹד:	And thus they heard from behind the Veil of Mystery:
וְאִם תִּשְׁאֲלוּ בְּמָרָה זוֹ תוֹרָה וְזֶה שְׂכָרָה,	And if you ask in your bitterness, "This is Torah and this is its reward?"
תְּשׁוּבָתִי יְדוּעָה:	"My answer is known:
גְּזֵרָה הִיא מִלְּפָנַי	It has been decreed ...
וְאֵין לְהַרְהֵר אַחַר מִדּוֹתָי.	Don't dwell too much on what separates You from Me.

The author would like to thank David Zvi Kalman for typesetting the Hebrew and English poem.

וְכֵן קָרָה בְּמִקְדַּשׁ הַמְעַט שֶׁלָּנוּ	What occurred in our Holy Sanctuary that day
בְּבוֹא הַצָּר לָנֻסּוֹת אוֹתָנוּ.	As the enemy came to tread upon our holy space
חַרְבּוֹ שְׁלוּפָה לְהַכְרִית אֶת זִכְרוֹנֵינוּ מִמְּקוֹמֵינוּ.	His wielding sword to break apart our memories from that place
אֶת קְדוֹשֵׁינוּ מָצָא כְּמוֹת שֶׁהָיוּ:	The sanctified recalled a few that remained –
מֵהֶם פְּנֵיהֶם זֶה אֶל זֶה לִפְנֵי קַדִּישׁ דְּרַבָּנָן	Among some their faces turned to one another before "Kaddish d'Rabbanan"
וּמֵהֶם פְּנֵיהֶם כְּלַפֵּי חוּץ לְקַבֵּל אוֹרְחִים	Among some their faces turned toward the door to welcome new faces
מֵהֶם מְמַהֲרִים לַעֲזוֹר לִידִידִים לִמְצוֹא	Among some they quickly assisted their friends in finding
אֶת מְקוֹמָם בַּסִּדּוּר	their place in the Siddur
מֵהֶם מְכִינִים אֶת פָּרָשַׁת הַתּוֹרָה	Among some those engaged in Torah Study
וּמֵהֶם בַּמִּטְבָּח מְכִינִים אֶת הַמָּנָה הַבָּאָה.	And among some who were in the kitchen preparing the next meal.
וְאֶל אַחַד עָשָׂר אָמַר יְיָ בַּלַחַשׁ	And to the eleven, God spoke in a whisper
הִגִּיעַ זְמַנְכֶם לְקַדֵּשׁ אֶת שְׁמִי בָּרַבִּים	"The time has arrived to sanctify My Name in public.
וְיוֹדֵעַ אֲנִי שֶׁלֹּא בִּיקַשְׁתֶּם זֹאת	"And I know you did not ask for this." Even so, they would be remembered
וּבְכָל זֹאת זִכְרוּ וְהַבִּיטוּ לְעֲקֵידַת יָחִיד	and looked upon as personally bound to the Altar as one united.
כִּי בֶּעָתִיד יִזְכְּרוּ יְלָדִים וּקְהִילּוֹת	For in the future their children and congregations would remember
שֶׁאֲנַחְנוּ אֶת קְדוֹשַׁת הַחַיִּים בָּאנוּ לִחְיוֹת	That we are Sanctifiers of Life who come to live
כִּי קַמְנוּ עָמַדְנוּ הִמְשַׁכְנוּ בְּדַרְכְּכֶם	For we arose, we stood as your followers in your path
כִּי זָכַרְנוּ אֱמוּנָה וִידִידוּת כָּאן לְאוֹרְכֶם.	For we remembered faith and friendship here toward your light.
אֶת חַלָּלֵינוּ קָבַרְנוּ	We buried our bodies.
וְעֲלֵיהֶם בָּכִינוּ	And upon them we wept
וּבְכָל זֹאת לֹא נִשְׁבַּרְנוּ.	And even so, this did not break us.
וּבְכָל זֹאת אֲנַחְנוּ בִּמְקוֹמֵינוּ עָמַדְנוּ!	Nonetheless we were steadfast in our place
וְנַמְשִׁיךְ לַעֲמוֹד.	And we continued to stand.
וּבְכֵן, אָבִינוּ מַלְכֵּנוּ, עֲשֵׂה לְמַעַן הָרוּגֵינוּ	And so, Our Father our King, act for the sake of those who were
עַל שֵׁם קָדְשֶׁךָ	slaughtered for your holy name.
וְעֲשֵׂה עַל טַף וִילָדִים וְכֹל אַנְשֵׁי אֱמוּנָתֶךָ	And act for the babies and children and for all the people of your faith.
זָכְרֵנוּ אֱלֹהֵינוּ, כִּי זוֹכְרִים אֲנַחְנוּ לָךְ	Remember us, our King, for we keep You in mind.
עֶזְרֵנוּ מַלְכֵּנוּ, כִּי מִתְפַּלְלִים אֲנַחְנוּ לָךְ	Help us, our King, for we prayed to You.
וְהַצִּילֵנוּ יוֹצְרֵינוּ, כִּי עָלֶיךָ עֵינֵינוּ.	Save us, our Creator, for our eyes are upon you.
וְכָל עוֹד נְשָׁמָה בְּאַפֵּינוּ	As long as this breath is within us
נְבַקֵּשׁ עוֹלָמֵנוּ	We ponder the world you created for us
וְעֶרֶב וָבוֹקֶר בְּכָל יוֹם תָּמִיד	And evening and morning, each and every day.
נְקַבֵּץ וְנִכְרִיז כְּאֶחָד:	We gather and we cry out as one:
שְׁמַע יִשְׂרָאֵל ה' אֱלֹהֵינוּ ה' אֶחָד.	**Hear O Israel, the Lord our God, the Lord is One.**

references to the original tragic story that is embedded in the fast of Yom Kippur, of victimhood in the face of the antisemitic oppressor. The Eleh Ezkerah for that time was paired with the yizkor prayers, the "memory" prayers, dedicated not only to personal memories of one's family but to communal martyrs throughout the ages. More contemporary mahzorim (High Holiday prayer books) have added remembrances of the Jews slaughtered during the Crusades of Christendom, in imperial Spain, in the pogroms of the Russian empire, in Arab attacks on Jews in the twentieth century, and in the Holocaust.

That Shabbat morning was like every Shabbat
The twenty early risers from the three shuls
Came to read Parshat Vayera from the Torah
And they did not know nor could they see in the reflection of God's mystery,
That the portion would reveal what would happen to them.

The twenty early risers from the three shuls: The Tree of Life building on Wilkins Avenue held three congregations: Tree of Life–Or L'Simcha, Dor Hadash, and New Light Congregation. Each synagogue had their own group of persons who arrived at the starting time of prayer in different places in the building. Jews have a habit of arriving late; most synagogues don't get their full attendance until thirty minutes into the service. Tree of Life–Or L'Simcha started first upstairs in their chapel with twelve men and women; New Light was downstairs with six people. In a library on the second floor were three men who had come early and were waiting for the rest of their Shabbat Torah study group to arrive. Eleven people survived .

Reflection of God's mystery: Here we suggest, mystically: the Torah that waited for the congregants in the Holy Ark was a mirror to the events that were about to unfold that day. How could it be that the very story that describes God's command to Abraham to murder Isaac, as a test, could be played out among the martyrs who clutched their prayer books in fear? Why then? Why now? The Torah story called the Akedah is a great story of mystery, understood only as a great gesture of faith.

And they read:
Abraham rose early and brought his servant lads
And his only son whom he loved
They went to Mount Moriah together
His son Isaac by his side and two lads behind
They walked three days in silence.
They went in hushed voices for nothing occurred to them.
Finally they arrived at Moriah
And there God tested Abraham
And Abraham let the youths rest at the bottom of the hill.
God said to Abraham: Ascend to me on the hill and I will test you there.

And they read: Note that the first part of the Akedah is summarized as it is in the Torah. It repeats the cadences that we read in the Torah: the silence, the mystified characters, Abraham holding Isaac's hand in his own, Isaac trusting his father to move forward ahead of the lads.

And they saw:
And Abraham rose
He ascended the mountain of God, the hill of Moriah
And a cloud covered the mountain and God called to him, saying:
Thus will you say to the house of Jacob and thus will you tell the house of
Israel: You will be holy for I am holy
And everyone who wishes to enter my covenant and visit my Sanctuary
That time when the many will come to sanctify my Holy Name in public
And to the living God they will call
And unto the Sanctity of Life and of Love that is implanted in every heart
And then the group returned, Abraham leading,
And they walked separately to their homes
And they were silent all of them in reaction to the frightful vision their eyes saw.

And they saw: There is a difference between "reading" and "seeing." Here we have the men and women of the three congregations see with their own eyes what the story begins to tell in all its horror. They enter the story with all others who "sanctify my Holy Name in public," the martyrs' duty of "kiddush Hashem" (sanctifying the Name of God, the Hebrew phrase for what a martyr has done).

When the many will come to sanctify my Holy Name in public and to the living God they will call: In other words, what happens on Mount Moriah is not what is "read" in the narrative. The story of Isaac being redeemed by an angel and the sacrifice of a ram placed by God is obliterated by the cry of the martyrs. For centuries, Jews have returned to the Akedah as a kind of solace for God's taking the souls of his people to spite the terrible power of the enemy. It is as if the martyr is saying, "Please take me, God, as you took your beloved son Isaac! Complete the sacrifice and let us come to you in our purity and holiness—for You are Holy, let us be absorbed in your Holiness!" The Lord commands it to be so. So did many Jews leave this world with prayers on their lips and these thoughts in their hearts.

And they were silent: We refer here to the story of Aaron and his sons in Leviticus 10:4, another story of mysterious cruelty. When two of his sons play with "strange fire" at the altar, they are instantly killed. Aaron doesn't speak or protest. He is silent.

> *And thus they heard from behind the Veil of Mystery:*
> *And if you ask in your bitterness, "This is Torah and this is its reward?"*
> *My answer is known:*
> *It has been decreed . . .*
> *Don't dwell too much on what separates you from Me*
> *What occurred in our Holy Sanctuary that day*
> *As the enemy came to tread upon our holy space*
> *His wielding sword to break apart our memories from that place*
> *The sanctified recalled a few that remained—*
> *Among some their faces turned to one another before Kaddish d'Rabbanan*
> *Among some their faces turned toward the door to welcome new faces*
> *Among some they quickly assisted their friends in finding*
> *their place in the siddur*
> *Among some those engaged in Torah study*
> *And among some who were in the kitchen preparing the next meal.*

This is your Torah and this is your reward: We return to the story of the ten second-century rabbis who were martyred.[3] After the torture and killing of Rabbi Shimon and Rabbi Ishmael, the angels cry out to God: "Is this the Torah and this its reward?"[4] God silences the angels and threatens to destroy the world if the angels press Him to give reason for His decree.

Their faces turned: What were the faithful doing at the moment the attack occurred? We the survivors have tried to reconstruct what was happening at that precise moment. It is the stuff of midrash: memories that comfort us, memories that pull at our heartstrings and show normal gestures as the gestures of the righteous. Tree of Life–Or L'Simcha reciting the great Kaddish, the Kaddish d'Rabbanan, proclaiming God's holy name in anticipation of what would happen next. The "greeters" at the door, two of them, both killed, observing the Jewish law of hospitality. A man who could not read seated next to his friend who would turn the pages for him (he was shot fatally). The three Dor Hadash members in the library reviewing the words of the Akedah in their Bibles. The two men of my congregation, downstairs in the kitchen. It was their duty to ready the meal for the next day.

> And to the eleven, God spoke in a whisper
> "The time has arrived to sanctify My Name in public.
> "And I know you did not ask for this." Even so, they would be remembered
> and looked upon as personally bound to the altar as one united.

---

3. This is a section of the Yom Kippur morning service that includes accounts of the deaths of some of Judaism's greatest sages, such as Rabbi Akiva, Rabbi Yishmael, Rabbi Hannanya ben Teradyon, Rabbi Tarfon, and Rabbi Shimon ben Gamliel the Nasi. It opens with the words "Eleh ezkerah, these I remember and I pour out my soul within me / for evil ones have swallowed us, like a cake not yet turned—when during Caesar's reign there was no deliverance / for the ten martyrs of that empire." Translation by Rabbi Jonathan Sacks in *Koren Yom Kippur Mahzor* (Jerusalem: Koren, 2012).

4. Babylonian Talmud Menahot 29b, a story about Moses being shown the death of Rabbi Akiva, one of the ten martyrs.

And I know you did not ask for this: This is the most troubling sentiment expressed in the poem, for me. No one who suffers asks for suffering. No one who dies a terrible death anticipates and accepts his or her fate! I recall the 1947 poem by Israeli poet Natan Alterman that speaks of young soldiers "being served on a silver platter" for the sake of Israel.[5] We cannot ignore that Jewish souls have been eliminated and exterminated throughout the centuries. We didn't ask for it. We often hid from it. But when it confronted us, we died as one nation, a nation despised but beloved in God's eyes.

> *For in the future their children and congregations would remember*
> *That we are sanctifiers of life who come to live*
> *For we arose, we stood as Your followers in Your path*
> *For we remembered faith and friendship here toward Your light.*
> *And so, our Father, our King, act for the sake of those who were*
> *slaughtered for your holy name.*
> *And act for the babies and children and for all the people of your faith.*
> *Remember us, our King, for we keep You in mind.*
> *Help us, our King, for we prayed to You.*
> *Save us, our Creator, for our eyes are upon You.*

And we continued to stand: Whenever someone complains to me that we stand too much in synagogue during our prayers, I think of all the Jews in history who stood up to savage hatred. The State of Israel restored the dignity of every Jew in the twentieth century because we stood tall and proud. Much of the language here is prayer language calling for God to act on our behalf so that those who died did not die in vain.

---

5. "The Silver Platter" (1947), which reads in part, "Then a nation in tears / And amazed at this matter Will ask: who are you? And the two will then say / With soft voice: We— / Are the silver platter / On which the Jews' state was presented today // Then they fall back in darkness / As the dazed nation looks / And the rest can be found In the history books." Translated by David P. Stern. Rani Jaeger, "The Sacrifices Made in Israel for Independence," Shalom Hartman Institute, March 4, 2013, https://hartman.org.il/SHINews_View .asp?Article_Id=117.

Save us, our Creator, for our eyes are upon You: In the daily service, we bow in supplication to our Creator and ask God to forgive our sins. We sit up and pray, "Guardian of Israel, guard the remnant of Israel," and then in deft theological statement, we say "our eyes are upon You" as if to say, "We know the future is hidden from us, yet we trust in You for we are Your people."

> *As long as this breath is within us*
> *We ponder the world You created for us*
> *And evening and morning, each and every day,*
> *We gather and we cry out as one:*
>
> *Hear O Israel, the Lord our God, the Lord is One.*

This well-known creed (Deuteronomy 6:4) is said at the end of Yom Kippur and also at the end of life.

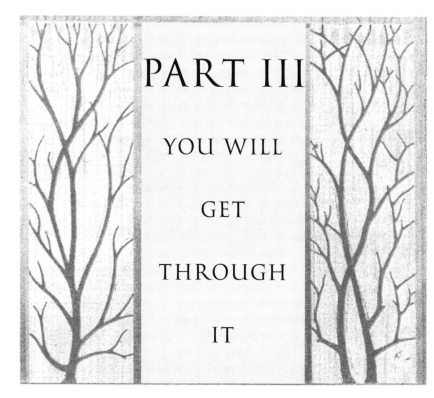

PART III

YOU WILL

GET

THROUGH

IT

KEITH WAY

Campbell Robertson

WE WERE AT HOME, savoring that brief blessed perch between the weekend's formlessness and the framing of the day's plans, when I got the call from New York. There's something on Twitter, the editor said, a shooting, or some kind of attack, apparently at a synagogue in Pittsburgh. Tree of Life.

I asked my wife where that was. We had been living in Pittsburgh for over a year, but I was on the road most of the time. I knew nothing at all about the city before we'd moved here and since then it had mostly been a place I passed through on the way to and from the airport; I still had to use Google Maps for any errand between the rivers. This would be typical in New York, where you're not expected to know much of the city beyond your narrow and crowded lane. But smaller cities are different. People here talked about long-retired politicians and old Steelers like *Of course you know about these things, you live here, don't you?* No, Pittsburgh was where I hung my hat. My wife and children had become far more of the city than I had.

Tree of Life was not the synagogue where my children went to preschool, though suddenly I wasn't sure about that, or even what day it was. They were sitting right there on the couch watching cartoons, but on hearing news like this, for a fleeting instant, you lose track of everybody. My wife reminded me: Tree of Life is the synagogue on the *way* to preschool, the big one on the corner. Right, I said, though I could barely picture it.

I drove through Frick Park, where the leaves were rehearsing for the big show, past the soundless cemeteries, then a right turn across from the building the New Light Congregation called home for nearly sixty years (although at that moment I had never heard of New Light). Three long and undulating blocks along Beechwood, boulevard of bygone mega-estates, and then left on Wilkins Avenue. It was quiet. I'd rushed to shootings and other disasters before but had usually arrived after the chaos had been snuffed out and the scene had already turned into the familiar set piece of police tape and camera stands and milling local politicians.

On Wilkins this morning, a handful of journalists were sprinkled on the block leading up toward the synagogue, two men with cameras, maybe two or three others. I don't remember exactly what time it was. I have since looked through the various modern fingerprints I've left behind—texts, tweets, emails—and can do little better than "sometime between 10:30 and 11:00." Late enough that someone in New York had heard about it. Early enough that it wasn't clear, when I first arrived, that anything had happened at all. But here came a police officer GET BACK GET THE HELL BACK WHAT THE HELL ARE YOU DOING YOU'RE GOING TO GET YOURSELF KILLED and then *pokpokpokpokpok* echoing over the intersection and then a group of people half-crouched being rushed across Shady Avenue. Halfway down the block a little alley juts off Wilkins. A dead-end passage, lined by fenced backyards, more driveway than street. I'd never even noticed the sign before. Keith Way. My home for the next half hour or so.

The scale of what you don't know is what weighs on a reporter's mind at moments like these. I knew nothing about Tree of Life. I didn't know that it was one of the city's oldest congregations, or that it was Conservative, or who the rabbi was, or that the families of colleagues and former colleagues at the paper had been members in years past. I didn't know a thing about its history, that it had broken off in the 1860s from Rodef Shalom—the synagogue where my children actually did spend their mornings at preschool; of its stutter-step migration across Pittsburgh, from rented rooms downtown to a building in the Oakland neighborhood—which later became a theater where my family had watched a musical—to that modern edifice in need of repair that was now under attack on Wilkins.

I didn't know that other congregations met there, had never heard of Dor Hadash or New Light. I had never heard of the Rosenthal brothers or Jerry Rabinowitz or Bernice and Sylvan Simon or Richard Gottfried or Rose Mallinger (did not know that her great-granddaughter was in my own three-year-old's preschool class) or any of the others I would soon learn about from eulogies and obituaries and relatives in such pain they could hardly speak. How many names would we learn when this was over?

There would be an official list, handed out at a press conference, there always was. I leaned against the brick wall, listening. The street was quiet, no indication of where things stood inside. A reporter at a desk in New York was following the police scanner; I was *on the scene.* To be clear: *on* the scene does not in any way mean *in* it. I wasn't crawling on the floor or holding my breath in a closet or cautiously moving in, heart pounding and service weapon drawn, just as I didn't share the particular burdens of the soldiers I walked alongside on Iraqi streets, or of the protesters in tense cities who shared the cruelties of their daily lives with me before I returned, eventually, to a clean room at the Hampton Inn. What I have seen as a reporter has always been from Keith Way.

These are moments of the strangest asymmetry. Nearly everyone who knew Tree of Life most intimately was either inside, enduring the most terrifying moments of their lives, or going about their Saturday morning with no idea that anything unusual was happening at all. Outside the walls of the synagogue things were abundantly mundane, Halloween pumpkins mugging on front porches, cars passing by unhurriedly on Beechwood. The people in those cars, as oblivious as they were right then, would soon have a much fuller picture of the horror at Tree of Life—what led to it, who did it, how it ended—than those whose lives were being cut short in the middle of it. At that moment there was a Pittsburgh where an unspeakable horror was taking place and a Pittsburgh where nothing was out of the ordinary, and from where I was standing you could still see both. They would collapse into one soon enough.

I walked up a little path between two houses to Shady Avenue to get a different look, but I was furiously waved away by a police officer. Back to the alley.

There was a colder asymmetry at work here as well, one much harder to digest. That a solitary man in a grubby one-bedroom apartment eleven miles away could pick a certain Saturday, turning it over in his head for who knows how long—a date that would soon become a national shorthand for mass murder, like 9/11, but the significance of which for hours or days or weeks beforehand this man alone knew—and when that day came, could drive through the calm neighborhood streets, walk inside and exercise the power of death over these good and decent people who knew nothing of this man's existence, much less wished him any ill will: that was the vilest imbalance of all. A whole city suddenly thrown into grief and fear by a single man and the grievances he'd hoarded in the lonely glow of internet chat rooms. What people would do with that kind of evil was something I didn't know yet either.

For the most part, the response would be similar to what it was after Las Vegas, Sutherland Springs, San Bernardino, and so on. Vigils were crowded to overflowing, strangers embraced and wept, funerals were packed. Lines that normally mapped out the city's different communities were ignored, and Muslims, Sikhs, Christians and Jews, Black Pittsburghers and white, mourned together. A man who had already made thousands of white crosses for shooting victims drove from Illinois and planted eleven of them with Stars of David affixed. A logo was drawn up, T-shirts made. The city promised not to back down. There is a template now, a crowdsourced manual: the incoming reporters are already familiar with the gun laws, the Justice Department with the grieving process, the mayors with the ways to commemorate, having learned from the experiences of their fellow chief executives in Orlando, Parkland, Newton . . . the list went on, and has gone on since, and it will go on.

Still, when you report on these things over and over you become attuned to the differences. The church massacre in Charleston: the reaction to that was different from what had come before. Yes, there was a template for grieving that horror, too. But it was a very old one, long kept but largely hidden from the eyes of white society, updated again and again and again. Violence is by its nature shocking, but white supremacist violence in particular, in this country, is apple-pie familiar. Just days after that massacre, I sat in the balcony of the South Carolina Senate chambers as lawmakers voted on whether to keep the Confederate battle flag flying just outside, right in front of the statehouse. This was violence with a prodigious history; what had happened at Mother Emanuel on a June night in 2015 fit onto a clear timeline that went straight back to the execution of church members in 1822 for allegedly plotting a slave rebellion, and went on long before that, too. Everyone understood this, even if they tried to deny it. It's still unknown what prompted the Las Vegas shooting, but as soon as you heard about Charleston, there wasn't any doubt. What was worse: a mass killing that made no sense at all, or one that did?

My wife is Jewish. I'd gone to years of Passover seders and mumbled gamely along to the Hanukkah blessings that my older daughter knew by heart by the time she was five. But I came from a family of devoted Baptists; the basic wiring is different. How you react to suffering, how you see your duty to respond, who has the duty to forgive, to what degree you feel that pain is inevitable, all of this is in the genetics of a person's faith, more nature than nurture. I have my instincts here and I don't see myself abandoning them. Still, my wife's were formed by priests in the temple of Solomon at the same time that my own ancestors, as Benjamin Disraeli put it to the Irishman, were "brutal savages in an unknown island."

Not long after the shooting I was walking through Squirrel Hill to a press conference a couple of blocks from the synagogue, stopping people on the sidewalk for short interviews. Many were returning from services and, without phones on the Sabbath, familiar with only the vague details of the morning, asking whether I had heard the whereabouts of this or that person (though by and large the Jewish community of Squirrel Hill would know the precise toll long before the reporters did, because it was known who showed up at the JCC that afternoon and who didn't, who always showed up early to services at Tree of Life and who didn't). They talked of the antisemitic episodes around Pittsburgh in years past, hate murders that took place thirty-two and eighteen years earlier, but also acts of vandalism, one-off assaults, things that at the time had seemed like outliers. *Had seemed*—in phrases like this there was an unmistakable dread. Not just anger, or sorrow, though one heard them as well, because they are the kinds of things one always hears on days like this, but dread. Things in the country were getting ugly, an older man said, his wife nodding slowly beside him. Echoes of what family members who had come over from Europe used to talk about. As terrible as this horror was, it might well be a vanguard of horrors to come. This was said with something like self-reproof: of course, this is the way of things; comforting and familiar as Squirrel Hill is, it is not apart from the world, it was naïve to think otherwise. I had never heard this kind of talk after other shootings, even Charleston. The talk this time was not of the return of some vile past, but of an age that never fully leaves, a darkness that inevitably comes back around again and again, the eternal recurrence of history. At other crime scenes one always heard that things in the country seemed to be coming apart; here it was that things, terrible things, might once again be coming together.

The following Wednesday was rainy and dreary. Little Spidermen and princesses carrying the spoils of trick-or-treating hustled along wet sidewalks past the people heading to the JCC for one of the week's shivas. By then, some order had settled in Pittsburgh. The funerals were being held, two or three a day and a giant multicolored cairn had begun growing at the intersection of Wilkins and Shady, tributes sent in from around the world. The president had come and gone, to the city's vociferous disapproval, and the day before the president's visit, the loner who had caused all of this had appeared, doughy and dispassionate, for a court hearing. It was a perfunctory appointment, brief and before a mostly empty courtroom, though two members of Dor Hadash sat quietly in the gallery. "To witness," one of them said to me in the hallway afterward. "That's part of Jewish theory, to witness and remember." Here it was, the ancient model of how to grieve, the template.

Pittsburgh had thankfully broken one part of the usual pattern, the part about how the gentiles behaved. The city had wrapped its arms around the Jewish community. This had virtually never followed violent antisemitism in its long, long history. The store windows on Forbes Avenue, from the Dunkin' Donuts to the Chinese noodle shops, were billboards of love and support—in another time, as I heard observed more than once, what happened to glass windows in Jewish neighborhoods would have been very different. Away from gentile eyes, the old template was carried out, with the *chevra kadisha*—those who wash the dead and prepare them for burial—collecting blood at the crime scene and the recital of the mourner's Kaddish at nearly a dozen gravesides. Shivas unfolded, one starting after another after the one before that, like a funereal fugue.

The shiva on Halloween night was for Dr. Rabinowitz, one of the most extraordinary men I've ever heard about. I had gotten to know him only in conversations and news articles after his death, seeing photos of his bow tie and kind smile, learning among many other things that he had helped men suffering from AIDS in the days when few others would. His name would come up in the most unexpected moments in the year that followed—one afternoon I overheard a sorrow-shaded conversation in a doctor's office about who was going to take on Jerry's patients—and it was jarring each time, to sense how diffuse his effect was around Pittsburgh. What to make of his life? What had HIV to do with it at all when he began treating the sufferers? What would have happened to him if he had observed the virus's death toll, voiced the appropriate concern, and moved on? The vast, vast majority of people did that, if they even took any notice at all, and they were fine, even morally untroubled. What had refugees to do with the lives of his fellow members in Dor Hadash, whose open embrace of immigrants had drawn the attention of the man who would come to Tree of Life to try and kill them? Attending to the pain of complete strangers is hard and potentially very costly work. Rather than committing themselves to this work, how much easier it would have been, and how completely justifiable in the eyes of nearly everyone, to sympathize, to pity, to offer support even, but from a *safe distance*.

I sat quietly toward the back of a meeting room as friends and family stood up front and talked about Dr. Rabinowitz but also about what had happened in a way that was, to me, surprisingly frank, stripped of false comfort. The story from the Talmud (Tractate Avodah Zara 8a) was told about Adam and Eve and the first sunset: how they believed that the darkening of the world meant a return to chaos and the coming of death, how they spent the long night weeping together, how with the breaking of dawn Adam came to realize that this, in fact, was the order of the world, that light is followed by darkness and darkness by light. I slipped out of the room not long after, walked past the wet and shiny trick-or-treaters, and I sat in my car in the dark, almost in a daze.

As I'm writing this, five hundred days later, an infectious disease is spreading over the world; the streets outside are empty and the stores shuttered. You, reading this many months from now, know what happens, how it all unfolds: the death toll, the economic damage, the societal disfigurement. For me, right now, it's all just beginning, and I don't know what you know. That asymmetry again. Right now, the phrase of the moment is *social distancing*. You never know who you are walking among, who is carrying a lethal pathogen, no matter how familiar your surroundings or routine the errand. Gathering for shul on an ordinary Saturday morning, for example. The courier of your death can show up anytime, anywhere. But the main reason for *social distancing* is so the hospitals are not overwhelmed. The idea is to slow and spread out the outbreak so that those who are most in need of help are able to get it before the hospitals collapse (again, this is the current fear, and you reading this know how it is realized). The whole system is terrifyingly vulnerable. Keeping it afloat, so it's there when we one day need it ourselves, requires a hyperconsciousness of everyone around us. You can go through life thinking you are at a safe distance from the dangers of the world, or from the suffering of strangers, but in either case you are perilously deluded.

On the last day before things started shutting down, I drove my daughter to school. I passed Keith Way, and I thought about Dr. Rabinowitz and about the midrash. Darkness falls everywhere when the sun sets; when it's night at the synagogue, it's just as much night in the alley across the street. But the dawn comes everywhere, too.

THE LAST DAY
I FELT SAFE AS
AN AMERICAN JEW

Toby Tabachnick

MOUNT LEBANON IS A MAYBERRY-LIKE SUBURB just south of the
city of Pittsburgh. It has a bronze-level designation as a "walk-friendly
community," which means that there are no school buses; children are
encouraged to walk to school instead. In the mornings and afternoons,
elementary through high school kids can be seen trekking along, their
book bags in tow, chattering away with one another, smiling, laughing.

The neighborhoods—which are lovely and tree-lined and filled
mostly with tasteful midcentury homes—are designed with safe sidewalks and patrolled by friendly crossing guards. Scores of children
skedaddle home at lunchtime for a quick bite with a parent or head to
a neighborhood pizza shop for a slice; after school, they stroll to the
locally owned ice cream parlor for a cone.

There is virtually no crime in Mount Lebanon. Years ago, when a
crooked contractor had absconded with a down payment for work on
our home, never to be heard from again, I called the Mount Lebanon
police for advice. Two officers appeared at my door within minutes to
take down a report. It might have been the most action they had seen
in weeks, or longer.

It's all very pleasant.

I moved to Mount Lebanon with my husband and children in 1993.
We came from Los Angeles, which is pretty much the opposite of

Mount Lebanon. Although I still miss the reliably perfect sunny days of Southern California, they were trumped by the appeal of suburban Pittsburgh's wholesomeness, its award-winning schools, its large yards, and its midwestern sensibility.

And I did not take those attributes for granted. As sappy as it sounds, I often would find myself driving back from the market or the library in our sweet little community, taking in the landscape and thinking how fortunate my family was, to live in such a picturesque and charming town.

I clearly remember thinking those very thoughts on April 28, 2000, as I drove on Cochran Road on my way back from the bank. I recall it was a particularly beautiful day, that winter seemed to have packed up its bags and taken off for good, that the grass in the perfectly mani-cured lawns was vibrant green and that the tulips and rhododendrons had already begun to bloom. I imagine now that the air must have smelled like spring, and I have confirmed with Google that the sun was indeed shining that day and that it was a delightful 66 degrees.

But I also recall that as I approached the intersection of Scrubgrass and Elm Spring Roads, not too far from my home, unveiled before me was a wholly incongruous scene: a harried SWAT team had as-sembled and was directing traffic away from Elm Spring, which had been cordoned off by the bright yellow police tape I recognized from television crime shows.

Mayhem.

There is a last time for most things in life. For me, there is a sad irony in the fact that for some of those things, I didn't realize it was the last time until it just never happened again.

What comes to mind immediately, for whatever reason, is bathing my children, who are now all adults. There certainly was a last time for each of them, the final time that I washed their little backs and rinsed the shampoo from their hair, their eyes squeezed tightly shut as together we sang songs from *Sesame Street*. "C is for Cookie." "Rubber Duckie."

So, what happened after that? Those mommy-supervised baths must have just ended, my children must have declared one by one that they were able and ready to take full responsibility for their own daily washing, or that they wanted privacy, or both. But I do not recall the final time I shared that experience with any of them. If I had known,

I might have savored each of those occasions more, I might have been deliberate in imprinting them into my memory. Now, those last baths are just vague shadows of the amalgams of thousands of baths, none more special than another.

There are other last times, though, where there is almost a hyperconscious awareness of finality.

The last time I felt complacently secure and safe in my identity as an American Jew is one of those last times, and I can name precisely the final moment I was confident that something horrific, something truly beyond the pale "couldn't happen here."

It was April 28, 2000, 1:30 p.m., as Richard Baumhammers, a racist, antisemitic immigration attorney, knocked on the front door of the sixty-three-year-old Jewish woman who had lived next door to his family for decades. When she opened the door to let him in, he shot her and left her for dead. Anita Gordon was a congregant at the same synagogue I attended with my family, Beth El Congregation of the South Hills.

After murdering Anita—and setting her house on fire, by the way—Baumhammers got into his Jeep Cherokee and drove to Beth El, where he fired shots into the doors and painted red swastikas on the bricks, along with the word "Jew." Then he drove to Congregation Ahavath Achim, a couple miles away, and did the same. His rampage included shooting two men at an Indian grocery not far from my home, then killing two more people at a Chinese restaurant.

He was still on the run when I first encountered the SWAT team, then finally made my way home and turned on the television to hear what was going on, around 2:00 p.m.

I had three children in the neighborhood elementary school around the corner. My oldest son had just turned ten and was in fourth grade.

Now, my children were on lockdown, their classrooms barricaded.

The only exception was my toddler, who was home with me only because his nursery school was on break for Passover. If it had not been a vacation week, he, and about forty other children, would have been at Beth El when Baumhammers opened fire on the building.

My oldest son told me later how scared they all were, huddled beneath their desks in that fourth-grade classroom, how they didn't know what was happening, only that it was something terrible and dangerous.

I was watching the live reports in my family room with my neighbor when we heard the news at 3:15 that the police had finally caught up with Baumhammers and arrested him. By then he had shot and killed another victim, a Black karate student at a studio in Beaver County.

He is currently on death row at Greene State Correctional Institute in Franklin Township, Pennsylvania, having exhausted his appeals.

For weeks—maybe months—after the Baumhammers rampage, it made me nervous to walk down the streets of Mount Lebanon on Saturday mornings on the way to shul, feeling vulnerable and identifiable as Jews, my husband and son donning *kipot*. I knew it was important to wear our identities proudly, but I also couldn't help looking in the windows of passing cars, scanning the faces of the drivers and passengers for signs of hate, or worse.

Mount Lebanon had, for me, morphed from a conclave of beauty and old-fashioned American goodness into a suspicious and ominous hamlet, like the one in the early nineties television horror drama *Twin Peaks*. While I previously marveled at the golden sunlit afternoons, now I just seemed to notice the shadows.

Logic and common sense eventually prevailed: Baumhammers was a one-off. It wasn't as if the world had turned against us. At some point, my children resumed walking to school, although I insisted on driving them for weeks. I slowly regained some sense of comfort and confidence. But the certainty of being safe as a Jew in Pittsburgh was gone. Baumhammers stole that from me on April 28, 2000.

And he stole it from at least one of my children.

When you are in the middle of a crisis, as a parent explaining the unexplainable to a child, you just want them to feel better. Now. You want them to go to bed at night without being afraid, to sleep through until morning. To not worry about being shot dead by a neighbor.

So, you somehow find the right words to say to your child, and you hold them close. And most of all, you resume a life that can pass for normal, even though everything may have changed.

On the morning of October 27, 2018, I was in bed with a bad cold and a high fever. It was Shabbat, and my husband also stayed home from shul to care for me. I was sleeping, on and off.

At 10:50 a.m., my telephone rang, unusual for a Shabbat morning. When I picked up the receiver, I heard the voice of my oldest son, then twenty-eight years old and living in Chicago. "Mom," he said. Immediately, I could tell by his tenor that something was very wrong. "There was a shooting at Tree of Life," he said, his voice shaking. Then, realizing that it was unusual that we were at home and not at our own synagogue, he said, "Dad needs to go warn the others. They are just sitting there, like sitting ducks."

None of this made sense. How could there be a shooting at Tree of Life, a synagogue just twelve miles from Mount Lebanon, and just three blocks from another synagogue, Beth Shalom, where I work at the *Pittsburgh Jewish Chronicle*? Tree of Life was the synagogue where my husband's uncle had served as president for years. We had celebrated numerous simchas in that building. We knew many of the congregants.

I turned on the television and saw friends and acquaintances, rabbis and other local Jewish community leaders, implausibly being interviewed by national news reporters. The scene was inconceivable. The news coming out—six dead, then seven dead, then eleven dead, several officers injured—was unfathomable. Working in Squirrel Hill, and immersed professionally in the Jewish community, that was my neighborhood, too.

Sick and unnerved, I stayed glued to the television until Shabbat was over and I got my assignments from my editor for the next day: write a recap of all that had happened; write bios for those murdered; head to the Jewish Community Center the next morning and interview the dignitaries from Israel who were on their way to Pittsburgh to lend their support. Less than twenty-four hours before, my assignments had been to write feature articles on party planning for a special section that we ended up not running for more than a year.

To say that the ensuing year was surreal would fall far short of describing how my life changed after October 27, 2018. I needed to very quickly find ways to talk to people who had watched their friends and family members murdered in the most brutal way, or who had barely escaped with their own lives by hiding in a closet, or who had been shot themselves and managed to survive. I struggled to find the words to open communication with them when there were no words adequate to do so.

If you are a living, breathing human being with a heart, there is only so much you can compartmentalize. I soon gave myself permission to cry during interviews, professionalism be damned.

The events of October 27, 2018, were horrific and shocking and life-changing. But for me, the hate that motivated them was something I had been keenly aware of since Baumhammers shattered my idyllic vision of my suburban community just a bridge away from Squirrel Hill in April 2000. And I came to realize on that rainy autumn day in 2018 that Baumhammers had forever changed the way my son would view the world as a Jew as well.

When he called to tell us of the shooting at Tree of Life, urging us to go to our congregation in Mount Lebanon to warn others that an antisemitic murderer might be on his way, he was recalling that day in 2000 that he had hid under his desk in his fourth-grade classroom. He was remembering the news reports he must have heard later about Baumhammers's murderous rampage, driving from one location to another, killing people because they were different from him.

Was the Tree of Life murderer planning to attack other congregations? I have been unable to substantiate reports that his car was filled with loads of ammunition and maps to other shuls. Perhaps we will find out when he is tried.

In the days immediately after Baumhammers's killing spree, there were solidarity dinners at the home of our close Catholic friends, and larger interfaith gatherings of support for our Jewish community. Then, for a few months, we followed the murderer's arraignment and his trial and his ultimate conviction. Then, his appeals.

As time passed I mostly stopped thinking about Baumhammers the man, despite the fact that he had forever altered my sense of security. Life goes on, and all that.

But on the morning of October 27, 2018, I knew for sure that he had forever changed life for my son. And that is something completely different.

WALKING IS
MY TRIBUTE

Abby W. Schachter

WANTING TO BE IN TWO PLACES AT ONE TIME is familiar. But when I found myself in a taxi in Manhattan on the same Shabbat morning that eleven people were gunned down at the Tree of Life synagogue in Pittsburgh, I didn't want to be in two places at all. I felt strongly that I was in the wrong place entirely. I needed to be back in Pittsburgh where I live and make my life. As soon as I got to my parents' apartment, and after alerting them to the news, I immediately got on the phone to the airlines to turn right around and fly home to my city, my community, my family.

In truth, I was most desperate to get back to my husband and four children. It was not that I feared for their safety, though. We are regular shulgoers and they would normally have been at our Conservative congregation, but I knew my family was attending a bar mitzvah at an Orthodox synagogue a mile away from the carnage. I was in a fever to get back to my family, yes. The six of us are close and it was especially difficult for me to be separated from my husband. I married at thirty-five and before we got together, I was convinced that I was too old to find a perfect romantic ideal for a spouse. I learned from Ben that the ideal is to find both a love relationship and a strong, honest friendship. My husband is that kind of friend, and we have built a life where we spend a lot of time together, including enjoying coffee together every morning, before the children are awake, working together from home regularly and traveling individually seldom.

There was a parallel feeling as well. It was the strong conviction that I was in the *wrong* place, both physically and figuratively. Maybe if I had flown into New York on Friday before sundown and had not broken the rules of Shabbat observance, I might have felt differently. According to traditional Judaism, there are thirty-nine *melachot*, or creative acts, forbidden from sundown Friday to sundown Saturday, including driving. Yet, I *had* returned to Pittsburgh the same day I left and thereby I *had* broken the laws of Shabbat observance by driving and flying.

The rest of Saturday was spent in reunion with my husband and children and then worrying. What had really happened? Who was hurt, or, God forbid, killed? Talking with my cousin, I knew that Joyce Fienberg was missing. I tuned in on Sunday morning for the press conference when they were to announce the names of the victims and was utterly shattered when Joyce's name was read.

Pittsburgh is my fifth hometown after Montreal, Jerusalem, Washington, and New York. I moved here soon after I got married, in 2005, and was immediately warmly welcomed by my cousin and her husband but also by her female friends, one of whom was Joyce. I used to see these women periodically, mostly for lively lunches on birthdays or special occasions. They were at a different stage of life. Their kids were grown and many had grandchildren. Some were still working, while others were winding down their careers. Some of their husbands had died, while some were caring for sick spouses. Meanwhile, I was having my babies and trying to manage working. We didn't know each other that well, but I felt accepted and appreciated. They asked about my kids, our choice of school, and my work life. They offered help and advice if I asked about recommendations for books, plumbers, or restaurants. I just loved having the chance to hang out with a bunch of smart, witty, fun Jewish women.

The day after the shooting and in the days that followed, I learned something else about Joyce. She had a relationship to Judaism that I hadn't understood before. She had been at Tree of Life that morning because she was one of very few people at shul on time in order to "make a minyan"—the quorum of ten people needed to form the community of worshippers. Joyce's husband Steven had died in 2016 and she recited Kaddish—the mourner's prayer—at Tree of Life. But rather than stop there, after her personal obligation was fulfilled, she continued to attend synagogue because she'd become one of those members who helps others make a minyan. For close to two years, she was so committed to making sure other Jews could pray in community that she showed up week after week, including on that fateful Shabbat. It struck me very hard that she had paid for her commitment to Jewish worship with her life.

I saw that same devotion to Jewish ritual and practice expressed over and over again among other Jewish Pittsburghers in the days following the attack, and it filled me with emotion every time. I spoke to friends who were part of the *chevra kadisha*—the group responsible for making sure that the dead are properly prepared for burial. There were those who attended as many of the funerals as they could and some who walked behind the casket, if possible. Multiple appeals landed in my inbox for saying prayers for the wounded and providing support for the bereaved. Students were enlisted to join a minyan and recite special prayers.

Attending Joyce's funeral, I saw many of the women I was used to seeing at lunch come together instead to say goodbye to our friend. I heard all about what she meant to her sons, her extended family, her community. It was heartbreaking to listen to all that we'd lost with her death.

Over those terrible days, I also thought about my own choices. It felt like a personal moral failing that instead of being together with my family, I had boarded a plane to New York. I considered what it meant that such a routine decision—to fly on Saturday—had turned into a fault line in time. I began to consider what I wanted from my own response to the shooting. In response to that experience I've chosen as my tribute—an affirmation of the value of living as a committed Jew—to walk on Shabbat. According to traditional observance of the Sabbath, driving is prohibited from sundown Friday evening until twenty-five hours later, when it is dark enough for three stars to be visible. Joyce's model of Jewish living and fulfilling communal responsibilities was a strong motivator. But I also kept in mind the feeling I had when I learned of acts of Jewish commitment that others had performed and that had made such a strong impression on me.

Analyzing and examining my Jewish life was not new. For years, my family had been living a vibrant but not unchallenging religious life. Like just about every other Jew I know who spends time thinking about the meaning and quality of religious observance, I expended thought and energy considering and reconsidering whether the Jewish rituals and practices I was modeling were valuable to my children, and which ones gave me personal satisfaction. The kids are enrolled in an Orthodox school, while we regularly attend a Conservative shul. This places our family in two connected but decidedly separate circles of Jewish life in Pittsburgh. One of the most basic differences is whether you strictly observe the Jewish calendar or whether you massage it in order to fit more closely into the non-Jewish majority culture. We are lucky to have a wide circle of Jewish friends as well. As a result, rather than feeling a part of one Jewish community, we are connected to several.

We had slowly been changing our eating habits from keeping kosher at home but not at restaurants (Rabbi Shlomo Riskin—an Orthodox rabbi who both founded Lincoln Square Synagogue on the Upper West Side of New York and was the founding chief rabbi of the religious West Bank settlement of Efrat in Israel—once said about such an arrangement: "Your pots will go to Heaven"), to the compromise position of eating only vegetarian or pescatarian outside the house. In this way, we hope to be able to enjoy eating out but not be limited to only kosher restaurants. We always sat down to Shabbat dinner together as a family, often with guests. My husband had started learning Talmud, while I opted for a weekly class examining the Biblical text. Taking on a new mitzvah, a new Jewish commitment, maybe wasn't such a break from the past. In one way, it can be viewed as the continuation of an organic process of adaptation to a more traditional model. And yet, in my mind, it felt like a watershed. It was the first time I thought to add a Jewish commitment for a particular purpose; that is, to increase the potential perfection of the world through Jewish observance. Traditional Judaism defines the performance of commandments as the effort to fulfill God's will on earth, today, now.

The more Jews fulfill more commandments, the closer we come to achieving a perfected world, a necessary precondition for the coming of the messianic age.

In the fall of 2001, I was at my office in midtown Manhattan when I learned that a plane had hit the World Trade Center. When it became clear that something besides a terrible accident was going on, I called my parents, who were then living in Boston, to let them know to turn on the TV news. I told my mom, "Now maybe they'll understand what happens in Israel." What I meant was that Americans might have a bit better understanding of what it means to have terrorists who reject your very existence, attack civilians and symbols of your power in order to cause the greatest degree of bloodshed and fear. It seemed very possible that by having experienced such devastating carnage Americans might appreciate even more strongly the struggle that the Jewish state had been dealing with since its founding.

At the time, the outpouring of patriotism, pride, and love for America was heartening and strengthening. And indeed, for a while, there were those who became more hawkish about national security because of the 9/11 attacks.

Some years later, I learned that along with those Americans who had responded to 9/11 by joining the military or rededicating them-selves to public service, and those Jews—like myself—who became even more committed to a forceful foreign policy and support for Israel, some American Jews had another response entirely: they became more Jewishly observant and committed to tradition. I heard of a man who decided after the attacks on the World Trade Center and the Pentagon to only marry a Jewish woman, which he did. Someone else I met opt-ed to eat only kosher meat; still others started to wear a *kippah* (skull-cap), in public or to the office. I have to admit, before the shooting at Tree of Life, I didn't get it—the attacks of 9/11 weren't motivated by antisemitism, after all. I couldn't see the connection between terrorist attacks on US soil and Jewish commitment. Truth be told, I'm not sure I see it any better now. Funnily enough, I know I have friends and acquaintances who don't understand my decision to observe Shabbat more strictly by not driving. After all, I did not make this commitment as some kind of punishment for having broken Shabbat the morning of the shooting. The opposite is the case. I have chosen to celebrate and affirm my Judaism in the face of one man's attempt to destroy as many of my fellow Jews as he could. Observing the responses of other friends and Jewish Pittsburghers to the Tree of Life attack, though, I can see how my decision to walk might not seem logical.

In the days after the shooting there were multiple expressions of solidarity, creativity, and comfort. Yet there was also a strong and very public political response—to blame the massacre on President Trump and to "come together" against hate by protesting the current occupant of the White House. Such a response was predictable. Pittsburgh is a city run by Democrats, a city that hosts two distinguished institutions of higher learning that are strongly liberal. It is a city where the Jewish community, like all other American Jewish communities, is majority left. On top of that, opposition to President Trump had been obvious and commonplace since his election in 2016. Perhaps I should not have been surprised and yet I was—shocked, even. Worse still, as far as I was concerned, those members of the Jewish community who deliberately appropriated Jewish symbols and texts to conduct their protest campaign were doing the opposite of what those symbols and texts are meant for. I was told by one such protester that it was her Jewish values that informed her outrage toward the president.

I'm politically engaged and yet the protesters' logic escaped me. How could it be that the most important response to a son of Amalek killing our brethren was for Jewish anti-Trump protestors to read Tehillim aloud down the middle of Murray Avenue? The protesters didn't just want to yell at President Trump and tell him how little they thought of him, his wife, his family, his policies. They unapologetically used a Jewish text to reject the president. To such people, it was perfectly obvious that left-wing politics and Judaism—the religion, the traditions, and the texts—were inextricably linked. I was bewildered and hurt that so many people—people I know—would use a brutal massacre to score political points. It was especially painful that so many would use Judaism as a means to do so.

It took time for my family to get used to walking to our synagogue. In bad weather the distance is onerous. And even in summer it can be a trek, since it's uphill most of the way there. But not long ago I realized how much I'd gotten used to it. And our youngest child, six, has stopped asking if we are walking or driving to shul. He's also used to it, apparently.

Walking on Shabbat is just one way to mark a fault line. It is a means of delineating the sacred space of Shabbat as separate from the rest of the mundane week. The observance of Shabbat is filled with such separations and designations. At first changing behavior can be uncomfortable, and especially when it comes to religious observance it can seem downright strange. I don't think about walking in connection with the shooting anymore, if I ever did.

Our Shabbat experience changed because of the shooting, but that does not mean that it remains uppermost in my mind on any given Saturday. Instead, not driving on Saturday has become as integral to my family's experience as anything else we do to mark the separation from mundane weekday to holy Sabbath. It has positively changed our relationships, as we are invited for lunch after services more often now. Others have told us their door is open to us if we get caught in the rain walking home, or need a glass of water or to rest. On some occasions, we've stayed longer at synagogue to enjoy an afternoon program or to visit with our friends. When the weather has been particularly forbidding, we've stayed home entirely and spent time together as a family.

I believe that one of the deeply beautiful aspects of Judaism is the possibility of adaptation and change. My Jewish life is a work in progress and as of this moment, walking on Shabbat is a part of the whole fabric of my current Jewish life.

AFTER
THE
OUTPOURING

Jane Bernstein

ALMOST EVERY DAY I drive down Wilkins Avenue, past the Tree of Life synagogue. It's the route I choose for the three-mile drive from my house in Point Breeze to Carnegie Mellon University, where I teach. A dozen other ways, all equidistant, would get me to campus at much the same time, but this is the way I need to go.

I took this route the morning of the shooting, on my way to a panel discussion at the university, unaware of the bloodshed at the Tree of Life or the reason the street was blocked, and I took it on the next days when police barricades kept the road closed to traffic. From my car I could see the police and reporters, the small tents erected to shelter journalists in bad weather, the vans from news stations parked haphazardly along the curbs.

Because almost every day I continued to drive as far as I could down Wilkins Avenue instead of taking another street, I watched the memorial evolve, first the lush flower arrangements set out on the grass, then the large upright white Stars of David, each with the name of a person gunned down. I saw the guitarists, the pedestrians pausing, bowing their heads.

After two or three weeks, I noticed that the shooting stopped coming up in conversation. Shopkeepers kept the signs in their windows that say *Stronger Than Hate* with a Steelers logo and a Star of

David, and the barricades stayed in place, but for those not intimately connected to the victims the mass shooting was in the past. So much else is happening—in our own lives, in our community, the White House, the world.

Then one morning, the police barricades that had blocked traffic for a whole season were arranged around the perimeter of the main building and a blue mesh fence was put up to hide the boarded-up windows on the synagogue addition. At last I could continue all the way down Wilkins, past the sturdy brick and stone homes. When I first moved to Pittsburgh from a town with old clapboard houses, I told my daughters that the houses here were the kind the Big Bad Wolf could not blow down.

The street is so quiet. I rarely see pedestrians, even when winter ends and the leaves on the big old trees begin to unfurl. Sometimes I drive past a woman walking her dog in a handsome coat, or a couple of students waiting for a bus. I find the silence haunting. The houses look so closed-off, the one with the thick columns, the angular contemporary one, with window shades fully drawn. Never have I seen someone on a porch or in the yard. Only now, all these months later, do I find myself silently asking, every day, *How are you, grandson? How are you sister, cousin, friend?*

My phone pinged while I was driving down Wilkins on the morning of October 27, 2018. It was the last day of a fiftieth-anniversary celebration for the Creative Writing Program and seventy-five alumni had come to town. The police barricades were an annoyance that threatened to make me late—a car crash, I thought, or a water main break. It was only after I parked that I saw the text from my husband, who was at a conference in Brazil. *Active shooter in the area. Be careful.* I put the phone in my pocket and hurried toward the room where the panel discussion had already begun.

For my parents, in 1966, it was a late-night phone call. A police detective on the other end said that their daughter Laura, a college student in Tempe, Arizona, had been murdered. I was seventeen and still living at home, and the call that woke my parents woke me, too. I got out of bed and stood in my parents' doorway, listening. Someone had stabbed my sister to death while she was chaining up her bicycle outside a friend's apartment.

I listened and then I went back to my bedroom and waited until morning to tell the friend who drove me to school not to pick me up. The wait for daylight seemed endless, since I did not know what to do apart from turning in circles. At 7:00 a.m., I called my friend. The words I needed to say felt as if they'd come from someone else.

My sister's murder was a major news story in Tempe, where no university student had ever been killed, and in our New Jersey town. Even in those days, when news didn't spread as quickly as it does now, reporters were crossing our lawn by daylight and neighbors had shown up.

My parents had to fly to Arizona to identify my sister's body, and when they returned to sit shiva our house was crowded with family and friends. My sister's fiancé and some of her college friends had flown in, filling our living room with their frank grief and youthful energy. They made so much fuss over me that it took my mind off the itchy wool sailor-style dress I wore—my only black garment—and the reason for their visit.

When shiva ended I went back to school and my father drove to work. My mother was left in the empty house.

Whenever I hear someone say you never recover from the death of a child, and I do, often, I think of my father, who lived for thirty-four years after his daughter was killed, and my mother for forty-two years, and those years were marked by dinners and business trips, petty quarrels about household matters, parties and vacations. To say one never recovers reduces the complexity of loss to a flat, relentless state of grief, as if it's possible for a parent, for anyone, to sit on the edge of a bed and weep for thirty years.

No one in my family broke down, took to drugs or drink, crashed cars. My parents resumed their weekly poker and mahjongg games shortly after my sister's murder. I started an art scholarship in Laura's name and hung out with my friends and *got back into the swing of things*, as one was advised at the time, never allowing myself to feel the depth of the loss, or the discomfort I now felt when I was alone with my parents. My mother *kept busy*. She did not *dwell on the past*. She began to work outside the house for the first time since her daughters were born. She was proud of her job as a bookkeeper and fond of the couple who owned the small company where she worked. She put aside all the money she earned and she and my father began to travel overseas twice a year. Many years later she told me that these trips to Europe and Israel were the happiest part of her life.

A year after my sister's murder, almost to the day, I left for college. I did well in school, got married and had children, fulfilled my dream of becoming a writer. I *moved on*, just as I was supposed to do. I did not let myself think about my sister, whom I loved dearly, or feel how lonely it was to be funny and gregarious. For so many years I pretended to be the person I'd been before Laura's murder, that I lost everything—a sense of myself, memories of my sister.

My response to tragedy is often so delayed that even now I do not know if my driving down Wilkins, instead of taking another street, is a strange vigilance, as if I'm a security guard tasked with watching the premises, or just a habit, devoid of meaning.

Seven years after Laura's death I began to see a therapist and to understand all the ways our family life had been ruptured and never fully repaired. I began to dream about my sister, too, realistic dreams in which she was alive and we were cooking or quarreling and I could hear her voice, and she was so vivid that I woke to a powerful grief I thought would demolish me. And yet these dreams brought her back to me, at least for a while.

Years later, when I read studies theorizing the ways that trauma is passed down through the generations, I thought of what my mother had learned from her own mother, who'd lost two children and left behind her family in Moldova. *Your friends will cross the street if they see you crying.* My grandmother taught this to my mother, who taught it to me. My grandfather, whose mother had died when he was a boy and who was not accepted by his stepmother, "forbade" his wife and children from crying, which he deemed "European." Crying was not allowed.

An obedient child, my mother took all of this to heart. It twisted and deformed something in her, and when as a little girl I cried she mocked my ugly face, with its funny *upside-down mouth*, the sounds I made, *wah-wah-wah*, and the way I was always crying about nothing. Well before Laura's murder, I learned how unsightly and humiliating it was to cry.

We cut Laura out of our lives the way people cut divorced spouses out of family photos. And yet years later, when my children and I visited my parents, my older daughter, Charlotte, slept in Laura's bed, and my mother, who never spoke my sister's name to me, told Charlotte it was her aunt's bed. An aunt, who never was to my daughter, who did not see pictures of her or hear her mentioned in conversations. So "aunt," then was a blank, a wound with no name. *Your aunt.* But this trauma was not transmitted merely because Charlotte slept in the bed of the ghostly aunt. It is in my cells, in the wound I bear, in the particular way I bear it. It's in how cool I am when I hear alarming news—putting the phone in my pocket when I read *active shooter in the area* and continuing on with the day—and how distant I seem from what in time I will feel deeply.

This daughter of mine, a grown woman who lives in Brooklyn and is ambivalent about Judaism, was bat mitzvahed at Tree of Life and later took confirmation classes, which she loved. She was the first person to call when I was inside my building at CMU. While I was worrying about lunch for the out-of-town alumni, she began to weep. "Mommy, it was the Tree of Life." I held the phone to my ear for a long time. It was as if she had to cry for both of us.

I walked in circles in my living room on Tuesday morning, three days after the Tree of Life massacre, walked and walked, much as I had as a teenager the night the police called my parents. I had to say something to my students in my classes that afternoon and not a single sentence formed in my mind.

I drove as far as I could down Wilkins, trying to get my thoughts in order. At the detour, I turned left and continued to the parking garage. Nothing. I walked slowly across campus. I could think of nothing at all.

I stepped into my classroom, flushed and mute. The undergraduates were sitting around the seminar table, gazing at their open laptops. I scanned the room—Chinese, Indian American, from a rural area in the West. . . . My last name meant nothing to these students, nor did my face.

"I'm Jewish," I said, barely recognizing my own quavering voice. The silence was broken by a student, who said: "You CMU students need to stop working for a few hours and *feel* your grief."

I could never speak to my mother about my sister, although decades after Laura's death I tried. It seemed, though, that time did not heal the wound, as perhaps it had for my father, a gregarious man, receptive to simple pleasures, like schmoozing with the neighbors and walking the dog. In the years after my sister's murder, he found ways to enjoy life.

My mother, slowly, decidedly, became bitter and isolated. Maybe it started because I could not be two daughters for her, or after my second daughter was born with developmental disabilities, or when she and my father stopped traveling. She began saying, "We're cursed." In the last weeks of her life, she was convinced that the aides at the nursing home knew her daughter had been murdered, were glad of it and laughed at her.

She wasn't the only one whose grief manifested itself years later. Twenty-seven years after Laura's murder, the cousin who'd been closest to my sister sent me a scathing letter castigating my family and me for excluding her from the grieving process. This cousin, who had a husband, a son, and a good career, lived in the Northwest, so we hadn't seen each other in years. The letter seemed mean-spirited and distressed me deeply. Years passed before I could say, and then to myself: "But there was no grieving process."

And only now, fifty-four years later, can I see how easy it is to overlook the cousins and grandchildren and friends.

If I say I'm *over* my sister's murder and have been for decades, it isn't as if after therapy I packed away my sorrow forever. It's rather that this tragedy from a lifetime ago no longer shapes my daily life. I live with and around the wounds inevitable to all humans who dare to love. I feel no residual sense of loss, only the regret that I was pushed by history or family or culture, or by my own way of being, to forget my sister.

I am healthy, I am fine.

And I grieve her.

Both of these.

Artwork sent from around the world replaced the ugly fencing on the Wilkins Avenue side of the Tree of Life, colorful images, hands, trees, doves, *hope, peace, love.* Some of it comes from students at Marjory Stoneman Douglas High School in Parkland, Florida, from Columbine High School in Colorado, from Newtown, Connecticut. I admire the young artists, and the teenagers and parents who speak publicly against gun violence and push for legislation, but when I drive past I look straight ahead instead of at the art.

I pass the houses on Wilkins Avenue with their shades drawn and think of the silent ones at home.

Then a child or teenager is murdered and I see the photos in the newspaper, and the wound splits open, the long-buried grief rises, and it is not Laura, but rather the loss of her, and I feel: I will never get over it, never.

Eleven Jews arrive at a synagogue for morning prayers and are gunned down. I cannot articulate what I feel, cannot find a single word to console or explain. All I can do for now is pick this route and drive.

FALL
SEMESTER
2018

Shock and Fear Grip
a College Classroom

Barbara S. Burstin

FOR MANY YEARS, I have taught three classes for undergraduates at the University of Pittsburgh on Tuesdays and Thursdays during the fall semester of the year. My usual routine has been to have a late morning class on the American Jewish experience for an hour and fifteen minutes. Then I have about a half hour to gobble down a sandwich and digest my *New York Times*. After that I scurry off to get to my first class in the afternoon, on the United States and the Holocaust. I get a fifteen-minute break before my third class, on the same topic. Those teaching days are a challenge; I am tired at the end of the day, but it is a schedule I have chosen and one that works well for me. At the end of the day I feel fulfilled and proud that I have imparted meaningful knowledge and understanding to my students.

But that routine was shattered one Tuesday in October 2018, following the Saturday massacre at the Tree of Life Synagogue. I knew that whatever I had planned was not going to be. I worried about how I was going to handle the trauma and trepidation that I was feeling and that I knew my students were feeling as well. That Tuesday was one that I certainly had not and could not have prepared for.

When I walked into my first class I could feel the tension in the room. The students looked at me with an intensity I had not seen before. All eyes were fixed on me. The room was quiet; the students were waiting for me to speak. I knew that it would be virtually impossible for me to talk with any kind of detachment; it was too close to home, literally, because like so many others in our community I too had lost a friend.

I began softly, trying to hold my feelings in check. But once I started, the room very quickly erupted with an outburst of emotions. The Jewish students in the class cried out that they were afraid: they were afraid for their own safety on campus and afraid about what this meant for them in the future as Jews. Some questioned G-d. How could this have happened, and why? It made no sense to them. We had discussed antisemitism before and what it was like for earlier generations of Jews to be a tiny minority in a predominantly Christian country, but the emotion hadn't been there. How could it have been? That was in the past. Maybe it had affected their grandparents, maybe even their parents, but not them. They were home safe and then suddenly they weren't. The non-Jewish students listened with rapt attention. They too were confused, dismayed, and upset.

Everyone talked; there was no holding back—feelings were raw. The time flew by. The class was over and the last student had finally gone. I sat down feeling comforted that some of the tension in the room had been relieved, but I knew that it would take time for the students to heal, that their feelings of shock and trepidation would not dissipate overnight, that there would be scars. I hoped that I had helped the students by listening to them and telling them that people, especially Holocaust survivors, had suffered incredible trauma in the past and had been able to move on, but my own stomach was still tied up in knots. I had to get ready for my next class on America and the Holocaust. What was going to happen with this group?

In this second class we had been dealing with the unfolding of events in Nazi Germany and the United States as two men, Adolf Hitler and Franklin Roosevelt, had taken center on the world stage early in 1933, within five weeks of each other. The nature of their leadership and the actions they quickly took once in power were presenting a diametrically opposed contrast in style and values. We had learned how Hitler's attack on the Jews had begun immediately with dismissals, arrests, imprisonment, random violence, social isolation, and untold humiliations—it was a fury being unleashed. We were only two-thirds into the semester, before we had even really gotten into the horrific toll from the mass deportations, the liquidations of the ghettos, the killing squads, and the whole bureaucratic process of destruction, but we had already felt the terror of what Jews were experiencing. We were beginning to fill in the details of a picture that many students already had some notion about. But what the students hadn't known, that they were now studying, was what was happening on the other side of the Atlantic, in America. They had never learned how the American public, Congress, the Roosevelt administration, American universities, and religious organizations were responding to the crisis overseas. That dark picture was deeply disturbing, jolting them, perhaps even more than the terrible stories about Germany, because it was nothing they had expected and it hit closer to home.

In response to Hitler's nationwide boycott against Jewish businesses and the dismissal of thousands of Jewish civil servants in 1933, the State Department had urged Roosevelt not to respond. After all, we had been silent in response to the terrible plight of African Americans in our own country, so how could we criticize what Germany was doing to its Jewish citizens and not be derided as totally hypocritical? In response to the Nuremberg Laws of 1935, when Jews were denied German citizenship and left stateless without any police protection, America went to the Olympic Games in Berlin in 1936. An attempted boycott failed in a very close vote, a boycott that had been led by Jews and others (including Ziggy Kahn, athletic director of the famed Irene Kaufmann Settlement in Pittsburgh). The result was an economic and propaganda bonanza for Hitler. In 1938 Roosevelt called for a conference, which took place in Evian, France, to discuss the plight of refugees. The United States could not accept any more refugees given its drastically restrictive immigration act passed in 1924, but it hoped other countries would lower their barriers. It was not to be. In 1939 the telegrams to the president from the desperate passengers of the *Saint Louis*, the "Voyage of the Damned," went unanswered and the hopes of the nine-hundred-plus passengers to escape the Nazis and disembark on free territory were dashed.

Roosevelt had to face harsh political realities—preparing isolationist Americans for involvement in a European war he believed we would not and should not be able to avoid; congressional representatives who overwhelmingly were unsympathetic to the plight of Jews and who were determined not to liberalize our immigration law; a

State Department committed to keeping any of those they deemed "undesirable," particularly the Jews, from reaching our shores; and an American citizenry that viewed any refugees, let alone Jews, with suspicion and disfavor. People were being fueled in their prejudice by over one hundred antisemitic hate groups around the country, including the German American Bund, which got the materials it distributed nationwide directly from Joseph Goebbels's Ministry of Propaganda in Germany. They were listening to the likes of Father Coughlin and others who were spewing anti-Jewish vitriol. In a public opinion poll, over a fifth of Americans somehow considered Jews a "menace" in the early 1940s. How else can you explain why Congress jumped to bring twenty thousand British children to America in the face of the German bombing of England in the summer of 1940, but when it came to bringing twenty thousand German (Jewish) children to America, that bill didn't even make it out of committee? Didn't the congressmen understand the meaning of the Kindertransport—that for Jewish parents to willingly put their children on a train heading out of Germany with the expectation that they would never see their little loved ones again, reflected immeasurable desperation and despair? The list goes on. . . .

Students had been learning about all this. It had caused dismay, consternation, surprise, anger, shock. These students had been coming to grips with the inhumanity of a malicious and driven dictator, with the ravages of prejudice and the evil consequences of a diabolical racial theory. They had also been struggling to absorb the inaction and spreading net of prejudice in our nation, which was unwilling to respond to the disaster overseas. And now these same students had to face yet another bitter reality—that antisemitism was not solely a scourge of the past. It was in their backyard. Vicious notions about Jews and immigrants had unleashed mass killing just a mile or two down the road from their very own classroom. For all the students, Jewish and non-Jewish, that horrifying reality smacked them hard.

I shared their concern and fear as well. Where were the boundaries? Was any place safe? Were students safe taking a course listed under Jewish studies in the course catalog? Was I safe teaching classes that pertained to Jews? Did I and my students need to go through emergency drills like students were doing in Jewish day schools around the country? Did I need to carry an emergency device to call for help? And what could I really do if someone came with a gun into my classroom? Should a university be so open without any security?

Now, more than one year later, those concerns have faded in their intensity. But other feelings and thoughts have arisen that perhaps are just as strong. I am distressed by the constant drumbeat of the need for security and of the pervasive discussion of antisemitism. Yes, we cannot be blind to what is happening in America, the dramatic escalation of violent incidents and the climate of hate that the white supremacists on the right and the Jew haters on the left have exposed. I am not denying that we need to be vigilant. Keeping Jews safe is a major responsibility and is a necessary expenditure that the community must shoulder. But I would suggest that American Jews are in danger of being mired in the swamp of antisemitism, that it has too much paralyzed us, turning us into pessimists, seeing ourselves only as potential targets.

When I teach about the Holocaust, I caution that given the nature of the material, we are only going to see Jews as victims, targeted for death. So I deliberately spend some time underscoring the life Jews led before the Holocaust—their hopes and dreams, accomplishments, and disappointments—like anyone else. In my class on the American Jewish experience I offer a reading that asks the question, are we "over-Holo-causting"; that is, directing our educational energies to teaching about the Holocaust and not teaching enough about Jewish values, Jewish religious traditions, Jewish peoplehood, and the contributions Jews have made over centuries? In his book *Where are We?* Leonard Fein suggests that we should look to Sinai as our defining moment, not to the Holocaust. I raise the question especially in light of the results of a recent Pew Study that asked, "What is the most important aspect of being Jewish to you?" Over 70 percent of the Jewish respondents answered that it was remembering the Holocaust. This response topped other suggested answers including Jewish observance, leading an ethical and moral life, caring about Israel, and working for justice and equality. Should we view that response with equanimity? Is remembering how we were victimized the most important aspect of being Jewish?

The irony, of course, is that all this concern about antisemitism comes at a time when Jews arguably are accepted now more than ever. This was a point I raised with my students that first Tuesday after the shooting. All the barriers that were so high in the past have fallen. There are no more quotas at elite universities keeping Jews out. There are no more covenants keeping Jews out of certain neighborhoods and no more signs that say Jews shouldn't bother to apply for jobs in corporate America. Public opinion polls reflect the widespread acceptance of Jews into the American mainstream. In fact, Jews are touted as leaders and role models; they are readily elected to political office and hold important public positions. When Joe Lieberman was put on the Democratic ballot as a vice-presidential candidate in 2000, it was a stirring recognition that a Jew was seen as actually helping the ticket in Al Gore's quest for the presidency, an amazing testament to how far Jews have come in America. And the high intermarriage rate perhaps attests to the acceptance of Jews in American society more than anything else. (Whether that is good or bad for the future of the Jewish community is hotly debated.)

All of these thoughts are in my head as I drive by the Tree of Life building. It is still fenced off, still a stark reminder of the horror that transpired there well over a year ago. I had an Israeli visitor come to Pittsburgh several months ago. I took her past the Tree of Life and she was shocked to see the way the building looked, this foreboding hulk in the middle of a bustling neighborhood. In Israel they make sure that any kind of crime scene is cleaned up immediately so a signal is sent that the perpetrator has not won, that the community has been resilient and has not been paralyzed by the tragedy. That clearly has not been our response for any number of reasons, but the bottom line is that we appear to be a community that is still reeling from its victimization, still struggling to come to grips with what happened.

The Tree of Life site will become an important destination at some point in the future. What do we want people to feel and understand when they go there, which they most assuredly will do? Certainly, the Tree of Life congregation needs to reestablish its home. That synagogue needs once again to become vibrant and active. It is a house of worship first and foremost. But most people who come to the building will do so to pay respects and learn more about what happened on that fateful day in October. Of course we want visitors to understand the toll that antisemitism has taken on the Jewish world in the present but also in the past. That's why the Holocaust Center of Greater Pittsburgh is slated to move into the building when it is finally ready for occupancy. People should know about this longest hatred. But is that the only message visitors should be left with?

The outpouring of sympathy and support in the aftermath of the killing was extraordinary and historic. In the past, certainly in the time frame that I teach about, attacks against Jews were met with approbation or quiet indifference. But not this time. Heartfelt responses flooded in from near and far. The small Muslim community in Pittsburgh raised over $200,000 for the victims within days and volunteered to guard the synagogues. Other funds flowed in as well in bigger and smaller amounts, totaling in the millions of dollars. Other religious and ethnic groups expressed their consternation and solidarity with the Jewish community. Pictures, artworks, flowers, notes, all manner of objects and genuine expressions of support overwhelmed the community. That torrent of solidarity needs to be recognized. It shows a feeling about Jews far different from that of the past; it shows how America really can live up to its ideal of strength in diversity, that people of different backgrounds can come together. That reality can provide some counternarrative to the horrific loss of eleven innocent lives.

But there is another dimension to the site that should be incorporated in future plans as well. It should include some reckoning of the Pittsburgh Jewish community prior to the killing. It should portray the vitality of the community, the diversity within it and the contributions that community has made in its 180 years in this city. It should say something not just about what Jews have done but about Jewish core values, observance and prayer. We must remember that that was why the eleven victims and others were in the synagogue that Sabbath morning. They believed in Proverbs that the Torah is a "tree of life" to all who grasp it.

It is important to include this perspective in the new Tree of Life building, first of all, because it is a rich history that would make all Jews proud of their heritage and their role in building the larger community. Secondly, visitors would appreciate that there is far more to the Pittsburgh Jewish community than the terrible events we experienced less than two years ago. While Pittsburgh will be forever associated with the worst outbreak of anti-Jewish violence in America, nevertheless, that narrative could at least be put in the context of the normalcy and vitality of Pittsburgh Jewish life. And finally, many have pondered how to respond to the rise of hate crimes and the violent rhetoric against Jews. While that involves new gun laws, a dampening down of incendiary rhetoric, some monitoring of hate speech on the internet, and so on, another way to prevent the spread of antisemitic ideology is to acquaint people with who the Jews are—members of society who have contributed to the wellbeing of that society and who recognize the fundamental values of peace and goodwill toward all. Those who are susceptible to radical hate-filled messages are those who, more often than not, have not known any Jews and/or who know very little about them. They have never had a chance to see Jews as real people, with the same hopes and aspirations as they.

So let's take advantage of the opportunity to teach not just about the bad times but also about the good times, about the vitality of a people that has contributed to Pittsburgh and beyond for so long and who are part of the Pittsburgh mosaic. Let visitors, young and old, see Jews in all their various stripes—from profoundly religious to more secular, from poorer Jews to richer Jews, and to see Jews who have been engaged in all kinds of pursuits as businesspeople, artists, musicians, doctors, lawyers, politicians, sports figures, and more. Let them see Jews who have fought and died in America's wars.

In the teaching about the Holocaust that I do, one of the points I like to make at the end of the semester is that people can recover and grow even after profound emotional and physical trauma. I challenge the students to think about the survivors of the Holocaust and how, after all they had gone through, they could make new lives for themselves, raise families and become respected citizens in a new land. The lesson is not lost on the students—if these survivors could overcome unfathomable hardship, so can we. To my students, Holocaust survivors are heroes for their resilience and determination.

So as I have pulled my thoughts together in the aftermath of the horrific events of October 27, 2018, we cannot forget; we have to confront that tragedy in all its stark reality. But we also need to celebrate how Jews have lived and what they have accomplished. The Jewish community in Pittsburgh is alive and well. We have a greater story to tell, beyond the tragedy that so stunned us, a very positive and proud story. By doing that we will give real meaning and sustenance to the Tree of Life. We will offer to all those who visit the site of the worst antisemitic attack in American history a message not only of death and victimhood but also one of hope, inspiration, and life above all else.

"YOU WILL GET THROUGH IT"

Linda F. Hurwitz

"SHOULD WE GO TO SERVICES for Karen's yahrzeit this morning?" my husband asked on the dreary morning of October 27, 2018. It was twenty-nine years on this exact date since our precious daughter was murdered right in our backyard. Karen had her bat mitzvah in the chapel of the Tree of Life synagogue on May 4, 1985, her thirteenth birthday. She chose the intimate setting. She was a shy person, sensitive and serious. She liked to read and was a wonderful writer. Being an only child, she sometimes found it hard to take the teasing of her peers and often wound up being taken advantage of because she trusted others and wanted to help them. I remember the beautiful wood and the charm of that synagogue full of caring friends and family and teachers from Community Day School who knew her well.

At Shabbat dinner of October 26, 2018, with friends and family that knew her well, we shared good, sweet memories of Karen. My mother, a ninety-seven-year-old Holocaust survivor recalled Karen working as a hostess in Eat'n Park during her senior year and how proud she was to have her grandma see her in her uniform. A dear friend whose children grew up with her remembered Karen preparing for her college interviews at Emerson College and Boston University, helping her choose what to wear, and putting her on the plane just three weeks before her death. As part of her application, Karen had written about her summer internship at WQED working for *Mr. Rogers' Neighborhood* and how she loved to write and hoped to pursue journalism. I recalled how excited Karen was to go to the Cheers Bar and Restaurant after the Boston interviews, as she loved the TV show. Her aunt and uncle added memories of Karen enjoying their three children who grew up just around the corner from us. We all knew we never would forget that date, October 27, 1989, when Karen was brutally strangled and stabbed to death. This year, twenty-nine years since our lives were broken by the brutality perpetrated on her, we chose to recall finer times. We went to bed trying to focus on the long-ago images, on her goodness as a young woman with college applications on her desk and her future still ahead of her.

Now it was a month since we had all been together in the sanctuary of Tree of Life for the High Holidays. During the Yizkor memorial service, we each had reflected on those who were no longer with us. On this Saturday morning, I felt sad and tired, and the reality of the forever loss of her and her future made me feel listless. This bitter taste had me feeling lethargic; thus, I had not gotten dressed yet. My husband went up the street to put air in his bike tires and said that when he returned, we could decide if we felt like going up the four blocks to Tree of Life services. On his way home, he saw police cars and heard sirens in our neighborhood. When we turned on the TV, we were shocked: our Tree of Life was under attack. It was incomprehensible that where we had been just weeks before, fellow congregants were being murdered. I pictured us seated all together enjoying the High Holiday services midway down the main sanctuary. I pictured Joyce Fienberg handing me the prayer book and Irv Younger telling people when to be ready to come up for an aliyah. I recalled meeting and hearing this new Rabbi Jeffrey Myers trying to get to know his new congregants—now he was being thrust into the line of fire!

As the first responders stopped the killer, the details of the horrific loss of life, of people we knew having been shot and killed, were overwhelming. The reality I remembered so well was that I knew that each family member of each person shot, one by one by one, would suffer the shock and agony that we had endured twenty-nine years ago on this exact date. They too would feel the weight of these events and losses like an elephant on their chest—the inability to cry, and then the unrelenting tears, the shock and disorientation, the anguish and confusion, the void and the vacancy and then the publicity and intrusion into their privacy. They too would have to call their family members and hear the anguished screams and cries and pain that we inflicted on our parents, on our siblings and nieces and nephews and the entire community by having to give them this news of those who were killed.

The most traumatic call I have had to make in my life was to my Holocaust survivor parents: to my dad, whose first wife and two children had been murdered by the Nazis, and to my mother, whose parents and sister and most of her family and friends had been destroyed, to tell them that here in America, here in my own back yard in Pittsburgh, Pennsylvania, their first grandchild had been brutally murdered.

Reportedly, Karen had responded to the late-night call of a friend who wanted to talk with her about his breakup with his girlfriend. She had been asleep, and she said it was too late for him to come to the house. He begged until she relented. When he arrived, he coerced her to go out back to talk with him. Then with the nunchakus he brought, he strangled her. When she screamed, "Why?" he savagely attacked her with his samurai sword, stabbing her multiple times, extinguishing her life and silencing her sweet, helpful voice.

Like the Tree of Life murderer, Karen's killer brought his weapon intent on violence out of his own meaningless, distorted rage. For the rest of us, it is impossible to imagine that kind of violent intent toward good, innocent people. Even having studied the unspeakable torture and brutality of the Holocaust, when the violence happens to someone you know, in your home, in your world, you gain only a fraction of understanding of what others have experienced. You learn, like I did from the Holocaust survivors I knew so well, that each of us has resources deep within us that will surface to give you the strength to go on with life.

In response to this call I had to make, my parents, knowing from their own suffering and survival that we have a strong will to live, said, "You will get through it! You will get through it!" My mother was born in Lodz, Poland, to a large, very educated, financially comfortable family. Her father was the oldest of seven siblings and her mother one of eight. My mother was adored by her parents and grandparents and even had great-grandparents growing up. She believed that if you were loved and fortunate enough to have secure, happy, formative years, you had the self-assurance to rebound when you had to face adversity. She was very close to her father, particularly, and often quoted his philosophy of life. Her family was not religious, but they raised her to believe in herself and in the reality that under all conditions one had to be able to respect oneself for one's actions and decisions in life.

My mother was a wonderful storyteller, bringing her family, her grandmothers and cousins, her friends, and her school experiences to life. She told me about summers hiking and kayaking in the mountains, of her volleyball team beating the German team just before the war broke out. She told me about the antisemitism growing in her high school years and especially in the one year of university she had in Krakow in 1938 when antisemites, emboldened by what was being allowed in Germany, pushed Jewish students off the benches in lecture halls and made them stand in the back of the classrooms.

My mother had amazing self-discipline and strength. She told me of how she acted during the war. She did not look Jewish, and she used her height of five-feet-eight, her beauty and self-assurance, and her excellent German to confront the enemy in many situations. She saw how much her strong father needed her when he was devastated by the death of her mother, whom he adored, in the ghetto. She showed me her courage through her many experiences: escaping Warsaw and returning to Lodz to be with family whatever was to happen; working as a nurse in the ghetto, hiding her baby cousin when the Nazis were rounding up children; facing the transport to Auschwitz, where soap and her toothbrush were more important than soup. She stayed with her sister, who was five years younger and dying in Stutthof, rather than going on the death march so that her sister would not die alone and so she could live with herself. She bonded like sisters with her friends Frieda and Dorka and they stayed close until, after five days without food or water on a ship in the Baltic and finally docking in Neustadt-Holstein, they were liberated by the British. Fate, stamina, determination, and self-reliance helped her survive and then build a new life. Falling in love with my father in a Displaced Persons house, trying to get to Palestine, ultimately coming to America, sponsored by my father's aunt and cousin, life began again.

My father, a strong, handsome man, a mechanic who could fix anything, who could walk on his hands, who was passionate and loving, responded to the murder of his first grandchild by saying to me: "This is all I know in life. The cycle of love and loss." He lived through the death of his mother when he was four years old and was raised by his sisters and brothers and a stepmother in Riga, Latvia. He endured World War I and the Russian Revolution, and then enjoyed a period in his life when he was a metalworker, married, and the father of two boys. When the Nazis broke their pact with Russia, his beautiful Baltic city was invaded and occupied. My father was always valuable to the Nazis since he could work in their factories, fix a motorcycle or car, and had a knack for languages, speaking Yiddish, Russian, and then German well. He managed to survive Kaiserwald, Stutthoff, and Buchenwald, and the death march to Germany in the Holocaust even though his wife and two children were murdered. He did not speak to me of his hardships, not wanting my life to be burdened by his sufferings.

My father adored my mother and believed that marrying her, coming to America, having three more children, starting over at thirty-six years old gave him a normal, wonderful life. He said to me when he was dying of cancer at age eighty that the last fifty years had been a gift. He took joy in everyday life and said to me often that even though he had not had the opportunity for advanced formal schooling, he knew people and he knew life. Many nights at the dinner table he shared his observations of people and of what was important in life. When he arrived in Pittsburgh for the Karen's funeral, he hugged me and insisted, "You will get through this! You will."

Having been raised by such resilient, loving, and strong survivors gave me my deepest will to stay strong for my husband and for my family and for my friends and for the community. My husband and I wanted to help and support each other, which meant that when we went back to work we called one another several times a day. We met for lunch, which we never had done before this tragedy, on workdays. We did not blame each other. Each of us was struggling with the truth that we had not been able to stop what had happened. We had not been able to save our child. We could not dwell in the "what if" realm or we would have lost our ability to survive. We had to help each other not go crazy.

We had to find a future. We had to have something to give us a purpose in going on with life. My husband said, "I cannot imagine not having any children," and he inspired me to move forward. We soon both felt the determination to start a family again. We threw ourselves into the adoption process and were very fortunate to raise two beautiful children, Jeffrey and Julia. We stayed in our house, determined not to let the killer take that from us as well. We changed and rebuilt the area where Karen had been killed, transforming it into a playroom for the two children. From a site of death to a site of life. We lived with the tears, with the pain, but, gradually, with new pleasures as well. It took several years until the daily tears stopped and the enormous heavy weight eased and life with laughter and dancing and celebration returned. Just fifteen years ago, the main sanctuary of Tree of Life was the setting for the b'nai mitzvah for Jeffrey and Julia. On that sunny Saturday in March, light streamed through the stained-glass windows, creating a kaleidoscope of colors complementing the bright joy we felt to have the opportunity once again in our lives to celebrate our children and their milestone in their studies. I cherish these memories of Tree of Life.

The families of the victims of the Tree of Life massacre will find within themselves the strength to go on, to give themselves the time, time to grieve and mourn and eventually move forward step by step. They have had to face the initial publicity and will again have to face the press and the perpetrator if a trial does occur. We had two trials and many additional hearings to face over those thirty years, every time dredging up again the pain and anger and injustice of the situation. The people of each synagogue will have to decide, as we did, if they can rebuild their home and return to the facility where the actions occurred. Do they want to give the perpetrator the victory of taking away their place of worship? Can the sanctity be restored? Can it be cleansed and restored? Can one return?

We stayed in our home. We converted Karen's bedroom into a nursery. We transformed the area of the murder for our new family. Ultimately, we were glad we did not let the killer take from us the home and yard we had loved. We wanted our children to share this space with their sister. It was not always comfortable, but we stayed where, as a family, we experienced happiness, sadness, and happiness again. It held many memories.

If you are related to the victims, you will now be associated with them and this event into the future. We are forever marked as the ones whose daughter was murdered. The first few years after she was killed, we got a place outside of Pittsburgh so that we did not feel so conspicuous when out in public. On weekends we went there with friends and family with whom we could be ourselves. As we got better, we almost felt as though we had to apologize for not seeming to be grieving as much. We felt that people talked about us with the best and most compassionate intentions, but it made us feel self-conscious. People often call me by my daughter's name, which shows they think of the event and her in association with me. Today still this happens. I had to find the words that felt comfortable when asked by new people I would meet, "How many children do you have?" When people ask, I pause and say one deceased and two living. I could not answer questions simply and be truthful and inclusive. Did I owe an explanation to everyone I would meet in the future?

The survivors of the shooting and those related closely to those who died will feel this attachment and label as part of their identity forever. Choosing words carefully to honor those who are gone, deciding whether to say something to strangers, is always a challenge. The tenderness one feels on the initial anniversaries becomes easier with experience and acceptance of what happened. Always, certain dates, anniversaries, associations trigger a renewal of grief. However, as my wise mother and father said, "You will get through it." You will learn better coping skills, you will learn how to live with this trauma, forever changed but knowing that your loved one lives on through you and all who remember him or her.

Finding a way to honor the life of the loved one who was killed is important. Establishing something that reflects his or her values and interests helps to give you a sense of purpose for the future. Our daughter loved to read and write and we supported several literary magazines, and the library at her Jewish day school was named for her. A friend of ours who lost an adult child created a golf tournament in their daughter's honor. Another friend designs cards that raise money for scholarships in memory of her deceased child. Keeping that person in your life, sustaining the memories, honoring how one lived, not how one died, inspires and strengthens.

I hope each victim's family member and each friend is fortunate enough to have a support system and the inner strength and resiliency to overcome the shock of October 27, a date of dread and sadness. I hope, as with my loss and sadness, that each survivor finds the building blocks to go on and honor life with life.

AFTERWORD

As Well As Can Be Expected

Beth Kissileff

IT'S NOT REALLY A QUESTION with a definitive answer, so usually when someone asks how I am, my stock response is, "As well as can be expected." It is a catchall, that enables me to say that I am fine when I am feeling decent. If I am feeling grief over lives lost, and a community shattered, that emotion too is covered by my response. The phrase works as a formula when it is hard to know what to say.

One of the things I have found most awkward since October 2018 is going out of town and meeting new people who, when I say I am from Pittsburgh, ask whether I was affected by the shooting. At the parents' reception dropping my daughter off for her first year of college, all of us were in a stunned state in anticipation of the loss that would await us when we got in our cars to drive back home, leaving our children on campus, their home no longer shared with those who have raised them. When asked, I told the woman dipping vegetables in hummus next to me where I am from. She asked, was I connected to the Tree of Life shooting? I didn't want to lie, so I said yes, but then received a barrage of questions that I didn't necessarily feel like addressing, since I was already bereft from saying goodbye to my daughter, though I would be seeing her for Rosh Hashanah in a few weeks. Finally, I walked away from my interrogator, giving her my card if she wished to share the poetry she told me she wrote about the shooting. She did not get in touch.

As I write, we are getting ready for the Passover holiday, when Jews tell the story of liberation from the slavery of Egypt. In her recent book about the Passover Haggadah, professor and writer Vanessa Ochs says of the volume used in the ritual telling of this story that "a Haggadah comes to life when it leads those who are gathered to use it to ask hard questions about slavery, exile, redemption, and freeing the oppressed."[1] The story of the Exodus is present in the book of the telling ("Haggadah" means, literally, "the telling"), but only activated when people gather to transmit it, to each other when they are together and even to oneself, should one be alone on the evening of the Passover seder. It is my hope that similarly, the essays in this volume will bring the experiences of the community of Pittsburgh—how it felt to live through the attack, write about it, and cope with it—very much to life. The essays in this volume raise issues and ask tough questions—Can one heal after gun violence? Can any of us feel safe again? Did antisemitism really not ever go away?—with the anticipation that perhaps for those reading, there will be an impetus to think about these issues in a new way and even perhaps act to ameliorate the twin problems of antisemitism and gun violence that plague the United States at this moment, as well as the concomitant fear of the immigrant that is said to have impelled the shooter to his brutal action.

Or, put another way, the knowledge that eleven Jews were murdered in a synagogue on a Saturday morning in the United States in 2018 does not give a full story. We must tell a story alongside any counting so that the numbers themselves do not remain incomplete. As the interpreter of Jewish texts Avivah Zornberg reminds us, "As in English, the Hebrew words for counting and recounting are related: *li-spor* and *le-sapper* have the same root."[2] This volume is our collective attempt to tell that story both by counting those we lost and by recounting our own experiences around the incident.

I am currently getting ready to celebrate Passover in the midst of the 2020 COVID-19 pandemic; our state, led by those with wisdom to follow medical science–based recommendations, is under quarantine,

---

1. Vanessa Ochs, *The Passover Haggadah: A Biography* (Princeton, NJ: Princeton University Press, 2020), 4.

2. *Bewilderments: Reflections on the Book of Numbers* (New York: Knopf, 2015), 13–14.

so I will celebrate Passover with just my immediate family, without the family members, visitors, and congregants we usually celebrate with, without our larger community.

After the shooting, one of the things that was most helpful to my own family was the sense of community we were given by the many kindnesses shown us. People we did not know signed up to make meals for us, cooked us food just because they wanted to offer sustenance to nurture us, brought us brownies before the Sabbath, dropped off sizable monetary donations to be of assistance. We felt cared for and embraced at the same time that we were shaken and terrified by the violence that had entered our worship space.

We felt very much that we were not alone, from the first official vigil on October 28, 2018, at the Soldiers and Sailors Memorial Hall, when clergy of all faiths and individuals from all walks of life stepped forward to help. The vigils and assemblages throughout the year, at the Rodman Street Missionary Baptist Church in East Liberty, the Hindu Jain temple in Monroeville, the Shadyside Presbyterian Church, the Islamic Center of Pittsburgh in Oakland, were all meaningful to our family personally and to New Light Congregation members. Visits to members of the three synagogues from Polly Sheppard, a survivor of the 2015 Charleston church massacre, from a delegation of students and teachers from the Marjory Stoneman Douglas High School in Parkland, Florida, in April 2019, and from four men who drove twelve hours each way from their Quebec mosque where six worshippers were killed in January 2017 were of immeasurable aid to us.

Especially at this time of quarantine, when public gatherings are not possible, we are hopeful that this book can serve as a virtual gathering place, bringing to life the feelings and emotions of writers in Pittsburgh. While the rest of the world has moved on to the next news happening, our local community bears the marks of the 2018 shooting. Visitors can still see signs everywhere in the neighborhood saying *No Place for Hate—Squirrel Hill*, or *Hate Has No Home Here*, or *No Matter Where You Are from, We're Glad You're Our Neighbor*, in English, Spanish, and Arabic. The crocheted Jewish stars with hearts in their center, contributed by craftspersons from around the world, still hang, if a bit faded and forlorn, from a few places. One can see them outside the Squirrel Hill Post Office, decorating trees in the shopping district on Forbes, and on the fence outside the now desolate and empty Tree of Life building.

On a purely physical level, the neighborhood looks back to normal, with only those small telltale marks of the atrocity that happened here. That glance and observation are misleading: it is not the same.

The physical look of the place does not portend the way many Squirrel Hill residents still jump when they hear loud sounds of any kind, or communicate how they look around them in any crowded public place to be sure they have an exit strategy should there be a need to flee. Question the corporeal state of almost any Squirrel Hill dweller and one will find some physical manifestation of the stress of the worst antisemitic shooting on American soil, which happened here in our neighborhood, whether it is increased stomach pain, migraines, increased anxiety, or difficulty sleeping. In the language of trauma researcher Bessel van der Kolk, "the body keeps score."[3]

As I write this, we are at the midpoint of the second year since the shooting, I am aware of the rhythm since then in thinking about where we were a year ago and how and why it is different now. There was a flurry of activity around the time of the shooting's one-year anniversary. When a young reporter (and friend of my daughter's from their year in Israel before college) came to town in fall 2019 to write about the community a year later, the tea shop where we were supposed to meet was closed, so we walked a block to another.[4] And on the way, in front of the supermarket, we ran into a daughter of one of the victims. I didn't tell her that the reporter is a reporter, just that she is a friend of my daughter. And I just said that the bereaved daughter is a congregant, not family member of a martyr, while we were together, as I did not want to constantly point her out as a victim. She knows her father is gone and how he died; she needs no reminder. A similar thing happened when my coeditor, Eric, and I had lunch with visiting scholar James Young in September. As we were talking, the daughter and the niece of another

---

3. *The Body Keeps the Score: Brain, Mind and Body in the Healing of Trauma* (New York: Penguin Random House, 2014).

4. Shira Hanau, "Where the Pain Is Still Fresh, and the Loss Is Still Local," *Jewish Week*, Oct. 17, 2019, https://jewishweek.timesofisrael.com/where-the-pain-is-still-fresh-and-the-loss-is-still-local/.

of our congregants killed on October 27 came into the restaurant. Only afterward did we disclose to our out-of-town guest the nature of the relationship of the women to the shooting. For those of us who know and care about the families of the victims, there are real-time reminders of the event any time we see those immediately affected by it.

For those reading, we hope this book has been like bumping into one of the family members of the victims, a reminder of what has happened that will endure. A gathering of the thoughts and ideas and emotions of writers able to articulate what this event has meant as well as what they are not yet able to articulate even though they may have made the attempt.

"You never really get over it," Chavie Levine Knapp told us about her experience of being in a bus that was blown up on April 9, 1995, killing her friend Alisa Flatow, whom she had invited on the trip to Gaza before the Passover holiday.[5] I was glad to hear her say it and to have my husband hear it, too. No one, least of all the survivors, needs the false comfort of relentlessly cheerful narratives galloping forth full of inspiration and confidence, to find meaning and power in roles chosen for them as being in wrong place at wrong time and yet surviving. It was sobering as well as relieving to know that in December 2018, over twenty-three years since that day, Knapp still felt it shaped her life and experiences; there was no rush for any of us to get over it either, then, if she had not, after so much time. We met Knapp by chance at the Carnegie Museum, waiting in the lobby after her youngest daughters performed at the Roots of Steel concert organized by Samantha Harris and a group of young people from Tree of Life, as a benefit for the three congregations. Knowing that the daughters had performed solos, my daughter told them that she too had been in the ensemble that performed a group number. The Knapps quickly understood why my daughter was included among the singers and Chavie shared her story.

Last year, the first Passover after the shooting, my parents took all of us to Jerusalem for the duration of the holiday. For three days in a

---

5. Abigail Klein Leichman, "We All Thought It Was a War," *Jewish Standard*, May 6, 2011, http://jewishstandard.timesofisrael.com/we-all-thought-it-was-a-war/.

row, well-meaning but obtrusively curious Israeli friends and relatives asked my husband for details about the shooting and his experience, and he felt that he should oblige their inquisitiveness. Each evening, after recounting his story, he was ill, an intense pain invading his stomach. I took action and emailed all those we were planning to see on the rest of our trip to let them know that questions about the previous October were off-limits. My husband simply could not stomach them without serious physical pain.

On the seventh evening of Passover, a holiday, we were invited for a meal to the home of our teacher Avivah Zornberg. Without asking questions, in her dignified and clarifying way she addressed my husband in the most gentle and respectful manner of anyone we encountered. Avivah told us that Rachelle Frankel, whose son Naftali was murdered in June 2014, when asked about her son, says that she misses him every day. But Frankel adds that, despite her grief over Naftali, there is still reason for simcha (joy), because she has six other children she needs to rejoice over. And then Avivah stopped. It was enough.

This collection, we are hopeful, is our contribution to that conviction that although eleven have been lost, there are still matters worth rejoicing over as individuals and as a community. We have collectively tried to present both the extent of the pain and the complicated emotions, but also the kindnesses that were shown. I am so grateful to each and every one of the writers for being willing to excavate and examine painful thoughts and experiences under what turned out to be a tight deadline so that this volume could be published for the second anniversary of the shooting.

The seventh night of Pesach, when we were with Avivah, does not have any commonly observed specific ritual or dramatic reenactment of what the day symbolizes: the crossing of the Red Sea, the finality of leaving Egypt, the certainty that slavery remains ensconced firmly in the past. In our discussion at dinner that night at Avivah's table, we decided that if the liberation of the Passover is a journey, the beginning is the important thing, the one we mark with a dramatic retelling in the Haggadah, not the stopping points on the way.

James Young expressed while on his visit to Pittsburgh that in order to begin to plan any kind of physical memorial, there needs to be an understanding of the meaning of the event it is commemorating. We hope this volume is a step in figuring out some of what that meaning might be. This book marks a beginning of Pittsburghers' being able to tell our story with the agency to direct the narrative. We are hopeful that this offering of words, this telling, will keep those eleven who were lost on October 27, 2018, the eighteenth of Heshvan 5779, firmly bound in the bond of our lives.

Squirrel Hill 13 Nisan 5780

ACKNOWLEDGMENTS

WE DID NOT COUNT HOW MANY of the essays here talk about the times the writer cried. Probably if we went through them, most of them have some reference to moist faces and overwhelming emotions. Not everyone we asked to write for this volume was ready to do so—perhaps someday there will be another volume, with a different set of writers, reflecting another level of grappling with the attack. For this one, we are grateful to all those who were willing and able to let their tears be exposed on the page and to share their experiences and emotions in writing. The writing was difficult for each contributor, and we are grateful that even under a tight deadline, those represented here were willing to do the necessary work. As veteran journalist Peter Smith told Beth, "The best muse is a deadline," and that proved to be true of all those asked to write. So first and foremost, we thank them. In many ways, this felt like a gathering of friends, getting together to swap stories and help each other through coping with the event.

We wish to acknowledge everyone at the University of Pittsburgh Press. They expressed immediate enthusiasm about this project and worked diligently to enable us to have an October 27, 2020, publication date.

Beth wishes to acknowledge her husband, Rabbi Jon Perlman, who knows how to make quick decisions. After thirty years of marriage, he is still the only person she has ever wanted to share her life with. She thanks their children, Tova, Yael, and Ada, for their support and encouragement of this project. Also, she would like to thank her friends Sheva Zucker and Adam Cohen, who read and improved her essay with judicious comments and cuts. Mostly, she would like to thank her coeditor, who made this possible both with his many ideas and with his knowledge of Google Docs that she has just not mastered. Not just on the page, but in their many conversations about the event and how to process and conceptualize, as well as how to put this all into book form, Eric was a wonderful and understanding friend and coeditor.

Eric wishes to thank his wife, Julie Weinrach, who was his fiancée when this undertaking began. Her daily kindnesses eased the burden of holding all the sorrow on these pages. He would also like to thank his coeditor, who brought so much heart and intellect to this project.

Being able to tell our story, as we choose, is a privilege, and having those interested in reading and hearing our stories even more; thank you to our readers for opening your minds and hearts to take in our experiences. On this day when we commemorate the deaths of six million Jews, we are glad that the deaths of eleven are of significance as well. We hope, one day, there will be no more martyrs of any faith or background.

Yom Hashoah 27 Nisan 5780
April 21, 2020

CONTRIBUTORS

Brooke Barker is a writer and illustrator, and the author of the *New York Times* bestselling book *Sad Animal Facts* and the book *Sad Animal Babies*. Her work has been translated into nine languages and she is a contributor to the *New York Times*, the *Stranger*, *Lenny Letter*, and the *Guardian*.

Ann Belser has a master's degree in journalism from Columbia University. She founded *Print*, Pittsburgh's East End newspaper, in 2015, after working at the regional metropolitan newspaper, the *Pittsburgh Post-Gazette*, for more than twenty years. She now runs the newspaper with her wife, Jan Kurth. She has a daughter and a son who is the 2017 National Marbles Champion.

Jane Bernstein is the author of five books, among them the memoir *Bereft—A Sister's Story*, and her new novel, *The Face Tells the Secret*. She is a lapsed screenwriter and an essayist, whose grants and awards include two National Endowment for the Arts Fellowships for creative writing and a Fulbright Fellowship in Israel. She is a professor of English and a member of the Creative Writing Program at Carnegie Mellon University.

Barbara Burstin is an instructor at the University of Pittsburgh and Carnegie Mellon University, where she teaches courses on the Holocaust and American Jewish history. She is the author of several books, including *After the Holocaust: The Migration of Polish Jews and Christians to Pittsburgh*, *Steel City Jews*, and *Sophie! The Incomparable Mayor Masloff*.

Lisa D. Brush is professor of sociology at the University of Pittsburgh and a member of and former vice-president for ritual at the Congregation Dor Hadash.

Laura Zittrain Eisenberg is on faculty in the History Department at Carnegie Mellon University, where she specializes in modern Middle East history. She holds a PhD in modern Middle East history from the University of Michigan in Ann Arbor. Her areas of research, publication, and teaching focus on the Arab-Israel conflict and peace process. She sits on the board of the Tree of Life Congregation, where her family are third-generation members.

Andrew Goldstein is a staff writer for the *Pittsburgh Post-Gazette*. He was part of the *Post-Gazette* team that received a Pulitzer Prize for coverage of the October 27 shooting.

Kevin Haworth is a novelist, essayist, and literary translator and winner of a 2016 National Endowment for the Arts Fellowship in creative nonfiction. His most recent books are *Far Out All My Life*, an essay collection, and *The Comics of Rutu Modan: War, Love and Secrets*, a book-length study of Israel's most prominent comics artist. He lives in Pittsburgh and teaches at Carnegie Mellon University.

Linda F. Hurwitz is the former director of the Holocaust Center of Pittsburgh, from 1988 to 2005. Under her supervision, the all-volunteer project with many local Holocaust survivors produced the book *Flares of Memory: Stories of Childhood during the Holocaust* (Oxford), edited by Anita Brostoff with Sheila Chamovitz. She was an English teacher and head of the middle school at Community Day School for ten years, and a teacher at CMU Osher Lifetime Learning and other adult education programs at Chatham College and at in the University of Pittsburgh's Informal Studies.

Susan Jacobs Jablow is a Pittsburgh-based journalist, essayist, and grantwriter. She is a former staff member of the *Pittsburgh Post-Gazette* and the *Pittsburgh Jewish Chronicle*, and her work has been published in numerous other publications. She is a graduate of Yeshiva University's Stern College for Women and the Columbia University Graduate School of Journalism.

Beth Kissileff is the author of the novel *Questioning Return* and editor of the essay collections *Reading Genesis: Beginnings* and *Reading Exodus: Journeys* (forthcoming 2021). She has taught at the Universities of Pittsburgh and Minnesota, and at Carleton, Smith, and Mount Holyoke Colleges. Her writing has appeared in the *Atlantic*, the *New York Times*, *Tablet*, *Haaretz*, and the *Michigan Quarterly Review*, among others.

Eric Lidji is the director of the Rauh Jewish Archives at the Senator John Heinz History Center.

Tony Norman is a general interest columnist and the book review editor of the *Pittsburgh Post-Gazette*. An award-winning columnist and feature writer, he was the recipient of a Knight-Wallace Journalism Fellowship at the University of Michigan for 2005–2006. Tony is currently the vice-president of the National Society of Newspaper Columnists and a board member of both the International Free Expression Project and the International Consortium of Investigative Journalists. For nearly two decades Tony was an adjunct journalism professor at Chatham University. He's currently working on a novel and a book of essays.

Avigail Oren earned her PhD in history from Carnegie Mellon University in 2017, and since then has been an independent scholar, entrepreneur, and activist. She also serves as coeditor of *The Metropole*, the blog of the Urban History Association.

Molly Pascal is a freelance writer, native Pittsburgher, and member of Tree of Life. Her work has appeared in the *Washington Post*, *Lithub*, the *New York Times*, *Newsweek*, *Huffington Post*, *Salon*, the *Pittsburgh Jewish Chronicle*, the *Pittsburgh Post-Gazette*, *Fringe Literary Magazine*, and akashicbooks.com, among others. Her short stories and essays have received awards or honorable mention from *Glimmer Train*, *Profane*, and *Pen Parentis*.

Rabbi Jonathan Perlman has been the spiritual leader of New Light Congregation since 2010. He is also the chaplain and spiritual coordinator at the Institute of Palliative and Supportive Care at University of Pittsburgh Medical Center. A Pittsburgh native, he is known as an interfaith leader and a creative writer and teacher.

Campbell Robertson is a *New York Times* national correspondent based in Pittsburgh.

Abby W. Schachter is a research fellow at Carnegie Mellon University's Institute for Politics and Strategy. She is the author of *No Child Left Alone: Getting the Government out of Parenting*. Abby is raising four children with her artist husband, Ben Schachter, in Pittsburgh.

Adam Shear teaches religious studies, Jewish studies, and history at the University of Pittsburgh. His scholarly interests focus on early modern Jewish culture and thought, with a particular interest in the history of Jewish books and the impact of printing on Jewish culture. He and his family have lived in Squirrel Hill since 2002.

David Shribman was the executive editor of the *Pittsburgh Post-Gazette* during the Tree of Life massacre. A Pulitzer Prize winner himself, he led the coverage of the episode that won the 2019 Pulitzer. He has since become a scholar-in-residence at Carnegie Mellon University and visiting professor at McGill University. He writes a column nationally syndicated in the United States and a separate column for the *Globe and Mail* newspaper in Canada.

Peter Smith is the religion editor for the *Pittsburgh Post-Gazette*. He was part of the *Post-Gazette* team that received a Pulitzer Prize for coverage of the October 27 shooting.

Toby Tabachnick is the editor of the *Pittsburgh Jewish Chronicle*.

Arlene Weiner is a poet and playwright active in several poetry groups in Pittsburgh. She has been a Shakespeare scholar, a college instructor, a cardiology technician, and an editor. Ragged Sky published two collections of her poetry, *Escape Velocity* and *City Bird*. Arlene earned her PhD in English and American literature at Brandeis, and has held a fellowship to the MacDowell Colony.

Rabbi Daniel Yolkut studied in Yeshivat Har Etzion in Israel, and in Yeshiva University's Yeshiva College, Bernard Revel Graduate School of Jewish Studies and Rabbi Isaac Elchanan Theological Seminary, where he was ordained. He has served in the rabbinate since 2000, and since 2010 as the spiritual leader of Congregation Poale Zedeck in the Squirrel Hill section of Pittsburgh, where he and his wife, Anna, are raising their six children.